The
POWER
of Hope

Overcoming Your Most Daunting Life
Difficulties—No Matter What

ANTHONY SCIOLI, PH.D.
HENRY B. BILLER, PH.D.

Health Communications, Inc.
Deerfield Beach, Florida

www.hcibooks.com

To Erica,
THE GREAT HOPE PROVIDER
IN MY LIFE.

—*Tony Scioli*

To Suzette River,
THE LIGHT AND LOVE OF MY LIFE
AND HER TALENTED DAUGHTER SOLEIL.

—*Henry B. Biller*

Library of Congress Cataloging-in-Publication Data

Scioli, Anthony
    The power of hope : overcoming your most daunting life difficulties—no matter what /
by Tony Scioli and Henry B. Biller.
      p. cm.
    Includes bibliographical references and index.
    ISBN-13: 978-0-7573-0780-5
    ISBN-10: 0-7573-0780-9
    1. Positive psychology.   2. Hope.   3. Optimism.   I. Biller, Henry B.   II. Title.
BF204.6.S254 2010
158–dc22

                                                  2010002240

Publisher: Health Communications, Inc.
                3201 S.W. 15th Street
                Deerfield Beach, FL 33442–8190

Cover design by Larissa Hise Henoch
Inside design by Lawna Patterson Oldfield
Formatted by Dawn Von Strolley Grove

CONTENTS

PART THREE: THRIVING WITH HOPE

ACKNOWLEDGMENTS

Like hope itself, the birth and growth of this book has been a collaborative process, involving higher aims as well as trust, openness, and patience.

Beyond our personal collaboration, our students have been a big help, scoring questionnaires and entering data for the research reported in this book as well as doing library searches for the reference section. Phil Scioli assisted in the development of the first versions of the hope test that you will find at the beginning and end of this book.

We would like to thank our editor, Michele Matrisciani at Health Communications, Inc., for her enthusiastic support of this book, her dedication and wise counsel in crafting an accessible manuscript, and her unending supply of wit and humor. Judith Antonelli did a brilliant job of copyediting and fact checking. Carol Susan Roth, our literary agent, supported our vision from the start, and generously shared her time and experience with us.

Finally, we would like to thank our families and friends for their many years of love, support, and understanding.

PART ONE:

UNDERSTANDING HOPE

We designed Part One of this book to provide you with a deeper understanding of hope. In Chapter 1 we explain why hope may be our most important emotion, as fundamental to human life as the air that we breathe or the water that we drink. In Chapter 2 we introduce definitions of hope offered by psychologists, philosophers, and other experts, culminating in our own integrative understanding of this complex emotion. In Chapter 3 we explore the dangers of losing hope, and describe the nine types of hopelessness that can plague an individual. Chapter 4 deals with cultural and spiritual factors that influence the development of hope. We review the hopes of different cultures and religions, while also addressing forms of spirituality that are not necessarily religious in nature. We highlight the centrality of faith in the development of hope and include a spiritual assessment tool that can give you a greater insight into your particular spiritual needs.

1

Why Hope?

We live in a world that is in desperate need of hope. You cannot turn on the television, click on the radio, or browse the Internet without being inundated with more doom and gloom about the economy, renewed hostilities in the Middle East, violence at home and abroad, another scandal involving a religious leader or a politician, or further warnings about food safety, fuel supplies, or global warming. In short, there seems to be increasingly little chance of securing the feelings of community, prosperity, and peace that make life worth living. In the past, one could find comfort and trust in a cloistered village or a well-established neighborhood, empowerment through the monarchy or government, and security in the fold of an ever-present savior. For those living in oppression or poverty, there was always the possibility of traveling to greener pastures. In contrast, today it seems that there are few, if any, safe harbors.

In this darkest of times, a true sense of belonging is hard to find, governments and other institutions appear increasingly impotent, and faith in a higher power has seriously eroded. Even in the most industrialized nations, many people have achieved great affluence without deriving any clear sense of purpose in life. Instant messages are sent around the globe, yet so many remain lonely and isolated. Occasional medical and political advances provide brief glimmers of hope. However, these scattered signs of light are dwarfed by ominous reports of resistant and deadly microbes and increasingly brazen acts of global terrorism. In short, the signs of hopelessness are everywhere.

Hope is about *mastery*, a feeling of empowerment, and a sense of purpose that is collaborative and focused on higher goals. In stark contrast, millions of adults are now losing their jobs. High school graduates and their parents are finding it increasingly difficult to pay for a college education. Others possess skills that are undervalued and undercompensated. Even for those who manage to remain in the workforce, many feel trapped in despised jobs or careers they cannot leave, worried that they may suffer an even worse fate.

Hope is about *attachment*, a belief in the continued presence of a loved one, a mentor, or an ally who fosters a sense of connection, trust, and openness. Clearly, such bonds of hope were not available to Eric Harris or Dylan Klebold, the Columbine killers, or Seung-Hui Cho, the Virginia Tech shooter. For countless other brooding youth who are simmering with hopeless rage, "hope providers" are badly needed. Many teens and young adults who are devoid of healthy role models will often join a gang as a way of securing a sense of belonging and mastery, however distorted and dangerous. The same crisis of connection defines the life of a forsaken individual with HIV or AIDS who is living on the streets or is relegated to a dark and lonely hospital bed.

Hope is about *survival*, a belief that you will be liberated from harm, that options will always be available to you, and that you can rest assured that everything will be fine. This dimension of hope is particularly elusive for the trauma survivor. Perhaps you are a war veteran, a victim of a violent crime, or an adult who was seriously hurt as a child. You might feel traumatized and trapped by an abusive or a controlling partner. Maybe you are facing retirement or can no longer live completely on your own.

Hope is often *spiritual*, not necessarily in the religious sense, but in terms of having faith, a sense of meaning in life, a connection to something greater, or a belief in a benign universe. In this period of great unrest, it is understandable if you or a loved one is suffering from a crisis of faith. If you have a religious inclination but find yourself stricken with a serious illness, a divorce, or being fired or laid off, you may be wondering where is God? If you are not religious but consider yourself spiritual, yet are now facing the foreclosure of your home, lack of funds to send your child to college, betrayal by your spouse, a close friend, or a business associate, your belief in a well-ordered cosmos may be shattered.

More than ever, the world needs hope, still the best medicine for overcoming feelings of helplessness, alienation, and fear. Unfortunately, we seem to be living in a hope-challenged world. You might even describe our current state of affairs as the culmination of a perfect storm that has been brewing for years to undermine every aspect of hope: mastery, attachment, survival, and spirituality.

The freedoms that have come with single parenting, no-fault divorce, air shuttles, and the Internet have their downsides, most notably in the realm of relationships. Our bonds with family and friends are not what they were in the past. Half of our marriages fail. Job and career opportunities scatter us across the country. Few, if any, of our families will invest several decades in the same neighborhood, cementing a sense of community. Sunday dinners have given way to e-mail and Facebook updates. We find ourselves squeezing in hurried visits to relatives and close friends a few times a year, for Thanksgiving or New Year's.

Hopeful mastery comes from a sense of empowerment and purpose. How many of us feel supported in our work, and how many of us can truly say that our work represents a calling or a life mission? Too many of us feel underappreciated, that our skills and our talents are being wasted and that our dreams are being forestalled. Too many of us plod toward retirement, our hope narrowed into building a large enough portfolio to weather our final years with some semblance of dignity.

For the present generation of young people, it has become exceedingly difficult to feel any degree of inspiration. In some cases, their parents have let them down by failing to empower them with a strong but loving presence as well as a foundation of values to sustain a life of mastery. In other cases, it is their teachers, school officials, or coaches who have dropped the ball, allowing personal ambitions or shifting political winds to come before the real needs and interests of the child.

The ever-dwindling supply of heroes hurts all our children. Athletes, for instance, are no longer the worshipped heroes they once were but are seen as greedy negotiators, mercenaries for hire, or steroid cheats. In a media-driven world fed by lightning-fast communication, children are aware of every celebrity scandal or dark cloud on the horizon. In this age of dwindling hope, we have robbed our young of the protected innocence that allows tender hopes to grow.

True hope diminishes fear and brings a bounty of options, but today we are living in a frightened world that seems to be growing uncomfortably constrained. *Terror* is the catchword of the new millennium. Since 9/11 we have received daily updates in the form of a color code that ranges from green (which, coincidentally, is the color of hope) for a low risk of a terrorist attack to red for a severe risk. For the greater part of the past eight years, this terror meter has been at either yellow (elevated or significant risk) or orange (high risk). Will we ever see green again?

We are in the midst of the worst economic cycle since the Great Depression. Even if we manage to pull ourselves out of the current financial mess, is there any guarantee that our jobs, our homes, or our pension plans will be safe in a world increasingly filled with corrupt CEOs and a political system that seems mired in either complicity or incompetence?

Some kind of faith is necessary for hope. Your faith does not have to involve a deity or a higher power. However, we have found that hopeful individuals tend to have one or more centers of value: cherished people, objects or institutions that they trust and from which they derive a feeling of empowerment, an experience of connection, and a sense of safety and liberation from pain and suffering. Unfortunately, many of our potential centers of value are under siege.

Can you put your faith in God? Why does God permit the evils we see today? Can you trust organized religion and its officials to weed out the bad apples and keep your family safe from predators? Can you put your faith in the government? Why don't our political leaders actually lead by balancing the budget, eliminating wasteful spending, and staying clear of corruption or scandal? Can you put your faith in nature? Scientists argue that global warming is a reality, that nature can no longer be trusted to absorb and support our modern ways. Can you put your faith in science and technology? We once believed that MRIs, lasers, computers, and the Internet would empower, connect, and liberate us. The explosion in AIDS, Internet pornography, and identity theft has shaken our faith in even these modern marvels.

THE HOPEFUL INDIVIDUAL

Individuals who are hopeful possess something deeper and more enduring than merely a knack for goal achievement, problem solving, or crisis management; they have crafted a different way of being in the world. Hopeful individuals feel empowered, connected, and centered regardless of what is happening in the here and now. When confronted by obstacles, they remain confident and goal oriented. When separated in space or time from loved ones, they remain at one with their family, their friends, or a higher power. When faced with a loss, an injury, or any other form of threat, they are not overcome by fear. They believe that there are always adequate resources within and around them to meet any challenge, and they never stop looking for options and alternatives. No matter how difficult, lonely, or stressful the journey, the hopeful individual is able to find a purpose and a reason for living.

Hopeful individuals are happier than unhopeful ones. We all want to be happy. Moreover, when we are asked what we wish for our children, our parents, or our friends, we invariably tend to reply, "I just want them to be happy."

Psychologists have known for a long time that objective well-being, which is measured in terms of money, status, or material possessions, is a poor predictor of subjective well-being. More recent scholarship on this topic reaffirms the wisdom of the ancient Greeks and indicates that a good life derives from having a sense of meaning and purpose. The rest, as the Book of Ecclesiastes puts it, may simply be "the vanity of chasing the wind." A hopeful disposition imparts a more lasting form of happiness because it rests on a life of purpose, a commitment to love, a resilient core, and a connection to something greater than oneself.

As you read this book, it is fine to look for remedies to address your present mastery, attachment, survival, or spiritual concerns. We have plenty of recommendations in this regard. However, we do not want to limit your potential for greater hopefulness. We want you to aim higher and further, toward the transformation of your character and toward becoming a true person of hope.

We have been researching, teaching, and practicing psychology for a long time. In fact, our combined years in the field total nearly eight decades. We have studied, taught, and treated individuals from all walks of life, including children and entire families. Later in this introduction, you will learn more about our personal journeys. Suffice it to say that we have shouldered our share of disappointments and losses. We know as much about hopelessness as we do about hope.

Moreover, because of our personal experiences as well as our professional work, we can assure you that you *can* always find, build, and strengthen hope. Sometimes this requires reaching out, but in other instances it comes from looking deep within yourself. Hope can come in the form of a lesson or a set of guidelines, or it may derive from an inspiring example of achievement, love, survival, or spiritual commitment. Hope is available to the young and the old, the rich and the poor, the healthy and the infirm, the devoutly religious, the staunch, or atheist. The old adage "There is always hope" is true.

If you have lost all or some of your hope or have felt hopeless for many years, this book is for you. Approach this book as you would any hope provider: with trust and openness. Read it slowly and complete the exercises and self-tests so that you can digest and internalize the contents more thoroughly. Rarely will you find just one answer or solution to a problem or a concern. Outline or jot down the alternatives that are presented in each chapter. Remember that hope is about options. Be patient with yourself and the process, particularly if you aim for the higher goal of becoming a person of hope. Be assured that if you commit to discovering and harnessing the power of hope, your life path will be forever elevated.

Not everyone is a fan of hope. There are self-proclaimed realists who believe that hope is tantamount to a form of denial or delusional thinking, that reality cannot and will not support a hopeful outlook. There are cynics who express disdain for the apparent naïveté of the hopeful, believing that more time or greater maturity will reveal the truth of a bleaker existence. There are New Agers who have embraced the wisdom of living only for today, believing that hope will spoil the moment and will perpetuate a life of delayed gratification for a tomorrow that may never come. There are those who believe they must take an active approach in dealing with the world, but they presume that investing in hope will bring a commitment to a life of passivity.

True hope should never be confused with false hope or blind optimism. True hope brings an enlarged life perspective rather than a narrow, distorted view of the world. True hope should never be confused with a stepping-stone or a wishing well; it transcends time and space. It is, as we have said, a way of living in the world, an attitude and an approach that is sustaining, in both the short run and the long run.

Moreover, in blunt philosophical terms, you can't actually live in the moment. There is not enough time or space in a moment for you to engage in the minimal amount of reflecting that it takes to have an experience. Trying to live purely in the moment would be like trying to catch dripping honey with a strainer; it is futile. In contrast, hope spreads a sense of empowerment, connectedness, and liberation across time and space. In this way, hope allows for a unique kind of happiness that is comparable to a beautifully extended version of a successful performer's flow state, a lover's sense of oneness, or a hiker's mountaintop tranquillity. Samuel Johnson, an eighteenth-century writer, offered, "Hope is itself a species of happiness, and, perhaps, the chief happiness which this world affords."

Hope is not passive. Hopeful individuals do not sit around waiting for good things to magically come to them. They are constantly engaged in the work of hope: plugging into sources of empowerment, building and sustaining connections, carving out paths toward liberation, and shoring up their terror management resources.

Indeed, the logic behind this book is that hope is a skill that can be learned, expanded, and refined. This is entirely consistent with the ancient categorization of hope as a virtue, which means a strength or a power that is developed to a lesser or a greater degree depending on the individual. Skills in any arena of life are not developed through wishful thinking, momentary flirtations, or passivity. You have to dig in and get your hands dirty. Likewise, to become a more hopeful person, you have to delve into the nature of mastery, attachment, survival, and spirituality and learn how to incorporate the subskills associated with these building blocks of hope.

WHY US?

How did we come to write a book about hope? For both of us, it is hard to completely separate our professional interest in hope from more personal factors such as childhood and family influences, idiosyncratic life circumstances, or interests and hobbies. Once you have read a little further, you will probably surmise, as we have, that our personal experiences have been a strong determining force, steering us in the direction of psychology, and specifically the kind of psychology that we teach, study, and practice with our clients. As we acknowledge this fact, we are keenly aware of how fortunate we have been to find vocations that have been so meaningful to us. This relates to another major theme that you will find in this book: that hopeful mastery derives from having a higher purpose in life, a calling or a mission.

One of us (Tony Scioli) is a clinical health psychologist with an interest in emotions, coping, and health, and the other (Henry Biller) is a clinical life-span psychologist with an interest in individual differences, fitness, and family development. Our passion for hope is reflected not only in the subfields in which we have chosen to specialize but also in how we approach these topics. Tony has focused his research on the positive role that emotions can play in an individual's life. He also does work in behavioral medicine and biofeedback, helping clients to learn more effective coping and self-regulation strategies. Henry's research on fitness is geared toward health-promoting strategies that foster greater resiliency across the life span. His work with children and families is geared toward maximizing the resources inherent in the family system, including much of the untapped potential of fathers.

We share a growing concern for what can only be called a global hope shortage. We see this most immediately in our clients. Few of them have ever felt empowered by a strong, caring presence. Rejection, abandonment, or outright abuse has made them guarded and unable to trust or be open with others. Trauma, oppression, or entrapment has reduced their perceived degrees of freedom. They feel completely trapped in their present circumstances.

We are aware that mainstream psychology has been slow to provide solutions for those who are mired in hopelessness. For most of the twentieth century, psychology seemed more preoccupied with unearthing new disorders or trying to figure out if our minds functioned like computers. There was little investment in understanding any human emotion other than fear and aggression. Resiliency was hardly ever discussed except in the context of positive temperamental factors among very young children. Interventions to foster resiliency, in children or adults, did not appear until the end of this past century.

Finally, we have written this book for personal reasons. More than a professional curiosity, our passion for hope is derived from our own experiences in confronting significant mastery, attachment, survival, and spiritual challenges.

EXERCISE 1: Reflecting on Hope

Before you read further, take a moment to reflect on your most memorable encounters with hope. Imagine before you a billboard with the word HOPE printed in giant letters. What was your most significant experience with this emotion? Perhaps it involved you or a close friend. Maybe it was a particularly inspiring story about an act of love, a heroic deed, or a tale of survival. Perhaps it dealt with your feelings in the aftermath of 9/11 or some other calamity. What kinds of thoughts, feelings, and images come to mind? Give yourself as much time as you need. Some hopes emerge in times of crisis, whereas others are actively pursued. Close your eyes and think about a few situations in which you strongly hoped for something.

List your three biggest hopes from the past:

1. _____

2. _____

3. _____

Were these hopes realized? If so, how much credit do you give to internal resources (your abilities) rather than external factors (family, friends, a higher power). If any of your hopes were not realized, how much of the blame do you place on personal shortcomings rather than external obstacles?

1. _____

2. _____

3. _____

4. _____

5. _____

6. _____

7. _____

8. _____

9. _____

TONY'S STORY

I was born in Cantalupo nel Sannio, a small town in the Molise region of Italy, about two hours north of Naples. Enclosed by forest-covered mountains dotted with tiny villages of clay-orange houses, Molise is the second-smallest province in Italy. In the late 1950s, Cantalupo could boast of having 5,000 inhabitants. Today the population has dwindled to about 800. As previous generations have passed away, many of the young have gone off to find hope in Rome, Milan, or Turin or have emigrated to the United States, Canada, or Australia. An increasing number of the once cozy stone and stucco homes are, I am sad to say, being abandoned. In their place one may find nothing more than a crumbling foundation filled with piles of brick and clay. Nearby, a few dried-out grapevines may be visible beneath the yellow and green overgrowth.

A 2008 travel guide described Molise as "remote and undiscovered." Indeed, time tends to forget places like Cantalupo. In the 1960s, while the United States was hosting the Beatles and heading for the moon, Cantalupo was more like a small town in the United States during the 1930s and 1940s. It was a farming community, and the widely separated neighborhoods seemed like semiautonomous villages, linked only by winding dirt roads half-hidden by tall fields of wheat, corn, and barley. Sputtering motorcycles mingled with horse-drawn buggies. Cars were a rarity.

In the pre-World War II era, educational opportunities were reserved for the more affluent Italians, primarily from the big cities and the northern provinces. My parents were fortunate to even attend a middle school. However, both of them never stopped learning and trying to expand their horizons. Instead of defensively devaluing education, as sometimes happens among the disenfranchised, my parents cherished what little formal education they received and always viewed it as the way to a better life.

My father became the town representative for the region and earned a reputation as a sharp investor, whether it was banking lira or trading livestock. Years later, when I came home for my college spring break, I shared a brainteaser with him that involved buying and selling a horse. About 20 percent of adults cannot arrive at the solution, and most need to spend a few minutes with pen and paper to figure it out. I read the problem aloud to him, and when I finished, he immediately gave the correct answer!

My mother had to balance caretaking with cooking, cleaning, and various farm duties. Many of the meals she made were cooked in a brick oven. She did not have a microwave oven, a washer, or a dryer. Even though she was allergic to many plants and grasses, she would sometimes spend hours in the fields, bringing the cows and the sheep to pasture, baling hay or taking corn to the village mill to be ground for polenta, and picking fruits and vegetables for sauces, preserves, and winemaking.

My parents had to be courageous; they had no choice. Both of them lost their fathers at an early age. As children, they experienced the Great Depression, and as teens their country was a major battleground for World War II engagements. My mother vividly recalls her family retreating into the nearby mountains to avoid the Allied bombings. My father was forced to join Mussolini's Black Shirts and was sent to Bolzano, near the German border, for boot camp.

In 1960, already in their thirties and unable to speak a word of English, they packed all their belongings into a few trunks and crossed the Atlantic with my older brother to settle in Boston, where my father was employed as a pieceworker in a factory that made switches for cars, railroads, and the military. He rode the two and a half miles to Arkless Switch on his bicycle, five days a week. In the winter, he would put folded newspapers inside his jacket for insulation. On weekends he cut, watered, and transported plants for a local greenhouse. My mother worked six and sometimes seven days a week at a dressmaking factory, in an old brick building that once housed the Waltham Watch Company.

With a family background characterized by dislocation and loss, hard-won mastery, and no shortage of traumatic encounters, I was perhaps primed to view hope in terms of mastery, attachment, survival, and spirituality. However, I am just as certain that my personal struggles to find love, success, and inner peace played a major role in my decision to become a psychologist who now studies hope for a living.

By the time I was four years old, I had twice been separated from my primary caregiver for extended periods: first my mother, while my parents were establishing roots in the United States, and then my aunt, who cared for me from the time I was six months of age to three and half years old. When I was five and reunited with my parents in Boston, my adopted "aunt" (my next-door neighbor) was stabbed to death by her boyfriend, the same man who drove me and her actual nephews to school every morning. At eight, I lost my best friend Eddie to a congenital heart defect. When I was twenty-four, my then mentor, psychologist Shula Sommers, died of cancer. At age twenty-five, just before I started graduate school, I went to Italy to visit my aunt, whom I had not seen for two decades. Five hours before I arrived in Cantalupo, she died of a previously undiagnosed bleeding ulcer.

It took me longer to form trusting relationships outside my family, compared to most of my friends and acquaintances. For one thing, I was more than a little gun-shy. In my experience, close relationships had become linked to abandonment as well as death, illness, and violence. In addition, I was straddling many worlds: the old world of Cantalupo and the new world of Boston, the blue-collar life of my parents and the intellectually charged atmosphere of higher education. I found it hard to feel at home or to develop a sense of identity.

For many years, I had to compartmentalize my experiences as I tried to follow multiple growth paths: an Italian, an American, a practical blue-collar man, and a clinician and an academic. Eventually, I was able to consolidate these various experiences of self into a meaningful whole. Not only did this bring a sense of inner peace, it also made it easier for me to be more present in my relationships with others and to be clearer about my attachment needs.

When I came to the United States, I couldn't speak a word of English. My family had settled in a lower-middle-class, blue-collar neighborhood. Back in those days it wasn't fashionable to be so Italian, to speak a language other than English at home, to bring pepper and egg sandwiches to school, or to have Neapolitan folk songs emanating from the patio. I worked hard to fit in, and when that failed, I found refuge in reading and sports, particularly baseball. When tennis became the rage in the 1970s, I wanted to find out what all the excitement was about. After playing one summer with a borrowed racket, I tried out for the high school tennis team. Unfortunately, all I could afford was a five-dollar racket with cotton strings, but much to my surprise, I earned a spot and eventually became captain.

In my senior year, I confided in my guidance counselor that I wanted to be a psychologist. He introduced me to the school psychologist, who told me that since I was an immigrant, I should pursue a business degree so I could elevate my family's "social standing." (Until my older brother entered college, not a single member of my immediate or extended family had ever gone beyond high school.) Nevertheless, I was very clear in terms of what I wanted to do with my life. Perhaps it was just my defense mechanisms, but I convinced myself that this school psychologist was an amateur at best and a fake at worst. Undaunted, I sought out a college with a strong psychology department.

Although I did well in my first few years of college, it took me a while to fully grasp the possibility of becoming a professional psychologist. I was helped by excellent mentors who were outstanding scholars yet down-to-earth. In retrospect, I can see that I gravitated more toward the modest Lieutenant Columbo types, the humble heroes who outsmart the entitled pseudointellectuals or elitists.

Role models from my peer group were especially important to me. In fact, I can still recall a pivotal day in the spring of my junior year when my hope for success was finally crystallized. I was walking with several classmates when one of them turned to another and asked, "What do you want to do with your degree?" The other replied, "I know exactly what I want to do. I want to be a psychology professor."

What a great idea, I thought. *Heck, if she can dream that, so can I.* Given my modest roots as an immigrant from a working-class background who had attended a large suburban public school that was not very conducive to promoting high achievement, I needed the inspiration of a classmate whom I saw as my equal.

Looking back, I can see that I have always been a hopeful individual, regardless of the circumstances. My family life, though sometimes disrupted by fate, fostered trust. My parents had never received much formal education, but they were highly skilled in practical matters and exceedingly wise. My older brother did go to college and then graduate school, showing me that it was possible for someone with our background to make it in higher education. Most important, perhaps, I witnessed my family and others persevere through dedication, support, and faith. In these manifold ways, I came to know the full meaning of hope.

HENRY'S STORY

I was born in a working-class neighborhood in Providence, Rhode Island, at the tail end of the Great Depression and just a year before the United States entered World War II. For economic reasons, our crowded household included my maternal grandparents, an uncle, my father, my mother, and my sister, who was almost eight years my senior. As a young child, I was in the unusual situation of having three adult males to interact with on a regular basis, and I developed an especially strong attachment to my father and my grandfather. Although my grandparents were immigrants from Russia who never went to high school and my parents did not go to college, they were all interested in reading and expressing their frequently diverse opinions. Freedom of expression was valued, whatever the topic or activity.

My grandfather, who was often unemployed, liked to talk about his days as a "cowboy in Arkansas" and sing the song "Don't Fence Me In." My dad, a furniture salesman who had been an air raid warden during World War II, was an especially kind and patient man. He and my mother, as well as my grandmother, were very sociable and had friends over for weekly card games. Our household always seemed filled with activity, with family members coming and going. Many of my fondest memories from this period are of frequent outings with my father or my grandfather. I was happy just to be with them, whether it was going on a mundane errand, tagging along for a work-related activity, or playing in the park.

This early bliss did not last long. When I was three years old, my family began to suffer a series of wrenching changes and losses. My uncle was drafted into the army. Initially stationed nearby, he was soon sent to Guam, halfway around the world. That was only the beginning. Even more disruptive, first my grandfather and then my father died within a span of less than eighteen months. My grandfather died rather suddenly when I was four and half years old. But my father, who had tuberculosis, spent most of the last year of his life in a hospital, where I wasn't allowed to visit.

In between these two great losses, I was hospitalized for a hernia operation. Neither my parents nor I were well prepared for this event. After entering the hospital and accompanying me to the door of the operating room, my parents were told to leave, while I fought and screamed to go with them. Forced down on the operating table, I was quickly given ether. Not fully understanding my circumstances, I awoke after the surgery feeling very thirsty, and I left my bed to find something to drink. In order to keep me still, the hospital staff put me into a straitjacket. Needless to say, I was quite terrified by the whole ordeal and greatly relieved when my parents came to get me a few days later, not yet aware of my father's serious health problems.

Before I had even turned six, I was the only remaining male in the household. My family had been greatly transformed. Beyond the loss of my father and my grandfather, my beloved and free-spirited grandmother remarried and moved away. My uncle, who had come back from World War II, relocated to New Jersey. By the time I entered first grade, my mother was already taking two buses each way to work, struggling in her role as the sole provider. I became a latchkey child who had to find both the will and the way to transform any perceived disadvantages into potential opportunities. Having an intense need to make my own choices and a seeming inability to sit still, I was a particular challenge to teachers and spent considerable time sitting outside the principal's office, especially during first and second grades.

Throughout middle childhood and adolescence, I struggled to retain a vital sense of paternal influence, relying heavily on my memories of my early relationships with my father and my grandfather and, in the process, becoming more and more my own father. Vowing to take care of myself, I was able to allay some of my feelings of loss as well as fears of illness and death. Although my father and my grandfather had not survived, I had.

Fortunately, I was blessed with a naturally assertive demeanor as well as athletic ability. Like many other boys growing up in working-class neighborhoods in the 1940s and the 1950s, I played sports as a daily endeavor; it often served as a buffer in the face of personal and family stressors. Also important for my developing sense of mastery, I managed to earn a little spending money by finding various part-time jobs. Nevertheless, I continued to have frequent difficulties adapting to those whom I viewed as unfair or unreasonable, including teachers, coaches, and employers. I hung out with boys two or three years older than myself, yet I was unable to tolerate bullies, so I shunned any type of gang activity and tried to limit myself only to those neighborhood opportunities that involved sports or card games.

When I was fourteen, my mother remarried, which meant that she and I had to move about sixty miles away, nearer to her husband's place of employment. Although I got off to a promising start, I became increasingly unhappy and would go back to my former neighborhood whenever I had the chance. When I was sixteen, I left home for good, much to my mother's dismay. As a result of these upheavals and because of my general dislike of the traditional educational environment, I attended seven different schools between ninth and twelfth grades without receiving a high school diploma. I did become interested in some schoolwork, but I was primarily focused on sports and girls. Eventually I began to think seriously about my future. I put my hope in college, believing that it might be more flexible and stimulating than high school, both academically and athletically.

Upon turning seventeen, despite my lack of a high school diploma, I presented my story to an empathic admissions officer at Brown University, Bruce Hutchinson. A navy veteran, Bruce had contracted polio during the Korean War, which left him dependent on crutches for the rest of his life. Perhaps he saw in me someone who was equally handicapped—if not physically, then at least socially and economically. In any case, Bruce advocated for me, touting my academic and athletic potential despite my lack of school-based accomplishments. To the surprise of all who knew me, I was accepted at Brown and found my niche in an environment that rewarded the drive and problem-solving ability that I had developed from being on my own.

During the first semester of my sophomore year, I woke up suddenly in the middle of the night with the sense that my "calling in life" was to help others by becoming a professor and writing books. I knew that I had to better organize my time and study diligently. Moreover, given my highly sociable and restless nature, I realized that academia was going to be a grind for me unless I could arrange for a kind of daily vacation from the isolated rigor of studying and writing papers. I began a ritual, which I have been committed to now for more than fifty years, to spend part of each day engaged in something playful, something pleasurable, and something family-oriented.

Given my need for family, getting married at twenty and becoming a father at twenty-two were crucial milestones in helping me to forge a more centered and purposeful life. Indeed, my experiences as the father of Jonathan, Kenneth, Cameron, Michael, and Benjamin have profoundly enriched my life. I am also very fortunate to be the grandfather of six (Connor, Emily, John, Sofia-Rose, Sammy, and Danny), an opportunity that my own father never experienced. My rather tumultuous early years prepared me to appreciate life, to remain balanced, and to thrive in the face of the inevitable vicissitudes of life.

As I approach seventy, I perceive myself as not even halfway through life, as I await all the wonderful things that the future holds for me and my loved ones, especially my soul mate Suzette, and her daughter, Soleil. I truly feel awesome, blessed, grateful, and hopeful.

COMMON THEMES

In many ways the deck was stacked against us. If we were starting out today, both of us would be considered at-risk youth. We came from humble immigrant stock. Our parents had little formal education. We suffered crucial losses at an early age and experienced multiple traumas. As latchkey kids, we had to create our own after-school activities. Although we can both attest to innumerable periods of sadness and stretches of time filled with frustration, loneliness, and anxiety, we did not languish or capitulate. We never felt compelled to withdraw from the world, or to numb ourselves with alcohol or drugs.

We had hope. We were empowered by the strong examples of our parents and other family members who persevered despite having many financial, educational, and social obstacles in their way. We were able to internalize that strength and combine it with our own talents and interests. Moreover, perhaps because our parents had not had the opportunity to succeed in traditional middle-class professions, we were forced to develop our own visions of mastery, but ones that were nonetheless consistent with our parents' transcendent dreams of noble possibilities and lasting progress.

We had family members and friends with whom we could be open and trusting. We knew that they would never abandon us, that they would always be with us, in one form or another. Raised by plain-speaking, no-nonsense elders, we developed a knack for recruiting peers as well as adults who had our best interests in mind and avoiding those who might prove dangerous, exploitative, or manipulative. Despite our early encounters with death and trauma, we never felt totally overcome by fear, and we always believed that we could find our way out of any difficulty. Sports and physical activities were very helpful in this regard, providing a powerful mechanism for reducing stress while boosting our self-confidence. Our families offered powerful examples of resiliency. Henry's widowed mother continued to work, to parent, and to live. Tony's parents, unable to speak English and without much formal education, managed to find and keep jobs, buy a home, and send their children to college.

We were both fortunate to develop a spiritual dimension in our lives. Tony's spirituality can be traced back to a very strong Catholic background; he served as an altar boy and then as a church lector. Henry grew up in a nonreligious family. Finding it difficult to place his faith in a traditional higher power, his spirituality is more grounded in nature and science. Nevertheless, we share two very strong spiritual impulses. The first is a belief in the interconnectedness of all life, from the smallest amoeba to the largest mammal. From this basic belief flows the related notion that we are all responsible for the universe and that the universe is responsible for us. We also share the unfailing belief that there is goodness in the world. It might not always be obvious, and sometimes you have to wait a while, but it will arrive, and when it does it will further nurture your hope.

WHAT YOU CAN EXPECT FROM THIS BOOK

As psychologists, we understand that people learn best when they are using the entire brain, meaning the right *and* the left hemispheres. The right side favors holistic examples, stories and analogies filled with emotion and drama, whereas the left side is analytic, partial to logic and step-by-step guidelines. In this book you will find many examples of hopeful mastery, attachment, survival, and spirituality. These are for your right brain. In addition, there will be plenty of step-by-step guidelines and suggestions to satisfy your left brain. To become a person of hope, you must rely on the light and fire of inspiration as well as the nuts and bolts of a hope-centered education.

Why is hope so important? In addition to relating our personal experiences and what we have gleaned from our clinical work, we will also provide you with the results of the research on the benefits of hope that we have been doing for more than a quarter century. Throughout the book, we will describe these studies in more detail, but for now we will give you a taste of what we have found.

Hope is a critical factor in mastery. More hopeful students get better grades in college. In fact, their hope scores, as measured by a standard questionnaire, are more predictive of their academic success than their Scholastic Aptitude Test scores. More hopeful individuals set more goals and work harder at achieving success. More hopeful individuals have higher pain thresholds and take longer to feel fatigue.

Hope fosters and sustains love, openness, and trust. More hopeful individuals are less likely to feel lonely or abandoned, even when they are by themselves or in a crowd of strangers. More hopeful individuals make better parents, friends, and lovers. Couples who share the same hopes and dreams are more likely to stay together.

Hope is crucial for survival and coping. More hopeful individuals recover quicker and with fewer complications from surgery or serious wounds, compared to less hopeful individuals. More hopeful cancer patients live longer than those with less hope. Hopeful cardiac patients are five times more likely to survive after an initial heart attack. More hopeful HIV-positive individuals demonstrate significantly stronger immune systems.

Hope is essential for a healthy spiritual life. Hopeful individuals derive greater job satisfaction, viewing their work in terms of a calling or a life mission. Hopeful individuals are more likely to discern a spiritual presence in their lives. For some this may even involve a mystical experience or a sense of oneness with something greater than themselves. More hopeful individuals are more apt to derive a sense of meaning from a loss, an illness, or another tragedy.

Ultimately, you can learn only so much from case histories or specific examples. Every individual has a unique personality, and each life situation is different. Instead of prescribing a one-size-fits-all formula, we provide a *basic philosophy of hope* that can help you to achieve a greater sense of mastery, attachment, survival, and spirituality. At the same time, we have tried to address a number of questions that may be on the minds of many hope seekers. These questions include the following:

- What is hope?
- How does one build and sustain hope in this age of anxiety?
- How can hope bring more love into your life?
- How can hope increase your chances of success?
- How can hope buffer your anxiety and bring peace of mind?
- How does hope relate to your faith and spiritual beliefs?
- How can hope aid your recovery from illness or trauma?
- How can hope increase your chances of a lifetime of good health?

EXERCISE 2: Take the Hope Pre-Test

To help you get further oriented and to aid you in monitoring your hope gains, we suggest that you complete the hope pre-test below. When you reach the last question, you will find a self-scoring key that will help you to create an initial hope profile. At the end of this book, you will find a second hope test that is very much like this one. The post-test will allow you to gauge how much of the power of hope you have absorbed and which sections, if any, you might want to review.

The Hope Test

Reflect on how you think, feel, and act *most* of the time. In other words, you should answer the questions below according to what is *generally* true of you. For example, if you have had an unusually good or bad week, put those thoughts and feelings aside and focus on your typical ways of thinking, feeling, and doing things.

Use the following scale to answer each question.

Not Me	A Little Like Me	A Lot Like Me	Exactly Like Me
0	1	2	3

____ 1. I believe that I am going to get what I really want out of life.

____ 2. I have a trusted friend or family member in whom I can confide.

____ 3. I can find ways to relax.

____ 4. I believe there are ways one can get in touch with a greater spiritual force.

____ 5. I give some credit to others for my successes in life.

____ 6. I find comfort in my spiritual beliefs.

____ 7. The future looks bright to me.

____ 8. I believe there is a positive force somewhere in the universe.

____ 9. I like to seek out new experiences.

____ 10. In pursuing my goals, I try to work hand-in-hand with God or a higher power.

____ 11. I'm capable of finding support from others when I need it.

____ 12. I have never felt close to any kind of spiritual force or presence.

____ 13. I have a purpose in life.

____ 14. I believe that the spirit lives on in some form after the body perishes.

____ 15. I have doubts about achieving those things that really matter to me.

Not Me	A Little Like Me	A Lot Like Me	Exactly Like Me
0	1	2	3

___ 16. I feel safe enough with certain people in my life to share how I really feel.

___ 17. By looking within yourself, you can find untapped sources of strength.

___ 18. Spiritual experience can occur at any time or place.

___ 19. When setting goals, I like to get feedback from others.

___ 20. My spiritual beliefs keep me calm during a crisis.

___ 21. I look forward to the future.

___ 22. There is too much evil in the world to believe in a just or caring higher power.

___ 23. I find it stressful to travel and meet new people.

___ 24. Accomplishments are due to human willpower, not prayer or spiritual guidance.

___ 25. In these stressful times, I'm fortunate to have a network of friends and family.

___ 26. I have the ability to connect with God, a spiritual force, or a higher power.

___ 27. My life has meaning.

___ 28. Every human being has an immortal soul.

Scoring Your Hope Test

Step 1: Reverse the values for questions 12, 15, 22, 23, 24

(i.e., if you put down 0, change it to 3; if you put 1, change it to 2; if you put 2, change it to 1; if you put 3, change it to 0).

Step 2: Calculate your Mastery Score: questions 1 + 5 + 15 + 19 = _____

Step 3: Calculate your Attachment Score: questions 2 + 9 + 16 + 23 = _____

Step 4: Calculate your Survival Score: questions 3 + 11 + 17 + 25 = _____

Step 5: Calculate your Positive Future Score: questions 7 + 21 = _____

Step 6: Calculate your Spiritual Hope Score: questions 4 + 6 + 8 +

10 + 12 + 13 + 14 + 18 + 20 + 22 + 24 + 26 + 27 + 28 = _____

Step 7: Calculate your Nonspiritual Hope Score:

Mastery + Attachment + Survival + Positive Future = _____

Step 8: Calculate your Total Hope Score: Spiritual + Nonspiritual = _____

Interpreting Your Scores

HOPE Score	Average	Low Range	Medium Range	High Range
Mastery	8	0–6	7–8	9 and higher
Attachment	9	0–7	8–9	10 and higher
Survival	8	0–6	7–8	9 and higher
Positive Future	4	0–2	3–4	5 and higher
Spiritual Hope	34	0–30	31–37	38 and higher
Non-spiritual	27	0–23	24–31	32 and higher
Total Hope	60	0–53	54–67	68 and higher

2

What Is Hope?

Love recognizes no barriers. It jumps hurdles,
leaps fences, penetrates walls to
arrive at its destination full of hope.

MAYA ANGELOU, *WRITER AND POET*

In the middle of the movie *The Shawshank Redemption*, the following exchange takes place between the two main characters. Andy says to Red, his friend and fellow prisoner, "You need it so you don't forget there are things in this world not carved out of gray stone. There is something inside that they can't get to—they can't touch—it's yours." Red asks, "What are you talking about?" Andy replies, "Hope."

At one time or another, we have all been witness to the "gray stones" of the world. For the two of us, Tony and Henry, there was plenty of hardship early in life. Would anyone have bet on us, two street kids from Boston and Providence, one an immigrant whose parents came to this country in their thirties without a penny and hardly any formal education, and the other without a high school degree and fatherless before the age of six? As Andy suggested, it was partly something that we felt inside, but also the points of light beyond the gray stones that offered us hope for a better tomorrow.

Although we did not openly talk about hope, it was clearly something we sensed internally and externally, and it made all the difference.

TONY'S EARLY HOPES

When I think back, most of my youthful hopes were rooted in mastery, survival, and spirituality. My attachment needs were essentially put on hold until I was in my late twenties. However, I did find ways here and there to make friends and satisfy some of my intimacy needs by being creative in my pursuit of mastery. It was only much later that I more fully developed my capacity for trust, openness, and hope.

I found great hope in education. Doing well in school and seeking advanced degrees gave me a sense of empowerment and purpose while also offering the promise of autonomy and freedom that my parents never enjoyed as factory workers. Whenever I grew tired of being in a library, staying up to write a paper, or turning down offers to go out on a Saturday night, I thought about how good it would feel to have options in the future, to be my own person, and to break free of my past.

Fortunately, my parents, despite their lack of schooling, were wise and placed a great value on education, supporting my studies in every way they could. I was always captivated by my older brother's description of higher education. When he went to graduate school, he considered becoming a professor. His description of the academic life filled me with hope. *What a life!* I thought. *You can get paid to think and talk about things that you learn!*

Sports also gave me hope. Succeeding in baseball and tennis made me feel stronger and more capable of prospering in other areas of my life. It also offset my feelings of being different or not good enough because I was an immigrant or because my parents couldn't speak English. I was especially lucky to develop a fondness and knack for tennis in the 1970s, when the sport was king. Always a fan of sports history, I was inspired by the story of Althea Gibson, probably because I thought that her experiences mirrored my own in some ways. Gibson was not a typical tennis professional. An African American from modest means, she grew up in Harlem and did not start playing tennis until the age of fourteen. For years, Gibson was prevented from playing in the white-only major tennis events. Nevertheless, she would go on to become the first African American to win a major tennis title, winning both the French Open and Wimbledon.

Sports were also a way for me to manage stress, to lower my anxiety, and to cultivate a sense of hopeful survival that was grounded in a more balanced and centered emotional state. Running, jumping, and lifting weights made me feel more resilient. I was not as afraid of what tomorrow might bring.

My spirituality was a strong source of hope, providing me with a more encompassing reservoir of assurance to manage my anxiety as well as a guidepost to enlighten my mastery efforts and nurture my attachment needs. I was raised Catholic, and for an Italian American growing up in the 1960s and the 1970s, this meant First Communion, catechism classes every Saturday morning, and an hour every Sunday serving as an altar boy and later as a church lector. My mother was deeply religious: attending Mass at least once a week, praying the rosary, and reading pamphlets in the evenings from various missionary groups she had supported. My aunt in Italy, the one who raised me till I was four, made regular pilgrimages to Lourdes in France. Thus, from a young age, I was immersed in a climate of religious and spiritual devotion. However, until I reached college, my own involvement in Catholicism was primarily rooted in ritualism and church-related social gatherings.

My spirituality started to deepen when I left home for the first time to attend a large public university. I found myself searching for deeper answers to the bigger questions. What is the purpose of my life? Does God exist? Given my early exposure to loss and death, I wondered if God would hear my prayers. Would He stay by my side and keep me safe? I committed myself to reading the Bible from cover to cover and to finding ways to integrate my studies with my spirituality. Initially a survival tool, my spirituality began to guide my mastery pursuits as well, including my professional development as a psychologist, in my twenties. My spirituality affected where I wanted to do my training and what kind of setting would be most conducive to my values. Finally, in my thirties, my spirituality became a matter of attachment. I simultaneously sought a deeper relationship with God and a greater level of self-understanding, so that I might forge a more soulful love when the right woman came along.

HENRY'S EARLY HOPES

My earliest hopes were strongly directed toward attachment and survival. Before the deaths of my father and my grandfather, there was a quartet of nurturing adults: my parents and my maternal grandparents. What I remember is how different they were from one another and yet how each one accepted me as an individual. For some reason, this made an enormous impression on me. It was as though the whole world were tolerant, forgiving, welcoming, and worthy of trust. I was not an easy child to handle or control. I hated sitting, being confined, or feeling trapped in any way. I loved to be outdoors, running, jumping, playing, and getting dirty.

My father and my grandfather, in particular, were very supportive of my need for freedom. When they passed away, my overextended working mother often got flak for not reining me in more. Somehow she sensed my need for autonomy and gave me the space I required. In this sense, she was a virtuoso hope provider.

Because of my early experience with loss, I put a premium on survival. In a short span of eighteen months, my father and my grandfather died. I felt vulnerable. Will I survive? To find a way to manage the anxiety and the fear that hung over me like a black cloud, I became even more focused on physical competence and sports. I needed to convince myself that I was superfit and superstrong. I would not succumb. I particularly enjoyed running-related sports like baseball and football, perhaps because this gave me the hope of developing great lung capacity—a 180-degree shift from the fate of my father, who died from tuberculosis. Developing my athletic skills gave me the sense that I could handle myself in the world. It made me feel confident that I had a physical edge rather than any kind of predisposed weakness.

Before I entered college, my sense of mastery revolved around being street-smart. I was a latchkey child by the age of six and used to making my own decisions. I did not like the structure of school, and I struggled with authority figures who seemed rigid and closed-minded. I was, in many ways, an at-risk youth. At the same time, I was buoyed by my mother's quiet but unwavering faith in my future prospects as well as by the sense that if I did succeed, I would deserve my success. There was no silver spoon in my kitchen!

I did not do well in school, did not have a high school diploma, and would need some help getting to college. Fortunately, this help did arrive in the form of Bruce Hutchinson, the generous admissions officer I mentioned in Chapter 1. Of course, I might never have given college a try were it not for the hope that it would be a different experience from high school—more interesting, more open, more passionate. Fortunately, most of my initial contacts with the faculty confirmed these expectations. I found the professors to be more open-minded as well as genuinely excited about their fields of study. This gave me a new kind of hope. If I committed myself, I might someday become an expert myself and blaze a path toward a meaningful future that would not compromise my need for an authentic existence.

Unable to connect with a traditional religious system, my faith and spirituality were derived primarily from memories of parental support and from nature. Even after the deaths of my father and my grandfather, they remained inside me as I confronted the challenges of childhood, adolescence, and adulthood. My mother managed to survive, despite many medical challenges, until I reached the age of thirty, and she provided me with an unwavering acceptance, no matter what my achievements. For the last five years of her life, she carried in her pocketbook a letter praising my accomplishments during my clinical psychology internship.

I became enamored of living things. I took great pleasure in being outside among the trees, the plants, and the wildlife—anything that was growing, blooming, flowering, or showing its vitality. Because my father had died so young, at the age of forty-two, I took a special interest in life forms that lived a long time. One of my favorites was the giant redwood tree—in particular, the sequoias of California. I marveled at their size: some were close to 400 feet high and nearly 10 yards in diameter. They could live more than 2,000 years, and nothing seemed to harm them. Even mighty floods that ripped away smaller trees had no effect on them. In fact, I learned that whenever huge floods came and then receded from their midst, the redwoods would draw on the silt left behind to grow even thicker roots. I also loved the fact that many of the biggest redwoods were located in the Grove of Titans, and honored with names like Apex, Helios, Hyperion, and Icarus.

THE ROLE OF PSYCHOLOGY IN OUR LIVES

Looking back, we can see that we were undoubtedly drawn to psychology because it provided a way of nurturing our growing hopes. Psychology offered a way of understanding and perhaps marshaling the positive forces that must intervene between hardship and success.

As beginning psychology students, we gravitated toward topics that would help each of us to better understand ourselves while also validating the truth of what we felt inside, what was important to us in our development, and what made it easier for us to navigate in a world filled with much gray stone.

Tony: The Validation of Emotion

After three years of studying psychology, I took a course on theories of personality. The professor, James Averill, a noted expert on emotions, discussed them like no one I had ever read or heard.

He critiqued the bias against being emotional, both within and outside psychology. Emotions are not primitive, irrational responses; they are not signs of immaturity or weakness. Emotions reflect personal and cultural values and priorities. You become angry because your rights have been violated, not because of an adrenaline surge or an overactive "rage center." You feel shame and guilt because you have a well-developed conscience and have internalized certain standards of moral action. If you are from a Mediterranean background, it is normal for you and your family to have a long and elaborate mourning period after the death of a friend or a family member.

These insights, taught by Professor Averill, rang true and deep for me. As an Italian American immigrant who was negotiating multiple realities, the idea that emotions were not fixed, irrational reflexes was both enlightening and liberating.

Henry: The Importance of the Father in Child Development

I did not like my first psychology class. Brown University's psychology department has always emphasized experimental research, primarily conditioning studies with animals or studies of memory and perception. In my introductory course we learned little about personality, psycho-therapy, or child development. At this point I wasn't sure whether I wanted to focus on psychology, anthropology, history, or philosophy.

Everything changed when I enrolled in my second psychology class. It was a course in child development taught by Professor Tony Davids. The moment I saw him up there lecturing, I knew that I wanted to be a psy-chology professor. Unlike my stereotype of an Ivy League–educated WASP academic, Professor Davids seemed much more like a working-class guy. He had a dark complexion, dressed casually, and spoke plainly. Later I learned that he had experienced a hardscrabble childhood, taken up wrestling for a while, and served in the air force before going to college. Rather than droning on, fixed to a podium, he paced back and forth across the front of the room, filling his animated lectures with anecdotes and clin-ical case studies. I guess the main thing was that he was a lot like me. *If he can be a professor*, I thought, *so can I.*

Although I enjoyed this class, I was disappointed that there was hardly any mention of research on the role of the father and relatively little about gender development. This just did not jibe with my own experi-ence. I had been very close to both my father and my grandfather. When they died, it was a huge loss for me. How could this be? Then one night it just came to me as I woke up from a deep sleep. I sat up, feeling very emotional, and told myself, *If no one else is going to write about the father, I'll do it. I know about close father-son bonds and the impact of losing your father at a young age.* Thus my frustration turned into hope as I realized that this untilled soil was available to be cultivated, perhaps even by someone like me! Not only would this bolster my personal sense of hope, in the process I might also be able to bring more hope into the lives of families.

Psychology and Hope

While we were trying to find our niche within psychology, we were amazed and disappointed at how narrow the field was in the 1960s and the 1970s. It was hard to find anything about any positive emotions, much less hope. One could count on the fingers of one hand the articles and books that dealt with the topic.

For some reason, the topic of hope would pop up once or twice per decade. In the 1950s it was from the psychiatrist Karl Menninger, who was trying to rally his colleagues to pay more attention to hope, the "indispensable flame" and the "divine fire."

In the early 1960s, it was from the psychologist Ezra Stotland, who argued that humans are not like rats or pigeons, acting on instincts, but are instead future-directed hope builders whose plans and expectations carry weight and affect their lives in real and meaningful ways. At the end of this decade, Jerome Frank reported on his exhaustive study of different forms of psychotherapy and concluded that they all were effective for one reason: they provided hope.

In the 1970s it was a Catholic theologian, William F. Lynch, who stated that hope requires the power of imagination and is strengthened by supportive relationships. In the 1980s, psychiatrist Louis Gottschalk demonstrated that more hopeful cancer patients live longer than their less hopeful counterparts. In the mid-1980s, with the publication of *Love, Medicine and Miracles*, Bernie Siegel touted hope while chronicling the lives of heroic cancer patients. Wrote Siegel, "Hope is a wonderful resource for the physician. Even when things seem hopeless, to give a family hope is never wrong. I am not talking about lying, but about hope."

In the 1990s, psychologist C. R. (Rick) Snyder showed that college students who were more hopeful did better in school, achieving significantly higher grades. Around this same time, Erik Erikson's last work was completed, a collaborative book that he wrote with his wife, Joan, and psychologist Helen Kivnick. Erikson suggested, as he had many times before, that trust and relationships allow a child to hope and enable the elderly to ward off despair.

Tony's own research on hope has covered much of the same ground. As a senior in college, he was most interested in the spiritual aspects of hope, especially the relationship between faith and hope. In graduate school, he started to focus on hope as a coping mechanism. For his dissertation, he studied the coping, or survival, patterns of children and adolescents who scored either low or high on a standard youth hope questionnaire. In the past decade, Tony has become more interested in the role of trust, culture, and relationships in the development and maintenance of hope. From his experience as a student of Jim Averill, he knows that there are multiple ways of looking at emotions, including hope, and this has given him the confidence (the hope) of pulling all his ideas together in this book.

True and False Hope

Our hopes might not always be appreciated by those around us. Some might even belittle or disparage our hopes. Frenetic go-getters may mistake our hope for passivity or for a willingness to forgo more immediate rewards, however less attractive. New Age, self-proclaimed Buddhists, ignorant of the real meaning of spirituality in either the East or the West, might chide us for pinning our hopes on relationships or for trusting so much in people and institutions. From their perspective, hope suggests an unbecoming clinginess. Cynical members of the medical profession may try to dissuade us from relying on hope in times of sickness, believing, like Ben Franklin, that it will cause us to "die fasting." Angry atheists may openly deride us for our more transcendent hopes, believing that we are simply too afraid to admit that there is nothing above or beyond the gray stones of the world.

These naysayers confuse false hope with the real thing. True hope is active rather than passive. It is the ally of human mastery and inspiration as well as the handmaiden of hidden dreams. As we understand it, hope is based on attachment and engagement rather than idle fantasy. Hope offers a real alternative to surrender borne of pain, suffering, or loss. It does not derive from blind optimism or a forced retreat from desire. Instead, true hope brings genuine assurance and lasting peace through psychological and spiritual transformation.

Hope is a powerful emotion that arises from the most basic longings of humanity. This includes our needs for mastery and protection, which are instinctive but highly subject to modification by experience. Hope also reflects the enormous impact of social and cultural attachments, the love and care that are required to achieve our potential as human beings. Finally, hope derives from our innate capacity to envision the future and create a better life for ourselves and our loved ones.

When blended into a full hope, these underlying motives result in a lifelong quest for love, success, and survival. In this sense, hope represents the most profound expression of the roots and the wings of the soul. Grounded in attachments to people, groups, and cherished objects (the roots), hope also serves the needs for discovery, mastery, and liberation from threats of annihilation (the wings).

Active Hope

Active hope is rooted in mastery, not submission. It is the kind of hope that helped to lift athlete Glenn Cunningham out of his hospital bed and into the Olympic stadiums of Los Angeles and Berlin. At the age of eight, Glenn was badly burned in a schoolhouse fire. His brother Floyd, who was with him at the time, died just two weeks after the accident. Glenn lost all the flesh on both of his knees and shins as well as all the toes on his left foot. His right leg was rendered two inches shorter than his left. At first the doctors expected him to die, then they wanted to amputate his legs. Always aware of what was going on, Glenn refused to accept their verdicts. Legend has it that Glenn literally dragged himself to recovery.

> When he wasn't in bed, he was confined to a wheelchair. One sunny day his mother wheeled him out into the yard to get some fresh air . . . he threw himself from the chair. He pulled himself across the grass, dragging his legs behind him. . . . He worked his way to the white picket fence bordering their lot. With great effort, he raised himself up on the fence. Then, stake by stake, he began dragging himself along the fence.

Glenn's parents also helped him. "It hurt like mad, especially when my father stretched my legs," Glenn told the reporter. "When my father would get tired I'd ask my mother to do the massaging and stretching and when she couldn't do any more I'd start doing it myself."

At first, all he could do was a fast hop, but eventually he was able to break into full strides. By the time he was twelve, Glenn had recovered well enough to race, and he was beating everyone in his age-group. He recalls that in the months and years immediately after the accident, he somehow found it easier to run than walk, "It hurt like thunder to walk, but it didn't hurt at all when I ran. So for five or six years, about all I did was run."

In high school and college, Glenn's racing prowess reached new heights. At age eighteen, he set the world high school record for the mile run. During his time at the University of Kansas, Glenn won six conference, two National Collegiate Athletic Association, and eight Amateur Athletic Union titles, and he set the world record for the mile run. In 1933 Cunningham was honored as the outstanding amateur athlete in the United States. In 1936, at the Olympic Games in Berlin, he won a silver medal.

Despite Glenn's contention that "it didn't hurt at all" to run, it did, and sometimes it was excruciating. In fact, he was in terrible pain during the Berlin Olympics because his condition was worsened by unusually cold weather. Moreover, because of limited circulation in his legs, he often needed an hour or more to prepare for a race, requiring extensive massage and heat. It is fitting that Glenn's favorite biblical verse was Isaiah 40:31: "Those who wait on the Lord shall renew their strength; they shall mount up with wings like eagles, they shall run and not be weary, they shall walk and not faint."

Connected Hope

A sense of connected hope is inspiringly illustrated by the relationship between Helen Keller and her teacher, Annie Sullivan. Beginning when Annie was twenty-one years old and Helen was seven, the pair lived and worked together for nearly fifty years. At public lectures, Annie read Helen's speeches word-for-word. Helen wrote a bestselling book about their collaboration entitled *Teacher*. Eventually their experiences were dramatized in a Broadway play and an Oscar-winning film, *The Miracle Worker*.

Anyone who has seen the movie or the play or has read about Helen and Annie knows of the events that took place on April 5, 1887. Desperate to teach young Helen the meanings of words, Annie poured water over her student's hands and then traced *w-a-t-e-r* on one of her palms. Helen later recalled, "Suddenly I felt a misty consciousness as of something forgotten, a thrill of returning thought."

In June 1960, nearly twenty-five years after Annie's death, a fountain was dedicated to her at Radcliffe College. At the dedication, when it was Helen's turn to address the crowd, she offered but one word: *water*. Working together, Helen Keller and Annie Sullivan demonstrated the power of relationships to create hope while bringing out the best in the human spirit.

Courageous Hope

The courageous hope of Christine King offers an especially poignant example of transcending adversity and fear. In her early thirties, Christine was diagnosed with breast cancer. Although the disease went into remission, her doctors warned her that there was a greater than 50 percent chance that it would recur. Nevertheless, she was determined to live a life of meaning and purpose. She even organized a large fund-raising event, Art for Hope, to increase public awareness about breast cancer. Upon her wrist she tattooed the word *hope*.

Spiritual Hope

The deepest hope is also spiritual. Anne Frank and Morrie Schwartz both found hope while staring death in the face.

During the Holocaust, Anne Frank and her family spent two years hiding from the Nazis in hidden rooms in her father's office building. Each day she lived with the knowledge that if they were discovered, she and her family would be transported to the concentration camps, forced into slave labor, starved and beaten, and then shot or gassed. For two years, she kept a diary, jotting down reflections on everything from her growing fondness for boys to questions about the nature of humanity.

On August 4, 1944, Anne and her family were discovered and sent to a prison, then transported to Westerbork, Auschwitz, and finally to Bergen-Belsen, a concentration camp in northwestern Germany. Weakened by years of hiding and months of abuse, she died sometime in early 1945, probably of typhus. Yet just nineteen days before her arrest and captivity, she was still expressing her confidence in the ultimate goodness of the universe and its inhabitants. On July 15, 1944, she wrote the following:

I still believe in spite of everything that people are truly good at heart. . . . It's utterly impossible for me to build my life on a foundation of chaos, suffering and death. . . . I somehow feel that everything will change for the better, that this cruelty too shall end, that peace and tranquility will return once more.

In the book *Tuesdays with Morrie*, Mitch Albom chronicled the last days of his former professor, Morrie Schwartz, who was withering away from ALS (Lou Gehrig's disease). Albom described Morrie as "realistic to a fault," noting he never spoke of a cure. He had bad days and terrible days. In the end, his tortured breathing was painful to witness. He cried a great deal, and each day he would lose control over another bodily function.

Despite all the difficulties, Morrie was determined to find meaning in his suffering. His hope was to make a difference in the world by imparting the lessons he was learning about living and dying, particularly about universality and spiritual integrity. In this regard, two comments by Morrie are particularly noteworthy. The first is a story that he related to Mitch about a wave that is terrified about crashing into the approaching shore. A second wave says, "No, you don't understand. You're not a wave, you're part of the ocean." Morrie's second bit of wisdom was uttered during his last *Nightline* interview. He told the host, Ted Koppel, "Ted, this disease is knocking at my spirit. It'll get my body. It will not get my spirit."

PILLARS OF HUMANITY

Hope is the pillar that holds up the world.

—PLINY THE ELDER

Hope is a vital force for humanity. In fact, we believe that the best art, literature, science, and philosophy are unconsciously (and sometimes consciously) meant to serve as ongoing lessons in hope, reflecting a perpetual investment in the importance of genuine success, true love, or hard-won survival. William Faulkner was acutely aware of this artistic mission when he took the podium in December 1950 to accept the Nobel Prize for Literature. In one of the greatest speeches of the twentieth century, Faulkner exhorted the aspiring writer to focus on "the old verities and truths of the heart. Until he does so, he writes not of love but of lust, of defeats in which nobody loses anything of value, and victories without hope. . . . His griefs grieve on no universal bones." According to Faulkner, it is the artist's "privilege to help man endure by lifting his heart, by reminding him of courage and honor and hope and pride and compassion and pity and sacrifice which have been the glory of his past." For Faulkner, the "poet's voice" was not merely "a record of humankind" but "one of the props . . . the pillars to help humankind endure and prevail."

Terror and Survival

If you reflect for a moment on the most enduring works of humanity, you will find that invariably they deal with one or more of the dimensions, or motives, that underlie hope. As one might expect, some of the earliest hope writings address survival. Consider *The Egyptian Book of the Dead,* already considered an authoritative funerary resource as early as 2000 BCE or the Tibetan *Book of the Dead* (eighth century CE). Both offered instructions on what to expect at the moment of death and ways to negotiate the afterlife. In *Antigone* (ca. 440 BCE), Sophocles celebrated humanity's "undying hopeful spirit." He eloquently captured the endless adaptations that mortals have made in negotiating the harshest environments, including their ability to "flee the arrows of the frost, when 'tis hard lodging under the clear sky and the arrows of the rushing rain."

If we fast-forward to the nineteenth century, we find that survival is still a primary focus. It was then that Fyodor Dostoyevsky wrote *Crime and Punishment,* a profound reflection on spiritual torture that also happens to include one of the most powerful reflections on humanity's hope for survival. After being jailed for his horrible deed, the murder of an unscrupulous pawnbroker, Raskolnikov is obsessed with his desire to remain alive:

> Where did I read about a certain condemned man, who, an hour before his death, says or thinks that if he should ever have to live somewhere on a height, on a crag, on a little square so narrow that only two feet can be put on it—and all around would yawn the abyss, ocean, eternal darkness, eternal isolation and eternal storm—and he would have to remain there like that, standing on a yard of space, a whole lifetime, a thousand years, an eternity, it would be better to live like that than to die right away!
> Just to live, live, and live!

In the twentieth century, George Orwell, the author of *1984,* wrote a powerful tribute to the will to live. As a policeman in India during the 1930s, he was obligated to witness a public execution. Deeply moved, Orwell wrote an essay that was simply entitled "A Hanging." Orwell quoted a boy who was present when the prisoner learned that his appeal had been denied. The boy told Orwell, "He [urinated] on the floor of his cell." Orwell followed the doomed man to the scaffold and studied his hair, the muscles in his back, and his profile. He remembered that a dog jumped into the middle of the procession and tried to lick the prisoner's face. The death march continued. Suddenly, "in spite of the men who gripped him by each shoulder," the doomed man "stepped slightly aside to avoid a puddle." Wrote Orwell, "When I saw the prisoner step aside to avoid the puddle, I saw the mystery, the unspeakable wrongness, of cutting a life short when it is in full tide."

In the latter half of the twentieth century, existentially oriented writers traced psychological distress back to life's ultimate concerns, including the struggle for meaning and personal responsibility as well as the fears of isolation and death. Psychologist Rollo May pointed out that for many individuals, much of the life force is inevitably directed toward the hope of warding off annihilation. In his Pulitzer Prize–winning book, *The Denial of Death*, anthropologist Ernest Becker argued that the primary motive of human beings was to defend themselves from the reality of their own mortality. According to Becker, a great deal of what we do, both good and bad, individually and as a culture, is ultimately designed for this purpose.

Love and Attachment

Love was very much on the minds of the ancient Chinese and Greeks. By 450 BCE, Confucius had already introduced the principle of *jen*, an ideal set of social ethics for relating to others. *Jen* was the linchpin of a philosophical system designed to inspire a "community of hope." It encompassed "benevolence," "humanity," and "moral goodness."

Plato's *Symposium* (ca. 380 BCE) was dedicated to the topic of love. Twelve men are gathered at a banquet in honor of a prominent Athenian.

One of the guests, a physician, suggests that they exchange thoughts on the nature of love. In the course of their discussion, they deal with a number of enduring issues, including the link between human and divine love, the potential healing power of relationships, and the existence of soul mates.

A few years later, Aristotle suggested that the need for kinship bonds surpassed even the desire for wealth and power: "No one would choose the whole world on condition of being alone . . . man is a political creature and one whose nature is to live with others."

Love and attachment rose to prominence in the Middle Ages with the development of the Sufi sect in the Middle East. Abu Hamid Muhammad ibn Muhammad al-Ghazali (1058–1111), a Persian philosopher-mathematician, rejected all earthly expressions of hope in favor of a mystical reunion with God. After al-Ghazali came the great Persian Sufi master and poet of love, Mevlana Jalaluddin Rumi (1207–1273). In his words, "Everything other than love for the most beautiful God is agony of the spirit . . . an advance toward death without seizing hold of the water of life."

At the close of the nineteenth century, the Indian spiritual leader Swami Vivekandanda challenged Westerners to reexamine their utilitarian social ethic. Speaking at the World's Parliament of Religions in Chicago in 1893, Vivekandanda called for a "morality of hope" that is not based solely on a logical analysis of costs and benefits. Instead, he argued that only a belief in the unity of all things can establish a basis for sympathy and altruism. He reasoned that people should be good to one another because they are part of a greater whole: "I do good to others because they are myself."

Throughout the twentieth century, the sociability of an individual appeared in the list of basic traits that was generated by psychologists who studied the makeup of personality. The strongest evidence that being able to relate to others is a basic component of human nature came from the works of psychologists Gordon Allport and Henry S. Odbert. In the 1940s they identified more than 18,000 words that could be used to describe a person's character. The largest category consisted of social adjectives such as *amiable, agreeable, difficult,* and *withdrawn.* Their findings indicated that the bulk of the personality lexicon focused on how well an individual can relate to other human beings. Within a few decades, psychologists began to carve out a science of human relationships and delve deeply into such issues as romantic love, attachment disorders, and social intelligence.

Courage and Mastery

For the ancient Greeks, true success derived from self-mastery. In fact, one of Plato's most famous dialogues (ca. 380 BCE) dealt with the nature of courage, an often ignored component of hope-centered mastery. In all ancient literature, however, it is hard to find a more poetic expression of hope-driven mastery than the following passage by Sophocles in *Antigone*:

> Wonders are many, and none is more wonderful than man; the power that crosses the white sea, making a path under surges that threaten to engulf him. . . . [He rules] the Earth, the eldest of the gods by turning the soil with the offspring of horses, as the ploughs go to and fro from year to year . . . man excellent in wit . . . masters the beast whose lair is in the wilds . . . he tames the horse of shaggy mane, he puts the yoke upon its neck, he tames the tireless mountain bull . . . speech, wind-swift thought, and all the moods that mould a state, hath he taught himself . . . yea, he hath resource for all.

Two of the most influential writings on empowered hope appeared in China between 500 and 200 BCE. Lao Tzu's *Tao Te Ching (The Way and Its Power)* challenged the orthodox recipes for mastery and offered a means of indirectly achieving one's aims through nonviolence, nature, and self-discipline. Sun Tzu's military masterpiece, *The Art of War*, written in the sixth century BCE, continues to fascinate generals, politicians, business leaders, and even coaches and athletes.

In the nineteenth century, the most passionate advocates of a power-oriented approach to success were the German philosophers Arthur Schopenhauer and Friedrich Nietzsche. Schopenhauer argued that philosophy, logic, and reason, as well as character, are ultimately by-products of the human will. As a young man in Frankfurt, Germany, Nietzsche was heading off to war when he came across the spectacle of an imposing military procession. He later wrote, "I felt for the first time that the strongest and highest will to life does not find expression in a miserable struggle for existence, but in a will to war, a will to power, a will to overpower!"

Most twentieth-century conceptions of human personality also included a mastery component. In *The Achieving Society*, David McClelland went so far as to examine the role of achievement motivation in fostering the "hopes of nations." His scope was broad, encompassing ancient Greece and modern India as well as the Protestant work ethic and various communist reform movements. McClelland presented data that an underlying need for achievement is a major force in promoting cultural as well as economic progress.

A closer look at Erik Erikson's conception of the life span reveals that after hope, the next three virtues that must develop are will, initiative, and competence. Harvard psychologist Robert White also challenged the prevailing Freudian and Skinnerian models of a passive humanity. In *Motivation Reconsidered*, he emphasized that humans and other primates have "an innate desire to play, explore, and master their world." In the 1990s, Richard Ryan and Edward Deci put forth a self-determination theory, stressing "the inherent tendency to seek out novelty and challenges, to extend and exercise one's capacities, to explore."

Defining Hope

Hope is a complex emotion. Psychologists such as Ezra Stotland and Rick Snyder have shown a bias toward goal-related explanations of hope. In their view, hope is a positive mind-set about achieving specific life goals in the not-too-distant future. Medical professionals, such as Karl Menninger and Kay Herth, have concentrated on the role of hope in coping and healing as well as in confronting loss and death. Philosophers and theologians like Gabriel Marcel and William F. Lynch have contributed greatly to our thoughts on hope's social and spiritual dimensions. As in the parable of the blind men and the elephant, each tradition has succeeded in grasping part, but not all, of what we call hope. For hope is all of these things and more.

To understand the way that hope is created and the way that it operates as an emotion, keep two images in mind: a network and a building. The network analogy will clarify how hope can be activated and used on a day-to-day basis, and the building analogy will help you to better understand the growth and development of hope.

Hope as a Network

According to psychologist James Averill, hope is most definitely an emotion. Like any emotion, it can be hard to control, it has a feeling tone, and it can motivate behavior. When the average man or woman is asked to rate a list of words to gauge whether they refer to an emotion, *hope* always emerges as a bona fide exemplar. To the ancient and medieval philosophers, hope was routinely listed among the passions.

What exactly is an emotion? We will spare you the details of the tortured debate that occurred throughout most of the twentieth century on this topic. Suffice it to say that there are two main approaches to the study of emotions: a core view and a construction view. Core theorists presume that regions or centers in the brain contain individual emotions. In contrast, construction theorists assume that emotions are systems or networks that draw on multiple areas in the mind and the body to form patterned responses. As our understanding of both mind and body becomes increasingly sophisticated, fewer and fewer emotions are being viewed as "cores."

We define hope as a future-directed, four-channel emotion network constructed from biological, psychological, and social resources. The four channels are the mastery, attachment, survival, and spiritual systems, or subnetworks. The hope network is designed to regulate these systems through both feed-forward and feedback processes that generate a greater perceived probability of power and presence as well as protection and liberation.

This sounds overly technical, so let's break it down. By definition, a network is just a system of interrelated parts. Viewing hope as a network makes it easier to understand how hope relates to mastery, attachment, survival, and spiritual needs. Each of these basic needs is served, respectively, by a control network, a social network, a safety network, and a spiritual network.

The four subnetworks, or channels, make up the larger hope network, and they develop in a semiautonomous fashion. When they work together, one channel can, like a television network, feed two or more other channels. For example, an individual with a strong spiritual foundation may have his or her mastery, attachment, and survival responses heavily influenced by his or her spiritual beliefs. Conversely, two or three channels can feed a single channel, much like a television set can be fed input from a cable box and a DVD player. In an analogous fashion, an individual's mastery, attachment, and survival systems may influence his or her spiritual development.

The hope network operates as both a feed-forward and a feedback system. Hope can be used for moving forward, growing, expanding, and amplifying our responses (feed-forward). This function is most often associated with the mastery aspects of hope, and it has been the primary focus of American psychologists who have studied this emotion. Hope can also be used as a buffer, to reset our physiology (homeostasis) when we are stressed or threatened (feedback). This function is most often associated with the attachment, survival, and spiritual aspects of hope.

Hope as a Five-Story Building

How does the hope network grow and develop? The building blocks of hope are comparable to a multilevel dwelling or structure of five floors or levels (Table 2.1). If you are oriented toward mastery, you may want to imagine an office or a cooperative. If attachments are most important to you, it may be easier to envision a social club or a community center. Those of you who are more geared toward survival may prefer the image of a retreat or a healthcare center. If you have strong spiritual tendencies, your building of hope may be your preferred house of worship. However, by the time you have finished reading this book, we suspect that you will be able to relate to each of these ways of thinking about hope: as a tool for success, as a relationship builder, as a vehicle for coping and healing, and as a spiritual passion.

Of course, there are no actual floors or stories in your brain and your nervous system. By levels, we simply mean separable developmental influences that can be ordered in a logical and temporal fashion, like the letters of the alphabet, and that then coalesce into hope. We identify the levels as follows: genetic and biological factors (level 1); early environmental influences in the form of family, community, and culture that affect you in psychological, social, and spiritual ways (level 2); traits or character strengths that grow out of this basic nature-nurture interaction (level 3); a faith system that arises when your character traits and experiences lead you to invest in particular objects, activities, or principles (level 4); and hope-generated beliefs, feelings, and actions that spring from the combined effect of the first four levels (level 5).

Like any structure, the strength of the upper levels depends on the firmness of the lower levels. For example, a favorable genetic background can offset an imperfect early environment, allowing for solid character development, which ensures adequate faith development and, ultimately, more adaptive hope-based responses.

LEVEL 1: The Genetics of Hope

The most basic level of the hope network consists of the genetic blueprints for mastery, attachment, and survival. There is overwhelming evidence that certain brain structures and pathways are primarily associated with particular motives. The hardware and the software for the mastery, attachment, and survival drives dominate the anatomical and physiological makeup of your nervous system. For example, the frontal lobe of the brain accounts for nearly 40 percent of the cortex, allowing for hope-associated initiative and planning. Damage to the frontal lobe, seen most strikingly in cases of lobotomy, produces apathy and indifference.

Research on the biology of attachment has isolated three important components: parts of the right hemisphere, the hormone oxytocin, and a walnut-shaped structure within the temporal lobe called the amygdala. The right hemisphere is involved in the recognition of emotions that are conveyed through the spoken word or facial expressions. Oxytocin, the "cuddle chemical," cements bonds by rewarding intimate encounters with feelings of warmth, closeness, and safety. The amygdala helps both humans and other animals to separate safe from unsafe encounters and to distinguish between appropriate and inappropriate social displays.

TABLE 2.1: The Building Blocks of Hope

5th Level: BELIEFS & BEHAVIORS Daily hope beliefs Daily hope feelings Daily hope actions	Help is near Empowered Collaboration	The universe is kind Connected Openness	Protection is available Safe Self-regulation
4th Level: THE FAITH SYSTEM	Centers of Value		
3rd Level: CHARACTER TRAITS Mastery-oriented traits	Goal-oriented trust Mediated (collaborative) control Sanctioned commitments		
Attachment-oriented traits		Relationship-Trust Connectedness Openness	
Survival-oriented traits		Survival-Oriented Trust & Care Recruitment Terror Management & Liberation Beliefs Resiliency & Self-Regulation Spiritual Integrity & Symbolic Immortality	
2nd Level: ENVIRONMENT (nuture) Psychological gifts Social & cultural gifts Spiritual Gifts	Empowering care Competence Purpose in life	Reliable care Social skills Benign universe	Coping skills Cultural survivor skills Salvation promises
1st Level: BIOLOGY (nature) Genetic roots and wings	Mastery-related genetics & brain circuits	Attachment-related genetics & brain circuits	Survival-related genetics & brain circuits

The self-protective system is composed of the immune system and a complex set of reflexes as well as the stress-related fight-or-flight response. The immune system includes the skin as well as specialized cells for destroying foreign invaders such as bacteria, viruses, and cancer cells. Examples of self-protective reflexes include the startle response to sudden noise, the reaction of the pupils to light, and the patellar, or knee-jerk, reflex. The human stress response consists of both a short-term crisis reaction and a long-term adaptation process. At the first sign of danger, adrenaline is released, increasing heart rate, respiration, and the concentration of glucose in the blood. If the stress is ongoing, the endocrine system comes into play, which results in the discharge of various stress hormones.

LEVEL 2: Early Environment

The second level (or phase) of the hope-building process involves early nurturing experiences. Human beings are among the most pliable of creatures, profoundly affected by early environmental influences. The quality of emotional, social, and spiritual input will greatly affect the development of the higher levels of the hope structure, including core hope traits, a personal faith system, and the ability to think, feel, and act hopeful on a daily basis.

True mastery is fueled by early empowerment experiences. Later in this book we will go into greater detail about the importance of having a strong presence in your life—be it a parent, a teacher, or a coach—and how this shapes your hope for goals and success. Mastery also requires competence in the form of skills like proper planning, discipline, and allocation of resources. These are the great mastery gifts that families and communities bequeath to their young. Empowerment and competence define how to be masterful, but the why of mastery requires a more transcendent sense of purpose, which is often derived from a religious or spiritual foundation.

Reliable care and love engender trust and openness, which are two critical components of hope. If parents and significant others are consistently available, we learn that our social world is predictable, ready, and willing to meet our needs. These potential hope providers can also instill hope by imparting social skills for appropriately engaging others and for disclosing our feelings, desires, dreams, and aspirations.

On a higher plane, an encounter with a spiritual presence can help to create a vision of a benign, perhaps even caring, universe. For some of us, this will come in the form of a traditional religious system such as Buddhism, Catholicism, or Judaism. For others it may derive from other spiritual experiences, such as spending time in nature, confronting a serious illness or loss, witnessing random acts of kindness, or even participating in sports and secular groups or clubs.

Family members and friends teach us ways of coping. They show us how to problem solve, gather support, plan for bad times, or distract ourselves when nothing more can be done. From our community and culture we learn additional ways of handling stress and uncertainty. Americans have traditionally espoused some form of rugged individualism in the face of stress (e.g., keeping a stiff upper lip or pulling yourself up by your bootstraps). More collectivist cultures—such as the Italians, the Jews, and the Chinese—have been more apt to encourage turning to the group for support and guidance.

Beyond family and community, we seek assurance in the great religious and spiritual systems of the world. While reflecting enormous diversity, all of them offer some form of hope for salvation. Perhaps it is a heavenly reunion with God and loved ones, or it may involve reincarnation or a final release from desire and suffering.

LEVEL 3: Character Traits (the Hopeful Core)

The third level of the hope structure consists of three types of personality traits. The first set of traits is forged from the mastery and attachment elements. *Goal-related trust* is invested in yourself and others. *Mediated control* is a way of experiencing the multiple influences that contribute to human action. At times, individuals may believe they are completely responsible for certain outcomes, but in other circumstances they may see themselves as the beneficiary or the victim of outside forces: human, divine, or both. In the scientific literature, these two ends of the perceived control spectrum are called, respectively, *internal locus of control* and *external locus of control.* In contrast, hope frequently stems from a psychological middle ground, an experience of control that emerges from a perceived association with a larger force or presence. The locus of control resides neither within the self nor outside the self completely but is mediated through a valued relationship. This sense of shared power is the backbone of a healthy physician-patient relationship, a good psychotherapy bond, or a positive student-teacher alliance. Hope is a shared burden, a team effort, guided by *sanctioned commitments* and higher aims.

The second category of hope traits emanates from the attachment motive. *Relational trust* is based on openness and disclosure as well as intimacy and appreciation. Hopeful individuals trust in the availability of a valued person or a transcendent presence. They maintain an attitude of *openness* toward the object of trust, striving for increasingly deeper levels of intimacy and strong self-other bonds. Hope confers a sense of *connectedness.*

The third set of hope traits is geared toward survival. These include *survival-oriented trust* and *care recruitment, terror management* and *liberation beliefs, resiliency* and *self-regulation,* and *spiritual integrity* and *symbolic immortality.* These traits provide a way of addressing the major challenges of the human condition: fear, pain, loss, and death. Survival-oriented trust is a general sense of assurance that your welfare matters to another person, a group, or a higher power. When you need help, care and protection can be found; you will not be abandoned. This notion is beautifully captured in a famous Irish blessing:

> MAY THE ROAD RISE TO MEET YOU,
> MAY THE WIND BE ALWAYS AT YOUR BACK,
> MAY THE SUN SHINE WARM UPON YOUR FACE,
> THE RAINS FALL SOFT UPON YOUR FIELDS AND,
> UNTIL WE MEET AGAIN,
> MAY GOD HOLD YOU IN THE PALM OF HIS HAND.

A capacity for terror management helps the individual to remain calm and centered in the midst of a crisis, preventing either overarousal or emotional paralysis. A liberation belief is the belief that there is always an exit, a way out of difficulty. Spiritual integrity is a sense of wholeness and continuity that can be kept apart from whatever physical insults and losses may be occurring. Symbolic immortality is acquired by investing parts of the self in more enduring aspects of reality. You will learn more about each of these survival skills in later chapters.

LEVEL 4: A Personal Faith System

Faith is the bedrock of hope. Khalil Gibran called it "an oasis in the heart." Mary McLeod Bethune, a daughter of former slaves who became a prominent educator and political activist, had this to say about faith: "Without it nothing is possible. With it, nothing is impossible." Faith can be developed through mastery, attachment, or survival experiences. Faith does not have to be religiously oriented, but it must be deeply felt and central to a person's way of thinking, feeling, and being in the world. If you are completely devoid of faith, you may find yourself plagued by a chronic sense of hopelessness.

Faith requires one or more "centers of value." These are typically people or institutions that you completely trust. It could be your family, one or more friends, God or a higher power, or your chosen vocation as a teacher (faith in education), a chemist (faith in science), or a politician (faith in government). In addition to these external centers of value, many people would add faith in oneself.

LEVEL 5: Hopeful Beliefs and Behaviors

The first four levels of the hope structure ultimately give rise to positive thoughts, actions, and feelings. These are the visible manifestations, or the exterior signs, of hope—the lights and outward flourishes of our genetic endowments, early support, character, and faith. When you have developed hopeful mastery, you always believe that help, in one form or another, is nearby. You feel empowered. You are ready to collaborate, doing your part but anticipating a helping hand.

The signs of solid attachment and healthy trust include a belief that there is a benign force somewhere in the universe. You feel connected to all that is good in the world, and you remain open, expecting an influx of more kindness and love. Hopeful individuals believe that they can access protection whenever they need it. They feel safe. In a calamity, hopeful individuals can remain centered on tasks and priorities without being cast adrift physically, emotionally, or spiritually. In contrast, hopeless individuals are often stuck in their tracks, frozen with dread. In *Hidden Spring*, Sandy Boucher chronicled her confrontation with cancer. Expressing her Buddhist beliefs, she wrote, "When I received the news of cancer, I understood that what is required of me now is that I be fully present to each new experience as it comes and that I engage with it as completely as I can."

FROM THEORY TO PRACTICE: HOW WE HOPE

At this point you might be asking yourself, "How do I put all these ideas into action?" How do you start the hoping process? Just as important, how do you sustain hope when the economy falters, when your health is compromised, when your spouse or partner and you grow apart, when your faith is shaken, or when your dreams and aspirations keep receding further into the night? How then do you keep hope alive?

In the remainder of this book, we will be laying out specific ideas and examples for dealing with the most pressing issues that we must all face. These challenges mirror the motivational building blocks of your hope network: mastery or success strivings, love and attachment needs, the survival instinct, and spiritual concerns. The hope prescriptions differ somewhat among these life domains, but invariably they involve developing and strengthening one or more aspects of hope.

As a way of readying your mind, heart, and soul for what is to come, let's consider, on a general level, how people hope. We can frame this discussion in terms of the four hope domains (mastery, attachment, survival, and spirituality). However, we must also consider where hope lies, biologically and geographically. As we noted earlier, hope is an emotion and a network, and it is linked to higher and lower brain areas and spans the left and right hemispheres. Thus, if you truly want to know how to hope, you need to learn about hoping with the left side of your brain as well as with the right side.

Mastery

In terms of mastery, our research suggests that hope, unlike a wish or a fantasy is reserved for an individual's big goals, the life-defining aims that simultaneously provide an anchor, a trajectory, and a legacy. In casual conversation we might tell a friend or a neighbor, "I hope it is a sunny day tomorrow" or "I hope the store has my favorite ice cream," but these are not heartfelt hopes; they are merely fleeting conversation fillers. When people aim for true success or mastery in life, they switch to the real thing—the genuine, stick-to-your-soul brand of hope.

Two strategies are used by people who want to enlist hope to achieve their highest aspirations. With the right side of the brain, they develop a sense of empowerment, a feeling of strength. If they have been blessed with good enough parenting, such individuals will have internalized the strength they felt from their mother or father. Over time, the power that was behind, beside, and in front of them becomes a part of their sense of self. Upon this foundation, some will add additional layers of strength by binding themselves with powerful spiritual and/or secular institutions, such as the Catholic Church, a Buddhist community, a political party, a civic organization, or even a sports team. Of course, many individuals are not blessed with good enough mothers or fathers. There is still plenty of hope, however. As we will discuss later in this book, it is possible to reparent yourself and your loved ones while also forging other empowering relationships.

With the more verbal and analytical left side of the brain, those who seek hope-driven mastery develop clear priorities; they take an honest inventory of who they are, what they can do, and what is important to them, and they use this information to forge a sense of purpose in life. With a clear direction, and an implicit mission statement, they are unlikely to be derailed, distracted, or defeated by ill fortune, unforeseen challenges, or temporary roadblocks. To use an analogy from the physical sciences: they behave more like gyroscopes than paper airplanes. The latter are blown here and there by the slightest waft of air, but a good gyroscope spins around a fixed axis and maintains its orientation regardless of any competing external forces that enter its field.

Attachment

Building and maintaining quality relationships is an enormously important hope task. This requires trust and openness. With the right side of the brain, those who are high in hope are able to maintain the basic feeling that there are "enough" people who are trustworthy. Because we are social animals, we are naturally wired to trust other human beings. However, as Erik Erikson pointed out long ago, some degree of mistrust is also likely to develop early in life. From the time we are infants, the world does not respond perfectly to our every need. Sometimes we are not heard or seen. We go without food when we are hungry and without water when we are thirsty.

If the world is responsive enough, however, we will trust that the majority of people we encounter in life are good, at least most of the time. This means that we can rely on them for support: to be there for us in good and bad times and to care for, listen to, and advise us. For those among us who have been victimized by abandonment or deceit, it is still possible to rebuild trust. We just have to know whom to surround ourselves with for this to occur. We will discuss this in-depth in a later chapter.

Openness is the other key relational skill for increasing and sustaining hope. More hopeful individuals cultivate permeable boundaries, allowing for the influx of good words and deeds from the outside world. However, as a left-brain activity, openness to hope is more like the biological process of osmosis and less like an open wound. An open wound is indiscriminately open; it must be covered, lest it permit dirt and germs to enter the body. In cell biology, which is governed by osmosis, only certain types and amounts of fluids and particles are allowed to enter, by way of a semipermeable membrane. In a similar fashion, more hopeful individuals seek out positive input but maintain a barrier against external sources of negativity. They seek out good hope providers, people who offer encouragement and a kind presence. At the same time, they learn to minimize their contact with dream killers and other mean-spirited individuals.

Survival

More hopeful individuals are able to stay centered, which means that they can remain emotionally self-regulated, regardless of external pressures. In part, emotional regulation involves physical regulation of the fight-and-flight system within the brain and the rest of the body.

Research is mounting that the right side of the brain may be more strongly linked to the limbic system, the area in the middle of your brain that acts like a sentry or a threat detector. The limbic system includes structures such as the amygdala and the hippocampus, which are implicated in producing states of fear, anxiety, and rage. This sentry in the brain has the potential to function like a rapidly rising and falling barometer—not unlike the homeland security code that is green when the country is considered to be at low risk but that jumps to blue (guarded or general risk), yellow (elevated or significant risk), orange (high risk), or red (severe risk) when terrorist activity looms.

When threats surface, more hopeful individuals are able to stay somewhere in the middle of the threat hierarchy. They are not off the chart in either direction, because too little reactivity would be just as bad as too much reactivity. How are the more hopeful individuals able to stay centered? We know that stressful events are harder to deal with if you think that the threat is completely beyond your control, that it is something that will never end, or that it is something that you cannot understand. In contrast, more hopeful individuals retain a sense of control, predictability, and meaning.

Spiritual beliefs give some people the sense that there is something inside and around them that is more potent than any present or future danger. Their spirituality assures them that "this too shall pass" and provides them with a larger worldview that imparts meaning to their stressful life events. For those who are not religious or even spiritual, control, predictability, and meaning may still be derived from memories of successful past coping efforts, from stories of others who have weathered the vicissitudes of life, or through the adoption of specific stress-management techniques.

With the left brain, more hopeful individuals are able to skillfully generate options and alternatives. Our research with children as young as seven years old confirms that more hopeful individuals generate more solutions to problems. More hopeful individuals never feel trapped, stuck, or cornered. They utilize multiple ways of coping, including logical analyses of the pros and cons of different game plans, social support, and the ability to weigh when to act as well as how to respond. They recall past strategies that worked in dealing with similar situations but may also borrow techniques that have been used by themselves or others for handling entirely different scenarios. They engage in anticipatory coping, which means that they plan ahead when they see trouble coming, and they imagine different possible courses of action. They build bridges and networks with family members, friends, and organizations that can provide release from otherwise inescapable dilemmas in the future.

Spirituality

As we noted previously, more hopeful individuals are not necessarily religious. However, they do share in common a spiritual foundation of some kind. Spiritual beliefs carry a strong emotional charge, and some psychologists believe that they are primarily associated with the right side of the brain. This would explain why it is often so difficult to put into words the nature of our spirituality. Of course, we also possess spiritual beliefs that can be articulated, and these are probably linked with the left side of the brain.

In terms of right-brain functioning, more hopeful individuals have a deep faith in one or more centers of values. As we noted before, an individual can center his or her life around a variety of things, including a deity, a family, a cultural heritage, a political party, or a vocation. Because of early exposure, genetic or historical links (in the case of family or culture), or simply repetition and total investment, these centers burrow into the right side of the brain, where they acquire a deep quality of unassailable truthfulness. Faithful dedication to these centers of value confers feelings of empowerment and a sense that there is goodness in the universe. For some people, there are the added benefits of experiencing moments of mystical oneness and a sense of symbolic immortality that is derived from being part of a larger, ongoing reality that will continue beyond this lifetime.

With the left brain, more hopeful individuals practice spiritual openness. They engage in rituals that will increase the chances of a spiritual experience. For the more religiously inclined, this may mean going to a house of worship, engaging in regular prayer, or singing and listening to hymns. For the nonreligious, it may consist of walks in nature, going on a spiritual retreat, or attending a gathering or conference of like-minded individuals.

More hopeful individuals also employ their spirituality for terror-management purposes. The religious pray for help, healing, and guidance. A Buddhist retreats into meditation, seeking insight and a sense of inner peace. A nature lover heads for the garden in search of remedies made from fresh herbs, pure water, and clean air. A scientist toils in the laboratory, convinced that this work will lead to a cure for a deadly disease. An economist crunches numbers, convinced that this will generate a recovery plan and avoid a national financial crisis.

EXERCISE 3: How Do You Hope?

Go back to Exercise 1 and review your three most significant hopes. What are you learning about the ways in which you hope? Are you primarily oriented toward mastery? Are attachment concerns more pressing? Is survival the dominant issue in your life? Perhaps each of your hopes is oriented around two or more of these motives. And what about your spiritual life? Are you satisfied with the time and energy you are putting into mastery, attachment, and survival or spiritual matters? List three short-term steps to achieve greater balance. Be as specific as possible. You are most likely to succeed if you stick to behaviors with at least an 80 percent chance of completion.

3

What Is Hopelessness?

Dante's portrayal of hell featured nine circles: spiritual torture chambers that contained little air yet plenty of fire and ice. Chronic hopelessness has been similarly described as "hell on earth." Moreover, like Dante's circles, the inferno of hopelessness is impossible to reduce to a single mode of suffering. Harriet Tubman, who is known as the Moses of her people, helped to liberate more than 300 of her fellow African Americans. Nevertheless, when she initially secured her own freedom, she felt cast adrift, like a "neglected weed" and a "stranger in a strange land." Virginia Woolf, plagued with debilitating mood swings most of her life, wrote in her diary, "It's like banging one's head against a wall at the end of a blind alley." Novelist William Styron, in *Darkness Visible*, described his own encounter with despair as a "toxic and un-nameable tide . . . most closely connected to drowning or suffocation."

Like Dante's circles of hell, it is possible to differentiate nine types of hopelessness. Three of them (the "pure forms") are doom, alienation, and powerlessness, and they can be attributed to breakdowns associated with, respectively, the mastery, attachment, and survival motives. These describe the experiences that plagued Tubman, Styron, and Woolf. The other six types of hopelessness are helplessness, captivity, feeling forsaken, feeling uninspired, oppression, and limitation; these can be characterized as "blended forms," because they consist of a disruption of both a primary and a secondary motive. Helplessness, for instance, is caused by a breakdown in survival (the primary disruption) as well as in mastery (the secondary disruption).

Before we delve any further into these nine varieties, let's consider the extent to which hopelessness affects our lives. You can think of the following section as a first look at these circles of hell. The remainder of this chapter will give you a more in-depth understanding of each variety of hopelessness.

The Impact of Hopelessness

It is hard to overstate the impact of hopelessness on individuals as well as on society as a whole. Hopelessness is everywhere. As we have already suggested, a variety of life circumstances can engender hopelessness, and multiple traps, obstacles, and minefields can cripple the mind, the body, and the spirit. Moreover, hopelessness shows no bias; it is an equal-opportunity syndrome. No one is immune, regardless of age, creed, color, or nationality. It can strike children as well as the elderly, the sick and the well, the prosperous and the poor.

The ancient Greeks as well as Dante portrayed evil as a nine-headed "monster." For the Greeks, the "many-headed" beast was Hydra, a serpentine creature that destroyed its victims with poisonous fumes and flaming arrows. Although some may view this as a mere coincidence, we may ask whether it represents a deeper insight into the varied nature of hopelessness. The snake-shaped constellation Hydra, which can be seen low in the southern sky in spring, even though it is the largest constellation, contains only one bright star.

After a lifetime of experiencing the highs and lows of being a public figure from a minority background, Sidney Poitier reflected on the universal nature of hopelessness:

> We suffer pain, we hang tight to hope, we nurture expectations, we are plagued occasionally by fears, we are haunted by defeats and unrealized hopes. The hopelessness of which I speak is not limited. It's in everything. There is not racial or ethnic domination of hopelessness. It's everywhere.

Consider depression and suicide. Hopelessness is a major factor in depression. When individuals lose faith in themselves, the world, and the future, they invariably become depressed. Depression affects nearly 15 million Americans and, according to the World Health Organization, is the leading cause of disability worldwide for people age five and older. Hopelessness is also the number one predictor of suicide. The American Foundation for Suicide Prevention notes that since the year 2000, more than 9 million suicides have been reported. In addition, "Each year approximately one million people in the world die by suicide. This toll is higher than the total number of deaths each year from war and homicide combined."

Even if the impact of hopelessness were limited to just depression and suicide, you would think that it would be viewed as a pressing public health concern. You would expect regular warnings from the surgeon general as well as intermittent public service announcements on television, on the radio, and in major periodicals. One or more celebrities might take on the cause to raise money for research and educational programming. Lobbyists and citizens' action groups would be clamoring for more federal spending. However, there is clearly no "hope crusade" in our midst. Why not?

Hopelessness is often invisible to the untrained eye. It can take a variety of forms, and the impact is sometimes not immediately apparent. To illustrate the insidious and the serious nature of hopelessness, we will draw a few analogies with medical conditions. When hopelessness saps your drive for success, it may be compared to an undiagnosed iron deficiency, the most common form of nutritional deficiency in the industrialized world. If your iron level is seriously depleted, oxygen cannot be transported efficiently from your lungs to the rest of your body, so you feel weak and tired. In a similar fashion, when the mastery motive is disrupted, it can seem as if the wind has been taken out of your sails; your ability to pursue goals is limited, and your zest for life is gone.

When hopelessness is clothed in decades of oppression, disability, or poverty, it might be likened to high blood pressure, a silent killer that slowly but surely destroys vital organs. It can be hard for a casual observer to understand why the oppressed, the disabled, or the poor sometimes appear to live for the moment, instead of planning for the future. What might not be obvious from a distance is that the perceived absence of a future is part and parcel of hopelessness. There is nothing to live for, to plan for, and to hope for. High blood pressure, if left untreated, can also give rise to a sudden stroke or a heart attack. Hopelessness, if left unchecked, can precipitate rage and acts of violent desperation. (Recall Columbine, Virginia Tech, and other cases of poor or alienated individuals who became easy recruits for suicide missions and other terrorist activities.)

When hopelessness hits early and often in the life of an individual, its impact is similar to a toxic substance that enters the body unnoticed, only to create health problems later. For example, the effects of asbestos exposure typically take fifteen to twenty years to surface.

The best medical analogy of all may be the immune system. Prolonged hopelessness can suppress the immune system, lowering the body's resistance to foreign invaders and diminishing the capacity for regeneration and repair. Over time, the perpetually hopeless are more likely to fall ill. Like hope, your immune system keeps you safe and strong. When it is working right, it is adaptive. When it is lacking, you are vulnerable. When it is overtaxed, your body may work against itself, perhaps leading to an autoimmune disorder. True hope is strong enough to weather all seasons, but false hope is maladaptive and even counter-productive. If you lack a functioning immune system, no supplement, no medication, and no miracle drug in the world will help you. Without hope, human beings cannot succeed, love, trust, or survive.

Hopelessness wears on the mind, the body, and the spirit. An individual without hope is unable to plan for the future or envision alternative ways of achieving important goals. He or she lacks drive, creativity, and flexibility. (This is what psychologist Rick Snyder labeled the "wills and ways" of hope.) Hopelessness is akin to a psychological lobotomy: it robs the sufferer of a willful, goal-oriented approach to life. Without a future and nothing to aim toward, the hopeless are lost, cast emotionally adrift.

Without hope, trust and openness are replaced by cynicism and withdrawal. Unable to trust, the hopeless pull away from others, reducing the odds of experiencing what philosopher Gabriel Marcel called the "fruits and pledges" of hope (i.e., present-day support and future commitments). Instead of intimacy and empowerment, feelings of abandonment, alienation, and anger take hold. A vicious cycle is created: mistrust is followed by a fearful retreat from society, which fuels further mistrust and self-isolation.

Depending on the type of hopelessness, one or more negative emotions will dominate the psyche. In some cases, the experience will be a prevailing sense of anxiety. Peace of mind will be replaced by a tense, vigilant countenance. For others, the problem will be fear, a gnawing concern that important outcomes will never be realized. Still others will languish in regret and exhaustive ruminations over "what might have been."

Hopelessness is literally a health hazard. If one has no hope, it is harder to maintain homeostasis, because it is much easier to be pushed out of your physiological comfort zone. For example, when your values and your priorities are in conflict or you experience role strain (e.g., being both a mother and a wage earner), your blood pressure and your heart rate increase and the stress hormone cortisol is released, which elevates your blood glucose level and increases stomach acid production while suppressing your immune system.

Those who are defensive or inhibited risk an increase in blood pressure, especially during and after stressful encounters. Highly defensive individuals produce fewer alpha waves in their frontal lobes, an activity that has been associated with increased natural (cancer) killer-cell output. If you have a heart attack and do not have at least one or two close friends, your chance of having a second, fatal heart attack is much higher. If you remain isolated, oxytocin, the "love hormone," will remain trapped within your pituitary gland instead of coursing through your body to diminish pain, depression, anxiety, and blood pressure. Fewer surges of oxytocin will make wound healing more difficult and drug-related side effects more serious.

The spiritual costs of hopelessness may be the most devastating. Hope is about transcendent aims, a higher calling that fills life with meaning and purpose. In contrast, a hopeless existence is marked by apathy and underachievement. Harold Kushner found in his forty years as a rabbi that "the people who had the most trouble with death were those who felt that they had never done anything worthwhile in their lives."

Psychologist Paul Pruyser asserted that hope rests on the belief that there is a benign force somewhere in the universe. When one loses hope, the world is no longer a good or safe place, and it may seem, in the words of William Shakespeare, as though "Hell is empty and the devils are here." The experiences of trauma survivors offer an especially powerful example of a faith-challenged worldview. In *Trauma and Recovery*, Judith Herman compared the posttraumatic experiences of female abuse victims to those of male combat veterans. For both groups, it seemed as though the world had grown dark and God was nowhere to be found:

Traumatic events call into question basic human relationships. They breach the attachments of family, love, and community. . . . They undermine the belief systems that give meaning to human experience. They violate the victim's faith in a natural or divine order and cast the victim into a state of existential crisis.

A deeply hopeful person assumes that life and the greater universe are moving in a positive direction. This kind of ultimate hope may be focused on one's final fate in the hereafter, on one's children and succeeding generations, on the planet, or simply on a better world. Without hope, there is no faith in the future, no sense that everything will someday be all right and that things will be resolved and unified, if not uplifted. In Marcel's words, there is no "hope in thee for us."

In Dostoyevsky's classic, *The Brothers Karamazov*, the cynical Ivan recounts terrible stories of child abuse to his brother, Alyosha. Ivan is convinced that the suffering of little children eliminates the possibility of any final harmony:

> When the mother embraces the fiend who threw her child to the dogs, and all three cry aloud with tears, "Thou art just, O Lord!" then, of course, the crown of knowledge will be reached and all will be made clear. . . . I can't accept that harmony. . . . It's not worth the tears of that one tortured child who beat itself on the breast with its little fist and prayed in its stinking outhouse, with its unexpiated tears to "dear, kind God"! It's not worth it, because those tears are unatoned for. . . . How are you going to atone for them? What good can hell do, since those children have already been tortured? And what becomes of harmony, if there is hell?

THE VARIETIES OF HOPELESSNESS

Fear is often considered the opposite of hope. In reality, however, the experience of hopelessness is typically devoid of fear. Hopelessness is beyond fear. In *Inferno*, Dante asked Beatrice, his deceased true love, how she could live in hell without fear. She replied, "Fear befits things with power for injury, not things that lack such power." When you abandon all hope, there is nothing left to fear.

If there is a single, unifying theme in the experience of hopelessness, it is a sense of entrapment. For example, in many folk traditions, a devil comes bearing locks and chains. In Greek mythology, those who upset the gods were ensnared, bound, or otherwise immobilized. Angry Zeus chained Prometheus to the side of a mountain. Ulysses, caught between a rock and a hard place, encountered a six-headed monster to his right (Scylla) and a deadly whirlpool on his left (Charybdis). Anyone who looked directly into the eyes of the snake-haired Medusa was petrified—literally turned to stone.

The need for freedom is as vital as the air we breathe. Near the beginning of the film version of J. R. R. Tolkien's *The Two Towers*, there is a powerful scene that affirms the soul's longing for liberation. It features the warrior Aragorn and the heroine Eowyn, two of the principal forces of light. As Aragorn prepares for a great battle against the forces of darkness, he tries to dissuade Eowyn from taking part in the fray. Eowyn refuses to sit idle in the face of encroaching evil.

Aragorn: What do you fear, my lady?
Eowyn: A cage. To stay behind bars until use and old age accepts them, and all chance of valor has gone beyond recall and desire.
Aragorn: I do not think that will be your fate.

The need for freedom can be taken for granted by those who have never felt trapped. In contrast, if you were to ask any man, woman, or child who has been enslaved by years of abuse, oppression, or imprisonment how it felt, they might very well say to you, "I can't fully describe it. You had to be there." Perhaps Pearl Buck put it best: "None who have always been free can understand the terrible fascinating power of the hope for freedom of those who are not free."

In the absence of hope, a variety of unwanted thoughts and feelings may engulf you. Like Scrooge in Charles Dickens's *A Christmas Carol*, you may be visited by any number of ghosts. Moreover, as Scrooge discovered, some of these ghosts may represent unfinished business from the past, whereas others will be more reflective of present or future concerns. Be assured that the darkness can be lifted.

In Figure 3.1, we have arranged the nine different types of despair into a circle of hopelessness. The first step in dealing with these various shades of darkness is to understand their origin, or developmental roots. If you lose an object of value, it helps to know how or where you lost it. Similarly, to restore hope you must grasp both the process of recovery and the motivational context, or life space, in which the loss occurred. If the hoping process were likened to a series of nine bridges that transport you from zones of darkness to areas of light, then you must know which bridge to take and how to cross it.

Figure 3.1. The Circle of Hopelessness

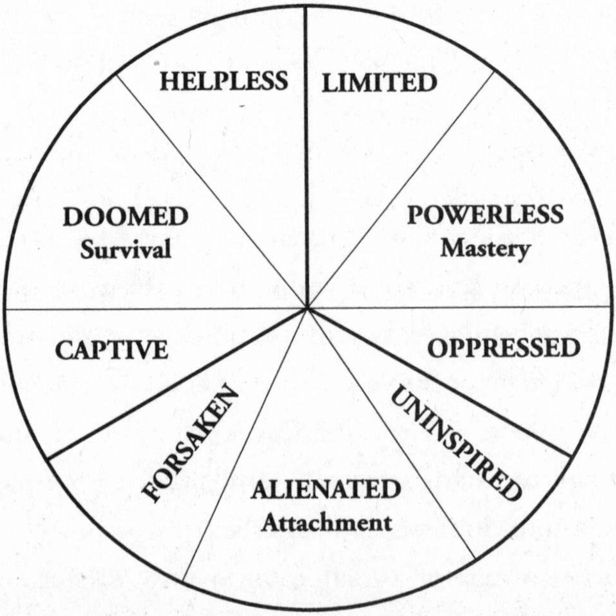

DOOM

Doom is a pure form of hopelessness that results when the survival motive is profoundly disrupted. Individuals who are weighed down by this form of despair presume that life is over and that death is imminent. Who, you might ask, is most vulnerable to sinking into this particular circle of hell? The most common sufferers are those who are diagnosed with a serious, life-threatening illness as well as those who see themselves worn out by age or infirmity. Such individuals feel doomed, trapped in a fog of irreversible decline.

In *Illness as Metaphor*, Susan Sontag provided more than a glimmer of hope for the physically ill. In her brilliant survey of medical history, she noted that a good deal of the hopelessness that surrounds illness is manufactured by the despair-laden metaphors that social institutions attach to certain diagnoses. For example, two centuries ago tuberculosis was dubbed the "thief of life." In the twentieth century, cancer meant death at the hands of a "secret invader" that "doesn't knock before it enters." Sontag also noted that in recent years, AIDS has become the "generic rebuke to life and hope."

One of the darkest depictions of an individual doomed by illness appeared in Leo Tolstoy's haunting novella, *The Death of Ivan Ilyich*:

He struggled desperately in that black sack into which an unseen, invincible force was thrusting him. He struggled as a man condemned to death struggles in the hands of an executioner, knowing there is no escape . . . he was being shoved into that black hole.

The aging process itself is enough to engender a sense of doomed hopelessness in some individuals. This is particularly likely when a person is plagued by a sense of regret for lost opportunities and times gone by. Aging well can be difficult, particularly in a youth-oriented society. The nineteenth-century Swiss philosopher Henri Amiel noted, "To grow old is the masterpiece of wisdom, and one of the most difficult chapters in the art of life." In *David Copperfield*, Charles Dickens's protagonist, weary from years of strife and disappointment, is shrouded in a "long and gloomy night . . . haunted by the ghosts of many hopes." Poet John Greenleaf Whittier wrote, "Of all the sad words of tongue and pen, the saddest of these: It might have been."

Like serious illness, advancing age can evoke feelings of entrapment, futility, and irreversible evil. Tolstoy, in middle age, was obsessed with death. Death appeared to him in nightmares, taking the form of a square room from which there was "no escape—no way out or in." An elderly female client of Tony's had been preserving fruits her entire life. Upon turning seventy-nine, she began having recurrent dreams of standing under a beautiful grapevine. She had just eaten a meal but remained hungry. However, each time she tried to reach for a cluster of grapes, it was beyond her grasp.

Arthur Miller's *Death of a Salesman* may be the quintessential American portrait of a failed life. Sixty-three-year-old Willy Loman made one bad decision after another and grew increasingly despondent. As one reviewer put it, his was a life enveloped in the "stench of hopelessness." When the present became too painful or the future appeared utterly bleak, Willy relied on comforting but illusory tales of previous successes. Grounded in nothing but false hope, Willy devised various ways of killing himself. He fashioned a makeshift gas pipe but ultimately staged a fatal car accident. The life of Willy Loman went up in smoke when he could no longer twist the past, cope with the present, or bear the future. "I'm not interested in stories about the past . . . the woods are burning. . . . There's a blaze going on all around. . . . The gist of it is that I haven't got a story left in my head. . . . I gotta go, baby. Bye! Bye!"

ALIENATION

Alienation is a pure form of hopelessness that results when the attachment motive is profoundly disrupted. Alienated individuals believe that they are somehow different from everyone else. Moreover, they feel cut loose, as though they have been deemed no longer worthy of love, care, or support. As a result they tend to close themselves off out of a fear of pain and rejection.

Alienated individuals may feel out of place for a variety of reasons. Sociocultural alienation occurs when individuals believe that their personally cherished ways of living are no longer honored by a larger group to which they formerly felt allied. Sociopolitical alienation can result when an individual's personally valued political beliefs are at odds with the ruling majority. Sociotemporal alienation may develop when individuals feel either ahead of their time, or as though time has passed them by.

Alienation is a perennial theme in world literature and religions. In Greek mythology, Oedipus was tricked into killing his father and marrying his mother. As punishment, he was driven from the city and spent the rest of his days alone, wandering from one lonely outpost to the next. The Qur'an warns that the afterlife of sinners will bring permanent estrangement from both Allah and loved ones. In the biblical story of Job, alienation from God and from family and friends—not the multitude of physical ailments devised by the devil—produced the greatest suffering. As a precaution, the Africans who practice Ifa hold regular blending ceremonies to prevent new community members from feeling adrift.

It is hardly a coincidence that the two greatest poems about hell were written by outcasts. Dante was banished from Florence for life and labeled an enemy of the state. John Milton, the author of *Paradise Lost*, was similarly ostracized. Like Dante, Milton spent much of his adulthood as a social and political insider who hobnobbed with the rich and famous. However, in his later years he found himself progressively marginalized, first by blindness, then by a new ruling party that he did not support.

In the nineteenth century Charles Darwin wrote of the human "dislike of solitude" and "the wish for a society beyond the family." He pointed out that solitary confinement is one of the severest punishments that can be inflicted on a human being. At the turn of the twentieth century, the sociologist Émile Durkheim demonstrated that many suicides derive from a lack of religious, domestic, or political integration. Half a century later, Erich Fromm suggested that humanity had been effectively "torn out of nature" with the evolution of "self-awareness."

Ron Kovic's *Born on the Fourth of July* is one of the most powerful and poignant autobiographies from the Vietnam War era. Kovic served two tours of duty in Vietnam, and during his second tour he was shot and left paralyzed from the chest down. Reflecting on his life before and after Vietnam, Kovic wistfully recalled growing up in an era of clearly defined social expectations, a foreign policy of good versus evil, and a cultural landscape in which Audie Murphy, one of the most highly decorated soldiers of World War II, and John Wayne, a movie star who made many war films, were revered. In stark contrast, Kovic felt profoundly alienated in a country that had grown deeply ambivalent about the war and the role of the United States in policing the world.

Kovic's most disturbing postwar experience came during the final night of the 1972 Republican National Convention. Kovic and two other disabled veterans were rebuffed for disrupting President Richard Nixon's acceptance speech.

All three of us took a deep breath and shouted at the top of our lungs, "Stop the bombing, stop the war, stop the bombing, stop the war." . . . Secret service agents grabbed our chairs from behind and began pulling us backward. . . . A short guy ran up to me and spat in my face. "Traitor!" he screamed.

POWERLESSNESS

Powerlessness is a pure form of hopelessness that results when the mastery motive is profoundly disrupted. From birth, human beings have an insatiable need to explore, manipulate, and control their environment. Infants will quickly learn to shift their gaze, kick their legs, or vary their cries if their responses can make any difference, from the presence of a smiling caretaker to the movement of a hanging mobile. Individuals of every age need to believe that they can author the stories of their lives.

In the film *Braveheart*, Mel Gibson portrayed the thirteenth-century Scottish hero-liberator William Wallace. Some of the most moving scenes dealt with the importance of having a voice. This was especially true of the film's climax. Wallace was betrayed, captured, and put on the rack for torture. Near death, he was nevertheless able to summon one last shout: "*Freedom!*"

Witnessing Wallace's last stand was his longtime nemesis, King Edward I of England. Once an imposing figure, Edward had been reduced to an impotent husk. Age and illness had left him mute, stripped of the powers of speech. The princess looked disdainfully at her moribund father-in-law and delivered the final deathblow:

You see? Death comes to us all. And it comes to William Wallace. But before death comes to you, know this: your blood dies with you. A child who is not of your line grows in my belly. Your son will not sit long on the throne. I swear it.

Sonny, a forty-year-old African American man, sought psychotherapy for performance anxiety. During his first session, he revealed a history of depression, low self-esteem, job stress, and thoughts of suicide. As part of his intake assessment, Sonny was given a sentence-completion test. The first sentence was "My dominant feeling is _____." Sonny filled in the blank with the word *hopeless*.

In Sonny's case, performance anxiety represented an inability to face life as an adult. Despite three college degrees and proficiency in several languages, Sonny found it impossible to function in a job that was commensurate with his ability. In fact, Sonny felt more like a ten-year-old child than a mature adult. His childishness was also expressed outwardly. For example, although he was more than six feet tall, Sonny was always stooped over; he seemed unable to rise to his full height. Sonny also spoke like a child. His tone was typically high-pitched. He squinted and strained when pronouncing multisyllabic words. Sonny's reduced stature was further symbolized in dream sequences: "I look so small, like a little kid, even though everyone else is grown up."

In therapy, Sonny traced his difficulties back to childhood and a father who was equally afraid of life. Sonny described his father as a weak, timid figure who had married a woman six years his senior. "I think he needed a mother to take care of him," said Sonny, with obvious bitterness in his voice. "My father never said much to me. He never encouraged me, never coached me, and never gave me a reason to feel good at anything. What he told me over and over again was 'You'll be like me—a nothing. You'll eke out an existence—that's it.'"

HELPLESSNESS

A feeling of helplessness arises when the survival (primarily) and the mastery (secondarily) systems are simultaneously thwarted. Helpless individuals no longer believe that they can live safely in the world. They feel exposed and vulnerable, like a cat that has been declawed or a bird that has been grounded by a broken wing. In the words of one trauma survivor, quoted by Judith Herman, "I was terrified to go anywhere on my own. . . . I felt so defenseless and afraid that I just stopped doing anything." Another defining feature of helplessness is an ongoing failure to take advantage of the most basic degrees of freedom. Herman related how a male trauma survivor lost even the ability to open doors or turn on lights.

Prolonged exposure to traumatic and uncontrollable life events puts individuals at risk for developing a profound sense of hopelessness. Psychologist Martin Seligman and his colleagues demonstrated the devastating effects of "learned helplessness" on animals. In a typical experiment, they restrained a dog or a rat and then subjected the animal to an aversive stimulus such as mild shock. After several trials, the animal learned that escape efforts were futile. In future trials, even though the animals were not restrained, they would lie passively and endure the shock.

In humans, repeated failure in dealing with adversity (survival) can also affect the mastery system. When survival is threatened, individuals rely on all their resources, including their capacities for problem solving, exploring, and manipulating the environment. However, when repeated efforts fail to produce any demonstrable change, they may forfeit their hope for mastery as well as their most basic survival instincts.

At the age of thirty, Barbara sought therapy for the first time. In the initial session, she made it clear that she did not want to spend months dredging up the past. What she wanted was help in dealing with chronic anxiety and her intrusive parents and in-laws. However, within a few sessions, Barbara began to open up and shifted the focus to her childhood. She was a trauma survivor who had been sexually abused by an uncle as well as emotionally abused by her alcoholic father and manipulative mother.

As soon as she turned eighteen, Barbara had moved a thousand miles away from home. Unfortunately, her parents continued to call her on a daily basis, second-guessing every decision she made. To make matters worse, both of them repeatedly tried to put Barbara in the middle of their own tortured emotional crossfire. Barbara longed for greater security and autonomy. In the course of therapy she became enraptured with the Oscar-winning film *Crouching Tiger, Hidden Dragon*. She explained to her therapist that "the woman in that movie is so free and strong. She doesn't have to take any crap from men. She can do what she wants. She's not helpless."

CAPTIVITY

So this is hell. I'd never have believed it. You remember all we were told about the torture-chambers, the fire and brimstone, the "burning marl." Old wives' tales! There's no need for red-hot pokers. Hell is—other people!

—JEAN-PAUL SARTRE, *NO EXIT*

A feeling of captivity arises when the survival (primarily) and the attachment (secondarily) systems are simultaneously thwarted. The psychologist William James observed that "no other stimulus has the power to affect me like another human being." His insight relates to two forms of hopelessness that can result from dysfunctional relationships. The first, other-imprisonment, is the more obvious, because it consists of physical or emotional captivity enforced by an individual or a group. Prisoners fall into this category, as well as those who are held captive in a controlling, abusive relationship. The second, self-imprisonment, consists of physical or emotional captivity imposed by oneself.

Consider Jean-Paul Sartre's classic play, *No Exit*. Three recently deceased evildoers find themselves in hell. At first they wonder, "Where is the punishment befitting our crimes?" Where are the pitchforks and the scalding flames so graphically illustrated in Dante's *Inferno*? As they begin to share their life stories, they discover something in common. All three of them failed to commit to love, having abandoned those closest to them in favor of a lesser aim. Finally, they understand. Hell can be an eternity with the wrong person, someone who brings out the worst in you, someone who tortures you day after day, hour after hour. In a similar vein, William James observed that "the hell to be endured hereafter, of which theology tells, is no worse than the hell we can make for ourselves in this world."

There is no more insidious form of entrapment than self-imprisonment. This occurs when an individual cannot leave a bad relationship because the person's sense of self will not allow it. Sometimes the problem is low self-esteem. In other cases there is an unconscious need to revisit and repair the past, what Sigmund Freud called *repetition compulsion*.

An even more complicated type of self-imprisonment derives from *projective identification*: one projects onto (or attributes to) the other person one's own bad qualities; leaving the other person thus becomes impossible without reclaiming the unwanted parts of oneself. Such individuals cannot leave because they would be losing part of themselves. The good parts can also be projected, to offset a fear of separateness or to protect valued aspects of the self from other negative inner qualities. These individuals cannot leave because they would be in danger of self-destruction.

Albert Camus' short story "The Adulterous Woman" is a classic existential tale of self-imprisonment. It is the story of Janine, an unhappy middle-aged woman who "goes through the motions of her uneventful life with her uneventful husband." Janine knew that her marriage was a loveless contract between "two frightened children" unable to face life alone. However, she could not bear the thought of living by herself. Indeed, she sensed that the reality of her existence rested on her husband's dependence on her. Despairing, Janine realized that "she was overcoming nothing, she was not happy, she was going to die . . . without ever being liberated."

Janine's act of adultery did not involve another man. Instead she flirted with freedom and possibility. One night on a business trip, while her husband lay asleep, Janine snuck away "to be with the cosmos." Standing high atop a terrace that surrounded her desert fort, she opened herself to the night sky, and for a few fleeting moments it seemed that the "sap again rose in her body."

Looking out at the limitless expanse of a dry, cold night, Janine was transfixed by the "drifting flares" of stars that fell like "sparkling icicles." She was "filled with such a sweet, vast melancholy that it closed her eyes." She knew that this kingdom had been eternally promised to her but that it would never be hers again. Reluctantly, Janine returned to her "icy room" and lay down. When her husband awoke, he was bewildered to find his wife "weeping copiously, unable to restrain herself."

Feeling Forsaken

My God, my God, why have You forsaken me?
Why are You so far from helping me and from
the words of my roaring? . . . You took me
out of the womb; You made me hope
when I was upon my mother's breasts.

—Psalm 22

A feeling of being forsaken arises when the attachment (primarily) and the survival (secondarily) systems are simultaneously thwarted. The word *forsaken* refers to an experience of total abandonment that leaves individuals feeling alone in their time of greatest need. Recall Job in the Bible, crumpled over and covered with sores, pleading with a seemingly indifferent God, or consider the plight of the *hibakusha*, the victims of the atomic bombing of Hiroshima and Nagasaki. The *hibakusha* were feared, isolated, and ultimately abandoned by the Japanese people during the years following the end of World War II.

In *Death in Life*, Robert Jay Lifton quoted some of the victims of the atomic bomb. One of these was writer Yoko Ota: "No one came to take care of the injured people and no one came to tell us how and where we should spend the night. We were simply left alone." Another victim, an engineer, lamented, "My children were treated very unkindly at school. Other children would taunt them and cry out: Son of a patient of the A-bomb hospital." A third victim, an elderly woman, recalled, "At that moment we all became completely separate human beings. . . . I thought, 'There is no God, no Buddha. . . . There is no help.'"

Time magazine correspondent Johanna McGeary recounted the story of Laetitia, a fifty-one-year-old single mother in South Africa who was diagnosed with AIDS in 1996:

> Laetitia's employers fired her . . . her children were ashamed. . . . Her mother ordered Laetitia out of the house. When her daughter wouldn't leave, the mother threatened to sell the house to get rid of her daughter. Then she walled off her daughter's room with plywood partitions, leaving the daughter a pariah, alone in a cramped, dark space without windows and only a flimsy door opening into the alley. When Laetitia ventures outdoors, neighbors snub her, tough boys snatch her purse, children taunt her.

FEELING UNINSPIRED

A feeling of being uninspired arises when the attachment (primarily) and the mastery (secondarily) systems are simultaneously thwarted. Feeling uninspired can be especially difficult for members of a minority. This is particularly true when there is a lack of positive role models within the group. For example, minority youth may find themselves gravitating toward the most high-profile members of their community rather than the healthiest ones. For instance, there is increasing criticism from within the African American community that the wrong role models are taking center stage. In particular, actor Bill Cosby and sportswriter Jason Whitlock have lambasted many of their brethren for disparaging intellectual achievement as a "white thing" while keeping the spotlight on certain rap artists who promote a cult of brute strength, intimidation, and unbridled hedonism.

Sports icons may be the single greatest source of inspiration for many African Americans. In 1947, Jackie Robinson broke the color barrier in major league baseball. In 1974, Hank Aaron grabbed the most coveted record in sports, overtaking Babe Ruth. In the 1980s and the 1990s, Magic Johnson and Michael Jordan ruled the basketball court. Nevertheless, this singular form of worship can pose a problem for those who are not interested in sports or who lack athletic talent. Hank Aaron, for his part, tried to make a distinction between serving as a specific type of role model and setting the more general example of living an honorable life. "I had to set an example for black children, and still do, because they need examples. A white child may need a role model, but a black child needs more than that in this society. He needs hope."

OPPRESSION

A feeling of oppression arises when the mastery (primarily) and the attachment (secondarily) systems are simultaneously thwarted. The word *oppress* comes from the Latin word that means to "press down." Oppression involves the subjugation of a person or a group. Often there is a political agenda, as in the oppression of an entire social class or ethnic group. As the synonym *downtrodden* suggests, there is a sense of being crushed under or flattened. The pressure builds, year after year, generation by generation, until hope turns to despair.

In *Lay My Burden Down*, Alvin Poussaint and Amy Alexander explored why suicide rates among black youths have more than doubled in the past two decades. In particular, the authors cited the work of Émile Durkheim. The famed sociologist had outlined various social forces that can contribute to suicide, including "excessive regulation . . . of persons with futures pitilessly blocked and passions violently choked." Adopting this perspective, Poussaint and Alexander concluded that the hopelessness wrought by years of oppression was a primary factor in the growing crisis of depression, hopelessness, and suicide in the black community.

Some individuals are doubly oppressed. With two strikes against them, they are especially prone to despair. Imagine being a noncommunist, religiously devout individual in the Soviet Union during the latter part of the twentieth century. Many Soviet government officials viewed religious faith as a political threat. Nevertheless, millions of Catholics, Jews, and Muslims preferred a life of oppression over membership in the atheistic Communist Party. Alternatively, consider the burden of being an African American female within a white, male-dominated society. Alice Walker has called her African-American sisters the "mules of the world."

It is not surprising that African American women have produced some of the most poignant literature on oppression. Writers such as Toni Morrison, Maya Angelou, and Alice Walker have drawn on their own personal experiences with discrimination and demoralization to fashion memorable sagas of disenfranchised and subjugated women, desperate for hope.

Alice Walker's protagonist Celie in *The Color Purple* is a poor African American woman who was physically and sexually abused by her stepfather, then given away to a man known simply as Mr.___. After years of suffering in a loveless marital prison, Celie told her husband that she was going to leave him. He replied, "You'll be back. . . . You black, you poor, you ugly, you a woman. Goddam, you nothing at all."

Celie's only source of hope was God. For decades, she wrote letters to God, seeking liberation as well as a greater perspective to make sense of her suffering. After decades of silence in response, Celie told her best friend, Shug, that she had lost faith in a "tall, gray-bearded, and white" God. "I don't write to God no more. . . . What God do for me? . . . He give me a lynched daddy, a crazy mama, a lowdown dog of a step pa and sister I probably won't ever see again."

LIMITATION

In the eyes of the people there is a sense of failure.
In the souls of the people the grapes of wrath are filling
and growing heavy, growing heavy for the vintage.

—JOHN STEINBECK, *THE GRAPES OF WRATH*

A feeling of limitation arises when the mastery (primarily) and the survival (secondarily) systems are simultaneously thwarted. Limited individuals experience themselves as deficient, as lacking in the "right stuff" to make it in the world. This form of hopelessness is all too common among the poor as well as among those who are struggling with severe physical or learning disabilities.

In *The Working Poor*, David Shipler gave readers a sense of the hopelessness experienced by those who "do not have the luxury of rage": the bank clerk with less than three dollars in his savings account, the carwash attendant without a car, the medical textbook editor who has not seen a dentist in a decade. Caroline Payne was one of Shipler's "working poor." Employed by a large department store, she repeatedly sought to be promoted to a managerial position. However, she was never chosen. At age fifty, she seemed resigned to stocking shelves for the rest of her life. Stunned by her lack of economic progress, Caroline reflected on a variety of personal handicaps that, she believed, had made it difficult for her to attain a better lot in life.

Caroline was a slow reader, born into a large and poor family that was too overwhelmed to offer adequate material or emotional support. After her parents divorced, Caroline had to contend with a stepfather who drank a lot and "tried to get fresh" with her. After graduating from high school, she married and had three children. She worked day and night to put her husband through college, only to have him commit repeated acts of infidelity.

Those who struggle with physical or learning disabilities are also apt to feel limited. For example, the rate of depression among people with spinal cord injuries is three times higher than among the general population. Individuals who have been diagnosed with epilepsy are twelve times more likely to commit suicide. Children and adolescents with speech, reading, or math difficulties often score significantly higher on measures of hopelessness than their nonimpaired peers do. Research indicates that more than half of all adolescents who commit suicide were once diagnosed with a learning disability. Similarly, adults with a history of learning disabilities are twice as likely to suffer from depression as the general population.

Exercise 4: Reflecting on Hopelessness

Answer the following questions:

1. When have you felt hopeless in your life? List as many instances as you can remember.
2. How many varieties of hopelessness have you experienced? How would you rate them, from least painful to most painful?
3. Which of these experiences of hopelessness are still burdening you?

4

What's in Your Hope Chest?

*The idea of a Hope Chest symbolizes so many hopes
and dreams—to me. It's about seeing the future unfolding
before one's very eyes. It's about preserving a lifetime of
memories and building a . . . legacy, a heritage.*

ALYICE EDRICH, *ARTIST*

Hope can be compared to an endowment, a hope chest filled with emotional, social, and spiritual resources for striving and connecting as well as coping with adversity and transcending the present. We have already noted that hopefulness is partly the result of an inborn capacity for mastery, attachment, survival, and spirituality. However, the ultimate depth and breadth of your hope foundation is largely determined by the cultural and religious or spiritual gifts that you acquire over the course of a lifetime.

CULTURE AND HOPE

The biological foundations of hope may lie in the fibers of your frontal lobe and your central nervous system pathways, but nature does not unfold in a vacuum. Strange as it may seem, the feeling of hope that is shared by most Americans is not identical to the way this emotion is felt by Israelis living on a kibbutz. Muslim hope is somewhat different from that of Native Americans. Buddhist hope can be distinguished from that of the Hindus. This is because cultural influences profoundly impact the manner in which members of a group express their mastery, attachment, and survival impulses.

Culture and Attachment

The manner in which we relate to others is affected by a variety of social factors, including the wider culture as well as our families, friends, and peer groups. Social influences can also impact how we relate to a perceived higher power. For example, in some cultures, including several in Africa, Eastern Europe, and South America, there is unquestionably a higher power that must be appeased and obeyed. In this worldview, there is the perception that human beings can do little to affect their fate or modify God's will. In contrast, the Chinese, the Japanese, and the Navajo seek harmony with natural as well as supernatural forces. In a third variation on this theme, most Americans and many northern Europeans tend to elevate the individual, believing that he or she can have a more collaborative, if not primary, role in shaping his or her destiny. Such differences in belief systems can influence whether we believe that hope comes from above us (e.g., through a higher power), through others, or from self-reliance.

In term of earthly relationships, some cultures are more collectivist in orientation, whereas others promote an ethic of individualism. For monks in Thailand, the meaning of hope derives from the collective, the strength of human bonds. For example, while participating in solemn graduation ceremonies, they pray in a large circle, holding one long string that symbolically binds them into a spiritual community. Before the intrusion of the white man, the Apache maintained an ancient system of clans known as the *gota*. These groups ranged in size from about a dozen to as many as forty individuals. Thus, the meaning of hope (*ndahondii*) in Apache suggests trust rather than potential goal attainment or survival expectations.

Similarly, the Navajo believe they are "glued together" with respect. In their cosmology, the Creator enlists the help of the "holy people" to create a natural world characterized by *hozjo*, or "balance." In Navajo the word *sih* means not only "to hope" but also "to take mercy upon" and "to take pity on."

The clan is the major source of Navajo identity. Before asking strangers any personal questions, they inquire about their clan of origin. For them, the source of hope is neither inside nor outside the self but lies in one's relationship with kin and nature. This is vividly expressed in their prayer to the sun: "Father, give me the light of your mind, that my mind may be strong. Give me some of your strength, that my arm may be strong."

Compare this communal hope with the privatized Western version. In *Das Prinzip Hoffnung* (*The Principle of Hope*), one of philosopher Ernst Bloch's primary goals was to show that hope could be achieved without recourse to God, angels, and saints. Friedrich Nietzsche similarly declared God dead, insisting that super-Earthly hopes were "poisonous" and that there will "cometh a time when man will no longer launch the arrow of his longing beyond man."

In the essay "Self-Reliance," Ralph Waldo Emerson (1841) celebrates American individualism, convinced that inspiration, guidance, and hope must come from within the person. In his words:

> [Human beings] should learn to detect and watch that gleam of light that flashes across [their minds], more than the lustre of the firmament of gods and sages . . . and accept in the highest mind the same transcendent destiny. . . . [Human beings can be] guides, redeemers, and benefactors obeying the almighty effort, advancing on chaos and the dark . . . [otherwise] there is no genius . . . no muse . . . no hope.

In many collectivist cultures, the beneficiary of hope is not the individual but a group, whose members may range from the nuclear family to the entire tribe, clan, or nation. A clear example of a kind of hope that is aimed at benefiting both the self and others is found in Islam. Muslims traditionally give away one-fortieth of their annual income to the poor, which reflects their deep concern for those who are less fortunate than themselves. The thirty-ninth sura of the Qur'an is a meditation on *companions*. The faithful are entitled to hope for a reunion with their family and with Allah. "He who is obedient . . . takes care of the hereafter and hopes for the mercy of his lord. . . . Those who are careful of their duty to the Lord shall be convened to the garden in companies."

Both the Navajo and the Hindus engage in rituals of hope for the protection of their homes and their families. One Navajo prayer reads, "This home, my home, shall be surrounded. . . . This fire shall be for the good of the family." Hindus construct altars within their homes to contemplate their various deities. Among the most important figures is the *gruhadevata*, the family godhead who is invoked to provide protection for all members of a household.

For many Christians, the ultimate hoped-for benefit is a reunion with God. Catholics who are free of mortal sin may receive communion. This ritual is considered a temporary fusion with the body of Christ, and it is viewed as a way of sampling heaven and maintaining an eternal connection with God. In Paul's Second Letter to the Corinthians, he described life on Earth as a deposit, a gift that must suffice until we are brought under the "heavenly tent."

The collectivist view stands in sharp contrast to the more individualized hope that is characteristic of American society and many northern European cultures. Near the close of *Atlas Shrugged*, Ayn Rand made a powerful appeal for the solitary hero in pursuit of individual dreams:

> Do not let your fire go out . . . in the hopeless swamps . . . the world you desired can be won, it exists, it is real, it is possible, it's yours. . . . I swear—by my life and my love of it—that I will never live for the sake of another man, nor ask another man to live for mine.

Culture and Mastery

Where can hope take us? How far can we go? Can we go forward, or will hoping simply result in "spinning our wheels"? In *The Gifts of the Jews*, Thomas Cahill wrote of the new conceptions of the world that were offered by Abraham and Moses. Prior to this time, life was conceived of as a giant wheel. The ancients were spellbound by the repetitive phases of the moon, the recurrent changing of the seasons, and endless encounters with life and death. The tradition of Abraham and Moses forever altered humanity's conception of life, substituting a forward-moving journey for a never-ending cycle. Cahill argued that this change was the basis for a new kind of hope based on the idea of a future that humanity could actively shape.

Belief systems are complex. For example, there are various strains of Buddhism; some feature cycles, whereas others espouse spirals or even a permanent heaven.

Nevertheless, most religious and philosophical worldviews can be characterized as primarily sequential or circular in their eschatology. These differences establish the bounds of "hopeful imagination." More circular cosmologies, such as those found in many parts of Asia, offer an experience of hope that differs from the Christian version. Followers of Theravada Buddhism hope to be reborn into a more favorable realm somewhere within thirty-one planes of existence. The spiritual guide-book Vinyana Pitaka instructs believers to meditate on both their past and their future lives:

> I directed my mind to the knowledge and recollection of former habituations. I remembered a variety of former habituations, thus: one birth, two births . . . or fifty or a hundred or a thousand or a hundred thousand births; or many an aeon of integration, disintegration, integration-disintegration.

In contrast to the cyclical course of Buddhism, the Jewish and Christian traditions are grounded in a more linear view of life, beginning with the epic biblical migrations. One of the great stories in the Hebrew Bible (the Christian Old Testament) concerns the exile of the Jews to Babylonia and their return to their homeland after the defeat of the Babylonian empire by the Persians. According to religious scholar Marcus Borg, the dominant biblical themes of exodus, exile, and return may be based on historical facts, but they also serve a larger symbolic function. Their purpose is to offer a perspective on the human condition. The notion of an exile speaks to a deeply felt sense of dislocation in the human psyche, whereas the return to the promised land reflects a desire for reunion and the repossession of a safe place in the universe.

Conveying a similar spirit of hope, the New Testament ends with the Book of Revelation, which refers to "a new heaven and a new earth."

With the triumph of good over evil comes the removal of every barrier to human fulfillment. A new paradise is created to house the resurrected Christian soul and to guarantee the hope of an eternal reunion with God and one's loved ones.

Culture and Survival

Psychologist Rick Snyder observed that hope can serve as a form of "reality negotiation," buffering individuals from painful life experiences. This process is complex, involving spiritual factors as well as aspects of the survival and attachment systems. To some extent, reality negotiation is an individualized process. It is partly derived from personal modes of coping, which are influenced by the level of an individual's emotional development. However, there are also culturally specific modes of escape and transcendence that can be accessed to offset personal threats as well as universal challenges.

For the followers of Theravada Buddhism, a good Buddhist can achieve escape from the endless cycle of transmigration through a kind of dissolution of mind, body, and spirit that brings complete release from all connections, spiritual as well as worldly. Although viewed positively by Buddhists, this spiritual progression is associated with greater and greater withdrawal and isolation. For example, upon reaching the twenty-eighth plane of infinite space, "his [the practitioner's] mind takes pleasure, finds satisfaction, settles and indulges in its perception of the sphere of nothingness."

In contrast, Christian salvation is a fusion of two promises: escape from suffering and a connection with God. Again, in the Book of Revelation there is an unambiguous expression of this great and final hope, a permanent spiritual reunion: "I heard a loud voice from the throne saying, 'Behold, the dwelling of God is with men. He will dwell with them, and they shall be his people, and God himself will be with them.'"

Culture, Time, and Hope

Time perception is another cultural gift that can profoundly impact the experience of hope. According to anthropologist Hoyt Alverson, time can be experienced as a *cause*, a *substance*, a *medium in motion*, or a *direction* in physical space. Each of these dimensions can influence our sense of hope. For example, the sense of time as a cause can give rise to faith in the future and the sense that time can yield something positive. The experience of time as a substance permits the feeling of "having enough time" to succeed, to find love, or to secure healing. This dimension of time is affected by an individual's age, health status, work style, and other daily commitments as well as by spiritual beliefs. Time is experienced as a medium in motion when individuals are hopeful and content; life appears to move at a comfortable pace, perhaps even to the point of resembling a continuous flow state. However, when there is a sense of desperation, time runs short, and when the future looks completely hopeless, time may appear to grind to a halt.

Spiritual beliefs also create different time-hope experiences. What can we hope to accomplish in the course of time? Can we hope for progress, love, or the elimination of suffering? These questions emanate from the sense of time as a potential cause. The substance of time is also constructed differently by the followers of various spiritual systems. Buddhists may use their time to perfect longer and longer periods of quiet detachment. Some Protestants might busy themselves in accomplishing the good works that are deemed necessary for their salvation. Hindus and Australian Aborigines have more than one temporal dimension to consider. A Hindu must address ethical shortcomings in the moment to generate a karma that will lead to a more elevated existence in the future (through reincarnation). Australian Aborigines prepare themselves for their Dreamtime ceremony, which allows them to access the past and make the necessary community reparations to ensure a more benign present and future.

Spiritual life also affects the perceived movement of time. In the Christian Bible there are many allusions to a "last day." In Paul's Letter to the Romans, it is written, "You know what hour it is, how it is full time now for you to wake from sleep. For salvation is nearer to us now than when we first believed; the night is far gone, the day is at hand." For Buddhists who contemplate thirty-one planes of existence and numerous rebirths, there is a different sense of time, a different level of urgency, and a different experience of hoping.

Time has a direction. It can also be expressed as a straight line or a circle. Linear time can be described as long or short, as here or there. Circular time may be perceived as the round of life, a circle, or a wheel of fortune. These aspects of time may influence hope by altering the perceived boundaries and limits of imagined possibilities. Where can one go? How far can one go? What is possible and what is impossible? Most of the major religions espouse either an escape from a cycle of suffering (orthodox Buddhism), a linear progression toward paradise (Christians and Muslims), or a combination of these two forms of salvation (Pure Land Buddhists).

EXERCISE 5: Hope Etiquette

Answer the following questions:

1. Where does your hope come from? Does it come from within? Do you find hope in a higher power? Does your hope derive from nature?

2. For whom do you hope? Do you hope for your own well-being? Do

you harbor hopes for your loved ones? Are you doing all that you can to realize your personal hopes or to facilitate the hopes you have for your loved ones?

3. What is your ultimate hope? Is it to achieve release from pain and suffering? Is it geared toward a permanent reunion with loved ones or a higher power? Is it focused on pleasure?

4. What aspects of time and hope are most relevant for you? Which of these time experiences would you most like to change? How could you alter this aspect of time experience?

Religion and Hope

Philosopher Huston Smith relied on the language of the performing arts to introduce his classic text on world religions. He encouraged readers to become "cosmic dancers" who are able to "leap beyond" a singular view of the universe. Smith fervently believed that there was much to gain by sampling the faith of others. Indeed, spirituality is a powerful hope conduit. Consider the hauntingly beautiful pop classic song "Question" by the Moody Blues. The spiritually loaded lyrics stir the soul with references to "a land that I once knew" (attachment), a "road that I must choose" (mastery), along with dreams of life-changing miracles and a safe passage (survival).

In the remainder of this chapter we discuss the enormous impact of religious and spiritual beliefs on hope. Like cultures, religious systems offer different kinds of hope. Based on our research on this topic, we have identified seven kinds of hope found in the major religions (Table 4.1).

Table 4.1. The Varieties of Hope Expressed in Different Religions

Varieties of Hope	Religious Systems
Attachment	Australian Aboriginal
Survival	Buddhist
Mastery & attachment	Hindu
Attachment & survival	
Religious subvariety (human bonds)	Jewish
Spiritual subvariety (nature bonds)	Ifa
Spiritual or religious subvariety (nature & human bonds)	Native American
Attachment & survival, with limited mastery	Muslim
Attachment & survival, with moderate mastery	Catholic & Eastern Orthodox
Mastery, attachment & survival	Protestant (most denominations)

African Ifa

Ifa is a belief system that originated more than 8,000 years ago in western Africa. Its beliefs and practices are designed to "preserve harmony with nature and the Creator," according to the *Ijo Orunmila*, the Ifa book of cherished prayers and parables. Although there is only one meditation on hope, it is the dominant theme in one of the longest and most important Ifa tales. The story clearly implies that hope flows from attachments

rather than from mastery or survival efforts. The narrative is about way-
ward ancestors who have attempted to strike out on their own without
community assistance or spiritual guidance. Lacking this support, they
aimlessly wander into isolation, suffering, and despair. Hope is restored
when the lost souls reestablish their bonds with loved ones.

> There was a time long ago when all was in harmony. . . . We started to do things counter
> to the law. . . . We lost the path. . . . After a century of parched dreams . . . the people
> were refreshed with the hope of faith. . . . They found the truth by returning to the arms
> of those they left behind.

Australian Dreamtime

The Aborigines of Australia value kinship ties and treasure the sacred-
ness of the natural world. There is a strong emphasis on totems, with
each family and tribe distinguished by a special relationship with a particular species of plant or animal. Despite variations in customs and
dialects, the Aborigines are united by a complex religious tradition
known as the Dreamtime or the Dreaming, a multilayered spiritual
ritual that is not to be confused with the simpler Western notion of a
nighttime reverie. Participants join in elaborate dances punctuated by
frequent foot stomping and interwoven with repetitive, hypnotic verses
that chronicle the lives of valued ancestors. The playing of a flutelike
instrument, the didgeridoo, provides a mesmerizing musical background
that is experienced as a veritable echo of the soul of Mother Earth.

The Dreaming allows the Aborigines to penetrate multiple dimensions of time and reality in order to contact spiritual protectors, celestial
guides, and powerful totems. Most important, by reaching into eternity,
they reconnect with long-departed ancestors and make reparations for
their sins.

The classic Aboriginal hope citation appears in the legend of Baiame, the Creator and a bountiful provider. This attachment-centered myth describes the hope of the world for peace, harmony, and a life managed in cooperative balance with the rest of creation. According to this legend, in the beginning, all was well in the world. However, when humanity violated its covenant with Baiame, it resulted in a rupture of hope that brought suffering and death. Rooted in bonded faith, hope was crushed by violating the Creator's trust. In his mercy, Baiame offered humanity another chance by establishing a safe harbor in the heavens. To this day, the Aborigines believe that the constellation of the Southern Cross is a place for them in the limitless regions of space, "the home of the All-Father Himself."

Buddhism

A form of hope based on survival rather than attachment or mastery might have been predicted for Buddhism, which is traditionally viewed as "the great salvation religion." One of the most cited sections of the sacred Buddhist text, the Pali Canon, is known as the "Book of Protection." Classic, or Theravada, Buddhism is marked by a renunciation of futile worldly pursuits and a diminished emphasis on the need for attachments of any kind. For these reasons, Buddhism has been adopted by many Westerners, some of whom are prosperous but aspire to go beyond materialism, and others who have a history of physical or emotional trauma and are seeking comfort and inner peace.

Christianity

A strong emphasis on community (attachment) and safety (survival) is rooted in the origins of Christianity, which flourished in the chaos of the disintegrating Roman Empire. Those who confronted the demise of a world order that had stood for 1,000 years were undoubtedly beset with profound alienation and tremendous fear. The traditions of the past could no longer be trusted, and the present was filled with terror. Early Christianity held out the promise of a lasting connection with God as well as the opportunity for salvation. When Protestantism arrived in the sixteenth century, it offered a greater dose of mastery. In fact, the so-called Protestant ethic has been implicated in the development of virtually every aspect of social, economic, and cultural progress in the West.

Islam

Most of the references to hope in the Qur'an relate to attachment or survival. This is enlightening, given the Western stereotype of an Islamic warrior heritage. The presence of far more references to an attachment-driven hope support the notion that the initial spread of Islam was greatly fueled by the binding power of socially and economically inter-dependent clans. In fact, nearly half of the hope terms in the Qur'an are associated with attachment. Muslims seek access to Allah or express hope that important relationships will continue to flourish. The other hope-related references are linked to survival. They are embedded in requests for mercy and forgiveness from Allah, who can be harsh in His judgment: "He [Allah] shows you the lightning, causing fear and hope."

Hinduism

Attachment and mastery define Hindu hope. There is considerably less emphasis on survival. In the Rig Veda, devout followers are encouraged to place their hope in Agni, the fire god who rules over Earth. Agni is described as the "adorable friend of man . . . found everywhere, including the vast offspring of the firmament that are the seven eternal and ever-youthful rivers. . . . Agni [is] their common embryo." This emphasis on relationships is not surprising in light of India's caste system, which influences every dimension of life, including marital choices and friendships as well as business opportunities and even available forms of rebirth.

For Hindus, enlightenment can be found through knowledge, love, work, or meditation. True spiritual success demands a great deal of effort and training. Various forms of yoga and other demanding exercises are practiced to increase strength through self-discipline and effect a union with the powerful resources of an inner god, or *atman*, while attempting to ascend to a higher rung of the spiritual ladder of samsara (the cycle of reincarnation caused by karma).

Judaism

The hope expressed in the Torah, or Five Books of Moses, focuses primarily on attachment and survival. In Genesis, God forms a covenant with Abraham that continues through his family: his son Isaac, Isaac's son Jacob, and Jacob's twelve sons, whose descendants form the twelve tribes of Israel. God's covenant is to make them a great people in a land that God has promised them.

In Exodus, survival is threatened as the Israelites are enslaved in Egypt, but they are eventually liberated by God and sent to wander in the desert, where they survive for forty years before entering the Promised Land. God's covenant with the Israelites is established at Mount Sinai with the giving of the Ten Commandments. The attachment of God to Israel through this covenant is described in the classical rabbinic commentaries as a "marriage."

Leviticus, the third book of the Torah, delineates the laws and rituals that are the foundation of the covenant and on which the survival of the Jewish people depends. The fourth book, Numbers, describes the forty

years in the desert and the many conflicts, disillusionments, and rebel-
lions that took place there, threatening the people's attachment to God
and their survival. It is also in Numbers that God promises vineyards and
a valley leading to a "door of hope" that will rescue them from Egyptian
domination. Finally, in the fifth book, Deuteronomy, Moses prepares
the Israelites to enter the land of Canaan. He reminds them that they are
a small people, and it is only their attachment to God's laws that will
ensure their survival in the land to which God is bringing them.

Native American Spirituality

Despite their differences, all Native American tribes express a devotion to kinship ties and a respect for nature (attachment). They also find
a common bond in survival—of both the perils of the physical environment and the dangers presented by hostile outsiders.

The Yupik of Alaska express their strong attachment hopes through an
elaborate naming ritual:

> Naming is a basic means of perpetuating relationships among the living and between
> the living and the dead, for those who share the same name may share a spiritual
> essence. . . . The dead person "enters" the new namesake, who acts just like the one
> after whom he or she is named. . . . The living namesake is called by the kin a term
> appropriate to the deceased and often treated if he or she were that person . . . creat-
> ing a dense social network among the living and the dead.

In terms of survival, the Yupik must grapple with some of the coldest
temperatures on Earth, an inconsistent food supply, and many months
without sunlight. Yupik tales focus on the awesome powers that lie
behind the blanketing snow, the crackling thunder, and the ubiquitous
mountains of unyielding ice.

The Navajo of the American Southwest have lived for centuries in matrilineal clans. For them, leaving one's territory is synonymous with forsaking one's identity. In fact, in their language there is no word for "relocation." The Navajo also cultivate a close relationship with nature. In the words of a Navajo elder, "We the five-fingered beings are related to the four-legged, the winged beings, the spirits. . . . We are all relatives."

"The River of the Separation" is an excellent example of a Navajo tale that links attachment and survival. The inability of men and women to live in harmony leads to both individual suffering and community disintegration. Another tale, "The Changing Coyote," offers a striking metaphor for an attachment-based hope. This tale depicts a selfish coyote that is threatening a clan's effort to build a better community just as people were trying to bring more light into the world.

The Innu, an indigenous group in Canada, have a classic survival tale called "The Wolverine," in which the main character must enlist the help of other animals to establish a safe haven. Against the backdrop of an ensuing flood, and perched on a few remaining stones, the wolverine implores his fellow creatures to search for soil. One by one, they dive to the ocean depths, until finally the muskrat surfaces with a plentitude of earth to save the day.

ATHEISM AND HOPE

For many individuals, hope and religion are intertwined. Religious faith provides them with a sense of empowerment, an unquestionable presence, and a fail-safe method for dealing with their deepest fears and frustrations. Does this mean that religion is a prerequisite for hope? Is hope within the reach of an agnostic or an atheist?

The philosopher and scientist Bertrand Russell was one of the most well-known atheists of the twentieth century. In one essay, "Ideas That Have Harmed Mankind," he openly derided any form of religious belief, and in another, "Why I Am Not a Christian," he dismissed classic arguments for the existence of God. Russell asserted that terror is the underlying source of all religious beliefs: "Fear is the basis of the whole thing—fear of the mysterious, fear of defeat, fear of death."

Russell's response to the human condition was to invest in a form of terror management that is based on the scientific method and human potential:

> Science can teach us, and I think our hearts can teach us, no longer to look around for imaginary supports, no longer to invent allies in the sky, but rather to look to our own efforts. . . . A good world needs knowledge . . . it does not need . . . words uttered long ago by ignorant men . . . it needs hope for the future, not looking back.

Some degree of hope that is based on progress and goals can be achieved through science and technology. Science provides a powerful means of exercising the drive for exploration, mastery, and control over the environment. Humans have commanded ships among the stars, plumbed the ocean depths, climbed Mount Everest, and traversed the North and South Poles. Nevertheless, hope is based on more than mastery. A full experience of hope also requires trust and a loving presence as well as potential solutions to the existential realities of human vulnerability and mortality. To address these greater challenges, we must go beyond dogma, religious or secular, into the realm of faith.

EXERCISE 6: Memories, Dreams, and Beliefs

Ask yourself the following questions:

1. Take another look at the lyrics of the Moody Blues song "Question." What images come to mind? What feelings? What memories? Has your life perspective changed as you've gotten older? Have your hopes changed?
2. After learning more about the hope content of the various religions of the world, have your opinions about these belief systems shifted in any way? Were you surprised by anything that you read?
3. Do you feel comfortable with your present religious or spiritual beliefs? If not, are you drawn to a particular faith system discussed in this chapter?

SPIRITUAL INTELLIGENCE

Faith is the very first thing you should pack in a hope chest.

—SARAH BAN BREATHNACH, *SIMPLE ABUNDANCE*

The most hopeful individuals possess a solid spiritual foundation as well as excellent mastery, attachment, and survival skills. The rest of this chapter is designed to help you to maximize your spiritual potential. To do this, we are going to systematically explore the meaning of faith and the concept of spiritual types. In essence, we are going to address the development of your spiritual intelligence.

In daily conversations, *faith* and *hope* are used interchangeably, as if they were one and the same thing. In private prayers as well as public pronouncements, the two words are uttered in a single breath. However, faith is not identical to hope; it is a precursor to or a prerequisite for hope. Think for a moment about the words used to describe someone's faith. There is usually an allusion to a foundation. For example, it might be said that someone is a person of "deep faith" or has an "unshakable faith."

Now reflect on the language of hope. The implication is that it is a derived virtue. For example, you can "pin your hope on science" or "place your hope in God." You might think that your hope rests on a particular leader or hero. In short, something is presumed to lie under or beneath hope. In the past, there were even references to hope as a "second soul" or as "nature's veil."

Faith is a critical ingredient in the development of hope. This is especially true of basic hope, which is a generalized sense of trust in yourself, the world, and the future. Basic hope can be distinguished from a directed hope, which points toward a particular goal or outcome. Basic hope is a personality disposition, a major factor in determining your response to life's greatest challenges. Individuals who lack this virtue find it extremely difficult to cope with the vicissitudes of life. Those who possess this spiritual infrastructure are much more likely to retain a hopeful attitude regardless of their circumstances.

An adaptive faith that can sustain hope is not blind, immature, lazy, or necessarily based on religious dogma. Some of the most astute observers of the human condition have argued that faith can be a positive and vital life force. Leo Tolstoy, for example, contrasted an informed faith with the hypnotism of slavish devotion. Likewise, he discounted the desperate beliefs of those who passively wish to be transported out of poverty, misfortune, or other conditions of misery. He declared, "This is not really faith, for instead of throwing light on man's position in the world, it only darkens it."

Theologian Paul Tillich characterized faith as a companion to truth-seeking. In his estimation, only a deep faith can give you the spiritual stamina to honestly examine the meaning and purpose of your life. Similarly, political scientist James Fowler presented a view of a maturing faith that is increasingly more engaged with the universe rather than disconnected or ego-centered.

The philosopher Huston Smith has emphasized that faith is a way of seeing rather than thinking. He suggested that faith allows believers to access the light of a transcendent reality that is veiled off to those without conviction. His views are reminiscent of the lyrics of the classic spiritual hymn "Amazing Grace": "I once was lost but now am found, was blind but now I see." Smith invoked the following words of the English poet William Blake: "If the doors of perception were cleansed, we would see everything as it is: Infinite."

THE VARIETIES OF FAITH

Faith is not necessarily religious. In fact, four of the five definitions of faith in Webster's dictionary have nothing to do with God or religion; they involve nonspecific references to beliefs, confidence, trust, or loyalty. Similarly, Fowler saw faith as a generic activity that is not at all dependent on religious content. In his view, faith involves a process of developing valued interests, spiritual or otherwise. Fowler called these faith domains *centers of value.*

Centers of value can encompass religious as well as nonreligious sources of faith. Individuals can either invest all of their faith in one center of value or cultivate a personal belief system that comprises two or more. These faith possibilities are rightly called centers because they tend to operate as hubs, or primary points of reference that ground thoughts, feelings, and behaviors. In essence, they lie at the center of human experience. This centrality confers upon each of these faith sources a spiritual dimension, regardless of their religious bearing. It is possible to order the primary sources of faith into eight major centers of value (Table 4.2).

Table 4.2. The Eight Centers of Value

Centers of Value	Expressions
Higher power	God-centered religions
Nature	Environmentalism; Earth-centered religions; natural health and healing
Custom and tradition	Confucianism; Hindu castes; Scouts; clubs and other social groups
Economics	Smith's "invisible hand"; Keynes's active governing
Diversity and equality	Political activism; communism; socialism; postmodernist thinking
Science	The scientific enterprise; technology; experts
Others	Teammates; family; friends; lovers
The self	Athleticism; conquests of nature; problem solving; creativity

Faith in a Higher Power

The demise of faith in a supreme being has been greatly exaggerated by many critics of traditional religion. Statistics from the late 1990s suggest that less than 5 percent of the world's population is atheistic. Europe and Asia claim the most nonbelievers, between 5 and 6 percent. In Africa, Australia, and Central and South America, only about 0.5 percent of the population appears to deny the existence of a higher power. A 2002 survey conducted by the Pew Research Council indicated that only 1 percent of North Americans considered themselves to be atheists.

The fullest development of faith requires knowledge and trust. If you choose to include faith in a higher power as one of your centers of value, then you must get close to that higher power. In this regard, spiritual writer Deepak Chopra suggested that there are seven potential ways of knowing God. According to Chopra, an individual's experience of God is a product of his or her current emotional needs and spiritual development. Early in one's spiritual growth, there is a tendency to project humanlike qualities onto God. As an individual's spiritual development progresses, he or she is increasingly able to grasp a more transcendent higher power. Chopra's sevenfold progression is as follows: God the Protector, God the Almighty, God of Peace, God the Redeemer, God the Creator, God of Miracles, and God of Pure Being.

Huston Smith took a different approach. He argued that there is a need for a knowable God to supplement our sense of an ineffable spirit. Since the human mind is unable to fully comprehend an infinite and eternal reality, there is a need for a personal God who demonstrates humanlike qualities. Although human beings can sense an even greater presence beyond these personal expressions of God, they must rely on more concrete representations for emotional assurance and communion.

From a hope perspective, Chopra's ranking of God experiences seems unwarranted. As we explained previously, different religions offer various forms of hope. Moreover, there are individual differences in faith needs. Some people desperately want to be strengthened or empowered, whereas others are seeking a mystical union or deliverance from fear and anxiety. If a seeker aspires to a fuller realization of hope, we would recommend that that individual broaden rather than narrow his or her faith investments to encompass a God who is simultaneously powerful, protective, and present.

Religious faith can take different forms. For a religious Catholic who is gravely ill, a visit to Lourdes may boost his or her faith. Lorraine Day, a bestselling author and former orthopedic trauma surgeon, combined her faith in religion with her trust in nature when a tumor was found in her breast. "I refused mutilating surgery, chemotherapy and radiation, the treatment methods all physicians are taught, and got well by using God's natural remedies instead."

Faith in Nature

There are subtle but important differences in spiritual beliefs among nature-oriented cultures. The practitioners of Ifa are a bit more Earth-centered, whereas Australian Aborigines and Native Americans place greater faith in human bonds. Followers of Ifa (which means "wisdom of nature") presume that all things possess consciousness and that one must cultivate empathy for every facet of nature. In contrast, the Apaches invest in matrilineal and matrilocal traditions while the Navajo believe that they are "glued together with respect." Likewise, the "Dreamtime ceremony" among the Australian Aborigines is geared primarily toward reconnecting with ancestors.

Nature worship has been reestablished in many parts of the industrialized world. The early 1970s marked a renewed faith in nature. Especially noteworthy were the introductions of Earth Day and the formation of Greenpeace, along with the first systematic attempts at recycling waste. Initially, the entire ecosystem was the focus of concern, underscored by the realization that the fate of humanity was tied to the survival of the planet. As more was learned about the dangers of pollutants and the origins of different illnesses, more attention was focused on natural health and healing. For example, in an effort to reduce the risk of cancer in the general population, large-scale efforts were undertaken to clean up toxic waste sites. Concerned about the quality of drinking water, many individuals purchased home filters or opted for bottled water. Traditional food stores started to stock "natural foods" to meet the ever-growing demand for soy products, whole grains, and organic produce.

More recently, some have turned to natural immune enhancers or organic cell protectors. In the United States, sales of such products soared from less than $2 billion dollars in 1980 to more than $50 billion in 2008. There now seems to be as much faith in naturopathy, or "nature's way," as in the practice of allopathic (Western) medicine.

Rachel Carson, author of *Silent Spring*, put her faith in Mother Earth while suggesting that being in nature was necessary for the full spiritual development of an individual:

There is symbolic as well as actual beauty in the migration of birds, in the ebb and flow of the tides, in the folded bud ready for the spring. There is something infinitely healing in these repeated refrains of nature—the assurance that dawn comes after night, and spring after winter.

Faith in Customs and Traditions

Individuals may place their greatest trust in time-honored traditions. A compelling example of a fully "communal faith" can be found in the works of Confucius. The great sage of China developed his codes of conduct in the early fifth century BCE. In the following centuries, Plato and Aristotle would come along to offer their own utopian formulas, placing their faith in government reform by "philosopher-kings." In contrast, Confucius put his trust in adherence to tradition and the virtue of living in communal harmony. Among his most important concepts are *li*, "right manners," and *jen*, "humanness," a combination of altruism and self-respect. His most famous treatise on these topics is "The Five Relationships," a guide for maintaining honorable relations between friends, the young and the old, parents and children, husbands and wives, and rulers and subjects.

In the modern era, most tradition-grounded faiths are highly localized, confined to isolated and dwindling tribes, remotely situated clans, or other small pockets of society. A striking exception is the caste system in India.

In Western societies, there is still a need for traditions and rituals. Many individuals in this age of anxiety are sorely lacking a sense of place or community. There is evidence that the incidence of clinical depression has risen tenfold since World War II; such a drastic increase cannot be attributed to any kind of genetic change. The most likely cause is a diminished sense of community. Studies of close-knit groups such as the Amish in Pennsylvania or the Kaluli in Papua New Guinea reveal a consistently lower incidence of depression.

Further evidence of the power of tradition comes from developmental psychology. Researchers have found that parents who maintain rituals such as regular dinners, holiday observances, and birthday celebrations are more likely to raise children who are happy and well-adjusted.

Today the need for faith in customs and traditions is often expressed by joining a civic organization, a club, or an interest group. With the advent of the Internet, there are also a slew of virtual communities. Sometimes these activities and affiliations supplement or combine with a deeper involvement in a religious or spiritual belief system, but for many individuals, these secular rituals become primary sources of faith. For example, some people invest great time and energy in organizations such as the Rotary Club or the Masons. Others prefer groups that provide resources for children and families such as the YMCA, the YWCA, or various national and international scouting associations. Sports enthusiasts as well as music and film buffs organize or join fan clubs and interest groups. Others gravitate toward ethnic-based organizations, veterans' groups, or workers' unions.

Faith in Economics

The writings of economists such as Adam Smith and John Maynard Keynes reflect a deeply held faith in a particular approach to managing the economy. Smith was certain that whenever individuals operated out of self-interest, an "invisible hand" would ultimately steer their actions toward the betterment of the commonwealth. In contrast, Keynes was convinced that governments should play a more active role in controlling the economy by monitoring spending and taxation.

Both Smith and Keynes demonstrated a quasi-religious fervor. The disciples of these economic "saviors" have continued to debate the relative merits of their respective "faiths." Those on the conservative side of the political spectrum remain faithful to Smith's invisible hand, whereas those with more liberal leanings put their trust in Keynes's plan to rescue the downtrodden through government interventions.

In the United States, the economic "faith wars" that receive the greatest attention are those fought between the Democrats and Republicans; the former party represents faith in government social programs and oversight, whereas the latter party puts more faith in the private sector and a more limited federal government. Clearly, there can be strong personal agendas that motivate allegiance to one party or the other (such as a desire for additional government funds or for greater tax breaks to preserve wealth). However, there are many Americans who deeply believe that the country (and the world) would be a better place if their party and, by extension, their preferred economic viewpoint, were in power. Ask yourself the following: To what extent are your political leanings shaped primarily by personal self-interest or a deeper faith in what you believe to be for the good of the country?

Faith in Diversity and Equality

In the eighteenth century, Jean-Jacques Rousseau was Europe's leading proponent for equal rights. Rousseau famously declared, "Man is born free, but everywhere he is in chains." In the nineteenth century, French philosopher Auguste Comte offered a "religion of humanity" to replace the "childish illusion" of Christianity. Comte chose the study of norms over doctrine, love of others over devotion to God, and faith in the social order over belief in a divine "chain of being."

Among the many who shared a faith in social reform were those who saw an opportunity to meld it with Marxist principles. Thus was born communism and socialism. Helen Keller was an avid supporter of the Socialist Party of America. This may surprise many readers who know of her only as the young heroine who overcame deafness and blindness in *The Miracle Worker*. Battling controversy and even ridicule, Keller passionately voiced her support for the alienated and disenfranchised. On December 31, 1920, she eloquently spoke before a crowd of marchers in New York who were prepared to celebrate the Russian Revolution:

Let us join the world's procession marching toward a glad tomorrow. Strong of hope and brave in heart. . . . All along the road beside us throng the people sad and broken, weeping women, children hungry, homeless like little birds cast out of their nest. . . . With their hearts aflame, untamed, glorying in martyrdom they hail us passing quickly. Halt not, O comrades, yonder glimmers the star of our hope.

Mao Tse-tung placed his faith in the oppressed masses of China. The China that Mao took over was on the verge of collapse. The country of 700 million was languishing under the control of a feudal political system and a badly outdated agricultural economy. Mao's greatest act of faith was the implementation of a five-year economic plan known as the Great Leap Forward. The plan was based on a massive steel production drive as well as the formation of semi-independent communes. "Everywhere, small backyard furnaces were built . . . there were around-the-clock shifts . . . cooking pots were smashed, door handles were melted down." As a prelude to this massive social experiment, Mao offered the following words of encouragement to his people:

> We must have faith in [ourselves] . . . there is great hope for this program. China can be changed, ignorance can be changed into knowledge, and lethargy into vitality. . . . I say this country of ours is full of hope. The Rightists say it is hopeless, they are utterly wrong.

In addition to Helen Keller and Mao Tse-tung, there were other prominent activists in the 1930s and 1940s who joined the crusade for equality. Bertrand Russell promoted a liberal philosophy rooted in logic. B. F. Skinner presented his blueprint for a utopian society that was based entirely on principles of behavioral conditioning. Mahatma Gandhi's faith in civil disobedience helped him to secure the freedom of an entire nation. Martin Luther King Jr. punctuated his struggle for equal rights with one of the great speeches of the twentieth century, delivered at the March on Washington on August 28, 1963:

> I have a dream that one day on the red hills of Georgia, sons of former slaves and sons of former slave owners will be able to sit down together at the table of brotherhood. . . . I have a dream that my four little children will one day live in a nation where they will not be judged by the color of their skin but by the content of their character. . . . This is our hope.

Faith in Science

Scientists may place their faith in Charles Darwin's theory of evolution, higher mathematics, or theoretical physics. For Carl Sagan, science was the ultimate center of value. In one of his last books, *The Demon-Haunted World*, he characterized science as "a candle in the dark." He noted the following:

Science is not only compatible with spirituality, it is a profound source of spirituality. When we recognize our place in an immensity of light years and in the passage of ages, when we grasp the intricacy, beauty, and subtlety of life . . . that soaring feeling, that sense of elation and humility combined . . . that is surely spiritual.

You do not have to be a scientist to put your faith in experts, technology, or the scientific enterprise. Psychologist Bruno Klopfer related the story of a man with metastatic cancer whose tumors would alternately grow bigger and smaller with each report of the failure or success of a new experimental drug.

Faith in Others

One of the most basic centers of value is faith in other people. This includes the blessing of a devoted family as well as the trust that develops among close friends. Faith in others is the emotional glue that underlies unit cohesiveness on the battlefield as well as team chemistry on the ball field.

Commenting on friendships, the Roman orator Cicero declared that "nothing better has been given to human beings by the immortal gods." In *The Art of War*, Sun Tzu praised the power of a closely banded fighting unit: "He will win whose army is animated by the same spirit throughout its ranks." Ralph Waldo Emerson called friendship "nature's masterpiece" and "a possession for all time." The great pro football coach Vince Lombardi elevated teamwork to a spiritual quest and engendered a champion's faith in a group of perennial losers. One of his former players confessed, "We'd go through fire for him."

Friends provide the greatest source of faith and hope for many people. One of the most impressive studies on this topic involved more than 40,000 *Psychology Today* readers. More than half replied that they would seek out a good friend in a time of crisis before doing anything else. In addition, nearly three-quarters responded that they would risk their lives for their best friends.

Psychologists Reed W. Larson and Nancy Bradney have provided additional evidence about the enduring significance of friendships. For their study, they devised a method of randomly paging volunteer subjects every day for an entire week. The participants filled out a mood and activity survey immediately after answering each page. The individuals reported being happiest in the company of a friend, regardless of what they were doing.

Unit cohesiveness is the military equivalent of team chemistry. According to Lieutenant Colonel Richard Hooker, effective military action requires both horizontal and vertical cohesion. The former addresses trust within a company of soldiers, whereas the latter deals with the amount of faith soldiers have in their unit leaders or higher-level commanders. Hooker argued that modern battlefield conditions require that military leaders pay particular attention to unit cohesiveness.

Max Edelman epitomizes a sense of faith in the goodwill of others. In the spring of 1944, while imprisoned at the Budzyn concentration camp in Poland, Edelman was severely beaten by a group of guards. Permanently blinded, Edelman was rendered unfit for most forms of prison labor. If word spread of his condition, he might be shot on the spot. Risking their own lives, the other prisoners did everything in their power to ensure his safety. Edelman showed complete trust in their words of comfort and advice. "I was left to die a bloody mess . . . my brother and my friends gathered around me to offer words of hope." He even found one of his German captors to be a source of faith and hope:

Without the help of Eric . . . I would not be here to tell you about it. . . . He lied to the guards about my whereabouts at every morning's head count, and kept me out of their sight. He warned the inmates in our barrack not to do me harm or steal my food.

Faith in the Self

For Carl Jung, the supreme archetype was the hero. As with all great myths, the hero story line was etched centuries ago. An individual of humble origins is chosen to undertake a journey. The obligation is non-negotiable, for the fate of both the hero and the society is dependent on a successful resolution of a sacred quest. The hero's path is arduous and fraught with peril. The hero suffers one or more serious wounds, but with the help of a benign sage or a great protector, he or she emerges transformed. In the words of Joseph Campbell, the hero is now prepared to "bring a boon to society that restores a valued way of life."

Whether viewed as an archetype, a spiritually inspired lesson, or a myth, the hero's tale is compelling because it reflects the hope of self-actualization. Personal growth is a journey of discovery that involves differentiation from others as well as an integration of talents and life experiences. It demands courage and entails risks. The process is difficult, if not impossible, without spiritual guidance. However, in the final analysis, the individual must assume the greatest responsibility for his or her self-development.

In Hermann Hesse's *Steppenwolf*, the fainthearted protagonist entered a dream world where a "supreme grandmaster" compared the process of personal growth to a game of chess: "This is the art of life. . . . You may as an artist develop the game of your life and lend it animation. You may complicate and enrich it as you please. It lies in your hands."

The hero archetype is especially relevant for those who have experienced great adversity or received little in the way of emotional support. This includes neglected children who surmise that they must fend for themselves as well as victims of abusive relationships or sufferers of a life-threatening illness. The hope of these faith-deprived individuals often derives from an attitude of self-sufficiency or from assuming the role of a battle-toughened survivor. Nevertheless, without a guiding myth or an inspiring role model, it can be extremely difficult for individuals to craft a heroic vision for themselves. Thus, it is common for the dispossessed to strongly identify with the hero's humble origins, wounds, and impulse toward transformation.

Heroes come in many forms. There are spiritual heroes such as Buddha, Jesus, and Mohammed. There are also war heroes, political heroes, and the "hero within." Even fictional characters can sometimes serve as role models to further a kind of heroic self-development. Many readers will undoubtedly recall a heroic comic book figure or television character who inspired them as children.

The hero myth can be viewed as a lesson in balanced personal growth. It suggests that where you finish is more important than where you began. It underscores the struggles and sacrifices that accompany character development while also acknowledging the need for a guide or mentor. It affirms the worth of the individual but simultaneously suggests that the greatest gains transcend even the self.

Crafting a heroic vision for yourself is not to be confused with hero worship. Some individuals who put all of their faith in perceived superhumans view themselves as incapable of dealing with the vicissitudes of life. Their sense of self may be largely derived from the success or failure of a particular entertainer, athlete, or politician. The media contribute to this problem of idle hero awe through slick marketing campaigns that generate unrealistic, idealized celebrity portraits. The point is to live and not merely observe a heroic existence. For example, even within the most Earth-centered or attachment-based faiths, there is the clear implication that the individual must bring the power of the exterior into the interior.

In *Little Girl Lost*, Leisha Joseph shared her inspiring story of courage and faith. Leisha's father died when she was very young. She was later sexually abused by several of her mother's boyfriends. Her psychotic mother attempted to burn their house down and went after Leisha with a knife. Nevertheless, Leisha persevered, became an honor roll student, and reached the finals of the Miss Teen USA pageant. However, a short time later Leisha was attacked by a serial rapist. Rather than live in fear, she chose to confront him in the courtroom. Leisha's faith is a great example of guided heroism, a spiritual meld of inspiration from above and fierce self-reliance. It is not surprising that she noted that "all of my Bible heroes are survivors."

Those who aspire to be rugged individualists often display tremendous faith in themselves. Two great examples are Amelia Earhart and Ted Williams.

Well ahead of her time, Amelia achieved a number of firsts as a female aviator. She was the first woman to fly solo across the Atlantic and the first woman to earn a Distinguished Flying Cross. When Amelia and her plane disappeared in 1937, she was attempting to be the first woman to fly around the world.

Her independent spirit was obvious from the time she was a young girl, and it never faltered. From the website dedicated to her memory (http://www.ameliaearhart.com/about/quotes.html), we learn that she constantly defied "conventional feminine behavior . . . climbed trees, 'belly-slammed' her sled to start it downhill, and hunted rats with a .22 rifle. She also kept a scrapbook of newspaper clippings about successful women in predominantly male-oriented fields, including film direction and production, law, advertising, management, and mechanical engineering." Amelia believed, "You can do anything you decide to do. You can act to change and control your life; and the procedure, the process, is its own reward."

Ted Williams was a proud man with as much right to boast as anyone. He was a Hall of Fame baseball player whose 1941 season marked the last time in the twentieth century that anyone finished with a batting average of .400 or better. He served in both World War II and the Korean War. With his excellent vision and superb coordination, he even set a gunnery record during pilot training. Williams had supreme faith in his ability, on or off the field:

> I lived a book on pitchers. . . . [My first coach] used to say that in seven years on the playground I never broke a bat hitting a ball incorrectly, that all my bats had the bruises in the same spot, like they were hammered there by a careful carpenter, right on the thick of the hitting surface.

EXERCISE 7: Test Your Faith

The following test will help you to determine your own sources of faith.

1. Describe your single most important source of faith.

_____

_____

_____

2. I have questioned or examined my faith:

Never	Rarely	Often	Very Often
1	2	3	4

3. Over the years, I have seen my faith increase or decrease:

Decrease Greatly	Decrease Slightly	Increase Slightly	Increase Greatly
1	2	3	4

4. I make time to practice what I believe:

     Never   Rarely   Often   Very Often
       1   2   3   4

5. Based on your answers to questions 2–4, where does your faith need work? Is it time for further examination? Perhaps you need to develop or restore your faith. Are you practicing what you preach?

6. How would you rank the eight different centers of value described in this chapter? You may want to refer to Table 4.2 on page 122. These were: a higher power, nature, custom and tradition, economics, diversity and equality, science, others, and the self. You might choose to rank these faith options in terms of your current faith status or your desired faith commitments.

a. _____   (Most cherished)

b. _____

c. _____

d. _____

e. _____

f. _____

g. _____

h. _____   (Least cherished)

Spiritual Wisdom

An intelligent faith requires a dedication to spiritual growth. The specific ingredients for developing a smart soul are the following: depth, honesty, openness, trust, and spiritual chemistry.

Depth

Spiritual depth is achieved through a significant investment in one or more centers of value. A shallow faith is revealed in superficial engagements with a higher power, the forces of nature, family and friends, or other faith sources.

Psychologist Gordon Allport's notions of intrinsic and extrinsic religiosity may help to clarify the difference between spiritual depth and spiritual superficiality. According to Allport, extrinsic individuals limit their investment in religion to public displays and social gatherings, filling their prayers with a list of personal requests. In contrast, the intrinsically religious are more private in their devotion, expressing a strong desire to develop a more intimate relationship with a higher power. Extending this idea, an extrinsically motivated scientist is primarily interested in fame and fortune, whereas an intrinsically motivated scientist could be characterized as a dedicated truth seeker.

Honesty

Spiritual honesty refers to your relationship with a particular center of value. Are you genuinely invested in a higher power? Are you truly devoted to social reform or equal opportunity? Is your investment in nature, science, or your own capacities based on an abiding respect for that center of value? To what extent are you merely going through the motions of "faithing"? It is critical to make sure that your faith is grounded in spiritual honesty rather than political correctness, peer pressure, or attempts to escape the past.

Spiritual honesty is reflected in a passionate commitment. The time spent in prayer, meditation, or service to your cause should be deeply engrossing, resembling the "flow experience" described by psychologist Mihaly Csikszentmihalyi:

> We have all experienced times when, instead of being buffeted by anonymous forces . . . we feel a sense of exhilaration, a deep sense of enjoyment that is long cherished and that becomes a hallmark in memory of what life should be like.

Openness

Openness is fundamental to faith development. According to Gabriel Marcel, "Openness allows the space for hope to spread." Openness helps the individual to fully engage the centers of value and allow the spiritual bounty of available resources to be more fully integrated into daily thoughts and actions. There are two main forms of openness: external and internal. Both involve a permeability of consciousness that is based on biological, social, and psychological needs.

Many of the world's faith systems include practices designed to foster openness. For example, the Africans who practice Ifa dance in front of a mat that symbolizes the interweaving of the natural and the divine worlds. Through this process, they open themselves to the possibility of spiritual guidance. Similarly, Hindus practice a form of yoga that is designed to open the various chakras or energy centers in the body. Jews face Jerusalem when they pray, and Muslims face Mecca; within each of these holy cities, Jews face the Western Wall and Muslims face the Kaaba, each religion's holiest site. Native Americans in the Southwest partake of peyote, which opens the senses to the spirit world.

There is also a need for an inner openness to reclaim hidden parts of the self. Over the course of an individual's lifetime, memories and images are imprinted in various realms of the mind, including "storage areas" that can be hard to access by using typical memory-recall strategies. Such psychic dispersion calls for a reintegration of experience. Sometimes these significant traces of life appear in dreams, during meditation, or while listening to music. Being open to such experiences is crucial for achieving greater self-understanding and ultimately for connecting with the wider self, or what William James called "the more."

Trust

Multiple centers of value, whether experienced as an internal or external faith source, are already prewired in the human psyche. It does not matter whether we refer to these emotional response patterns in terms of archetypes or instincts. The important point is that you harbor a vast reservoir of potential energy for connecting with multiple faith sources. Mystics understand this notion very well because it underscores their belief that each individual is part of a greater whole. Moreover, this is why many religious and self-help groups encourage their members to look within for their "inner god" or "wise mind." Faith arises from a satisfaction of the trust needs associated with the motives underlying hope. Goal-oriented trust engenders the belief that one is adequately empowered to achieve mastery. Relational trust fuels the expectation of continued involvement with a valued presence. Safety-based trust imparts a sense of security or the assurance of ultimate salvation.

The keys to developing trust in one or more centers of value are self-examination and patience. Begin with a spiritual inventory of your faith needs. Some individuals are primarily mastery oriented, while others seek greater intimacy or peace of mind. Perhaps your faith needs encompass more than one of the hope motives as well as multiple centers of value. Once you begin to understand your spiritual needs, adopt an attitude of active waiting, remaining patient but simultaneously mindful. Be ready for investment opportunities related to mastery, attachment, or survival.

Trust and openness are mutually reinforcing virtues. Without openness, you will be unable to engage with trustworthy others. Without trust, you will be unable to cultivate an attitude of openness. Summoning the courage to achieve greater trust and openness will create psychological space for you to engage one or more centers of value and will assure you what Marcel dubbed the "first fruits and pledges" of fundamental hope. The "fruits" include dependability (goal-oriented trust), intimacy (relational-trust), and security (survival-trust); the "pledges" encompass continued success, ongoing presence, and future wellness.

Spiritual Chemistry

Spiritual chemistry is the final ingredient for faith development. As an individual, you have a unique set of physical and emotional characteristics that impact your relationship with the outside world. You might be active and relish a brisk morning walk. Perhaps you are more sedentary and are happiest when lounging before a fireplace. You might enjoy the outdoors and delight in the changing seasons or prefer a climate-controlled interior. You could be someone who readily consumes ice cream, cheese, and yogurt or someone who suffers from lactose intolerance.

On a spiritual level, certain religious beliefs might be hard for you to digest, whereas others are particularly appealing to your tastes. You might find spiritual sustenance in nature or a social cause, or perhaps you are satisfied by indulging in the process of scientific discovery. Whatever your inclinations, you need some type of faith to live fully in the world. The key to a "good enough" faith lies in meeting the needs of your particular spiritual type.

SIX SPIRITUAL TYPES

Pay close attention to your faith needs. Do not settle for a particular mind-set or worldview because it is the current rage or politically correct. Bowing to such pressures puts you at risk for feeling powerless, alienated, and vulnerable. Instead, your goal should be to develop a faith that is consistent with your basic spiritual type.

Our research suggests that there are six basic ways of being spiritual. Each represents a culmination of many factors, including temperament and critical life events as well as family and cultural experiences. The following is a brief description of each type:

- *Followers* share a need to believe in a higher power and seek the presence of that being or essence in their daily lives. They desire external structure in the form of an ordered cosmos, a spiritual doctrine, and rules for living.
- *Collaborators* see themselves as joining forces to achieve important outcomes. They prefer to develop alliances and cultivate support for spiritually acceptable ends rather than adhere to a fixed code.
- *Independents* strive to analyze and explain the world. They prefer to place their faith in reason and logic. In addition, they are particularly apt to draw strength from the hero archetype.
- *Mystics* tend to be emotionally sensitive, intuitive, and primed to experience a union with a transcendent presence. They desire contact, merger, and oneness.
- *Reformers* believe in changing the world. They seek a pluralistic mosaic

or a spiritual cooperative. Most of them have personally experienced injustice, discrimination, or alienation of one kind or another.

- *Sufferers* are acutely sensitized to the pain and dangers that characterize the human condition. They seek liberation from distress, frequently through changing themselves rather than struggling with external constraints.

Depending on your spiritual type, you will probably find yourself initially attracted to a particular center of value. At the end of the chapter you will have the opportunity to take a spiritual type questionnaire. Table 4.3 pairs the spiritual types with faith possibilities. For example, if you are a spiritual follower who craves structure, you might gravitate toward a traditional religion, but if you are collaboratively oriented, you may prefer a Protestant sect that emphasizes a God who "helps those who help themselves," or you may also feel drawn to the Hindu concept of an *atman* (inner god).

Spiritual independents, who seek to increase faith in the self, thrive when provided with inspiring role models. These role models can be drawn from virtually any field of human endeavor, including the arts, science, business, politics, sports, and entertainment. Hope stalwarts, besides the ones that are listed in the table, might include Lance Armstrong, Carl Sagan, and Oprah Winfrey.

Spiritual mystics live for moments of transcendent connection. Do you seek a faith based on an emotional merger with a higher power or spiritual presence? If so, you may be a mystic. Christianity, Judaism, and Islam all have mystical traditions. If you are more interested in a merger with nature, you might want to consider exploring Native American spirituality, Ifa, or the Australian Dreamtime ceremony. Nature worship can serve as a source of mysticism as well as of collaborative spirituality. The determining factor is whether you are more invested in experiencing a sense of fusion and oneness or in seeking empowerment.

Table 4.3. Spiritual Types and Faith Possibilities

Spiritual Types (and Hope Motives)	Options for Jump-Starting Faith
Follower (Attachment and survival)	Catholicism (Roman Catholic or Eastern Orthodox); Evangelical Christianity; Islam (Sunni or Shiite); Orthodox and Conservative Judaism; Confucianism
Collaborator (Mastery and attachment)	Liberal Protestantism; Quakerism; Hinduism; Ifa; Native American religions; Reform Judaism
Independent (Mastery)	Ralph Waldo Emerson, Ayn Rand, Bertrand Russell; science-based hobbies or careers; athletic pursuits; skills-oriented education and training; Unitarian Universalism
Mystic (Attachment)	Jewish (Kabbalah, Martin Buber); Christian (Thomas Keating, Thomas Merton); Sufi (Rumi); nature-based (Rachel Carson, Jane Goodall)
Reformer (Attachment and mastery)	Sociopolitical activism; union membership; writings of Mahatma Gandhi, Martin Luther King Jr., Jean-Jacques Rousseau, Henry David Thoreau; postmodernism (Michel Foucault, Jacques Derrida)
Sufferer (Survival)	Buddhism; dialectical behavior therapy; relaxation, meditation training, biofeedback; massage, polarity therapy, reflexology; yoga

Christian mysticism has a long tradition, influenced by Neoplatonists such as Plotinus in the third century and St. John of the Cross in the sixteenth century. In its modern guises, it includes "the contemplative life" as described by Thomas Merton and the more recent "centering prayer" of Thomas Keating.

Some Jews who prefer a more mystical form of spirituality might look to the Kabbalah while those of a more secular persuasion might be more attracted to the writings of Martin Buber.

Muslims who seek a deeper bond with Allah can turn to the offerings of the Sufi sect, such as Rumi's inspired poetry of love.

Spiritual reformers are acutely sensitized to acts of injustice or limitations regarding equal opportunity. If this is true for you, your path to a stronger faith is likely to involve some form of activism. For example, you might want to consider helping children in need or getting involved in local or national politics. Other faith-building exercises for the reformer include volunteering at a hospital, a school, or a community shelter.

Gina O'Connell Higgins described the inner dynamics of activism that can serve to positively motivate victims of cruelty and abuse. In her interviews with resilient adults, she explored the process of "giving what one did not receive" and the gratification of fostering "symbolic corrections" to restore one's vision of a just world. For example, one survivor of severe child abuse became the head of a large human service agency. He described his work as a "crusade of joy."

Spiritual sufferers may find solace in Buddhist practices. Buddhism is the only major faith that highlights specific strategies for escaping the torment of pain, loss, and death. It promises a tranquil mind and a peaceful alternative to futile cravings. Many psychotherapists have begun to incorporate Buddhist principles in treating trauma survivors and other chronic-stress sufferers.

It is important to have some awareness of the many faith options at your disposal. Moreover, do not feel that you must restrict yourself to just one spiritual possibility. The human mind is multilayered. Just imagine all the data that is stored in the folds of the cortex that encases the deeper structures of your brain! As you grow in spiritual wisdom and integrate your inner and outer worlds, certain spiritual alternatives will inevitably move to the foreground, whereas others might recede into the background. Remember that openness to experience is one of your greatest resources for building faith and hope.

Tony's Faith and Spirituality:

I was not surprised by my results on the spiritual type questionnaire. I scored highest in "sufferer" and second highest in both "collaborator" and "mystic." Because I experienced a great deal of loss and trauma at an early age, this made perfect sense to me. It is also not a coincidence that I gravitated toward behavioral medicine as a subspecialty because it incorporates various mind-body techniques for reducing anxiety, pain, and other stress-related disorders. I can also relate to the concept of being a collaborator.

While I have some faith in science and experts as well as in my own abilities, I feel most comfortable when I forge a partnership, drawing on my own skills as well as the advice of others. I find myself doing this in just about every area of my life, from job-related tasks to home repairs and my personal healthcare. For example, when I am not feeling well, I will do some research on my own, pray for guidance, ask friends and family for advice, and also consult with my personal physician. At first I was a little surprised by my relatively high mystic score. But then I considered my early attachment disruptions and painful losses as well as my ongoing investment in prayer and meditation. Clearly, maintaining a continuing positive presence is important to me. In terms of my centers of value, I have looked to my Catholic faith, my family, and my friends as well as my profession of psychology to satisfy my need for healing (sufferer), connection (mystic), and empowerment (collaborator).

Henry's Faith and Spirituality:

My scores on the spiritual type questionnaire reflect my orientation toward independence as well as my desire to be a reformer, contributing to building a better world as a parent, educator, and scholar. Not surprisingly, my centers of value relate to athleticism, or more accurately in my case, a broader sense of physical competence. I also have a great deal of faith in my problem-solving skills and creativity, which I strive to blend with my faith in diversity by using my skills to be a kindly hope provider, to see the good in others, and to sustain a healthy respect for individual differences.

I was somewhat surprised that I did not score very high in the mystic category. This is perhaps because my particular brand of mysticism has been primarily humanistic and nature-based. Nevertheless, my sense of connection with loved ones, some no longer living, is very strong. For example, although my parents passed away decades ago, their inner presence is linked within me to my sense of connection with my own children and grandchildren. In addition, I have always felt a deep sense of oneness with nature. I find it extremely painful to see any living thing— human or nonhuman, plant or animal—taken for granted, mistreated, or destroyed. I suppose that my early experiences with the fragility of life and the reality of having to fend for myself from an early age heightened my sense of empathy for the welfare of all living things.

EXERCISE 8: Discover Your Spiritual Type

For each of the following questions, rate your agreement by using the scale below. When you have finished, total your scores for each of the six spiritual types and place your ratings next to each item in the spaces provided. Your highest score is your primary spiritual type. Your second highest score is your secondary spiritual type.

Strongly disagree	A Little Like Me disagree	A Lot Like Me agree	Exactly Like Me agree
0	1	2	3

_____ 1. My life is ultimately in the hands of God or a higher power.

_____ 2. I am often keenly aware of the presence of God or a higher power.

_____ 3. When I get what I want, it is usually because I have worked hard for it.

_____ 4. To prosper, I must be in harmony with the will of God or a divine force.

_____ 5. I am often amazed at how tense and anxious I have become.

_____ 6. I frequently go out of my way to make sure that a fair and just outcome will take place.

_____ 7. Without my faith in a higher power, I would feel lost and without direction.

_____ 8. I often pray or meditate to become closer to God or a higher power.

_____ 9. My life is primarily determined by my own actions.

_____10. I feel most satisfied when I'm working hand in hand with a spiritual presence.

_____11. I have a difficult time relaxing my mind and my body.

_____12. Everyone has unique gifts, and we need to ensure that this potential is released.

_____13. I often turn to scriptures or spiritual leaders for guidance and support.

_____14. My faith is based on developing a closer connection to God or a higher power.

Strongly disagree	A Little Like Me disagree	A Lot Like Me agree	Exactly Like Me agree
0	1	2	3

___15. Few feelings in life are greater than pride in one's own accomplishments.

___16. In dealing with life, I manage what I can and leave the rest to Mother Nature.

___17. Compared to others, I have had a rather painful life.

___18. I feel that one of my life goals is to work for justice and equality.

Score your type:

Follower:	1 ___	7 ___	13 ___	Total = ___
Collaborator:	4 ___	10 ___	16 ___	Total = ___
Independent:	3 ___	9 ___	15 ___	Total = ___
Mystic:	2 ___	8 ___	14 ___	Total = ___
Reformer:	6 ___	12 ___	18 ___	Total = ___
Sufferer:	5 ___	11 ___	17 ___	Total = ___

My primary spiritual type (highest score): _____

My secondary spiritual type (second-highest score): _____

PART TWO:

REBUILDING HOPE

Part Two provides suggestions for addressing hopelessness, anxiety, and fear. These three psychic disruptions are a source of misery for millions around the globe. In Chapter 5, an approach to overcoming hopelessness is outlined that combines cognitive therapy, a healing relationship, and a spiritual practice. In Chapter 6, you will learn specific coping skills that can be used to forge a more resilient emotional core. In Chapter 7 we discuss the major fears that can get in the way of a more hopeful life and provide strategies for transforming each fear into hope.

5

Dealing with Hopelessness

The truth I wished for came to my mind
in a great flash of light. . . . I could feel
my being transformed, instinct and
intellect balanced equally, as in
a wheel whose motion nothing jars.

—Dante, *Paradise*

In this chapter we introduce strategies for confronting feelings of hopelessness. You will recall that we began Chapter 3 with a quote from Dante's *Inferno* and his reference to the nine circles of hell. Fortunately for his readers, Dante envisioned an equal number of nine heavenly spheres. In an analogous fashion, we offer nine sets of solutions, one for each type of hopelessness introduced in Chapter 3.

Beyond addressing the various types of hopelessness, we also provide suggestions for dealing with depression and suicide, two of the most serious consequences of hopelessness. Dante imagined that heaven was akin to a sacred ladder whose rungs varied in brightness, from lower levels that were moonlit to the highest and brightest stations. Similarly, we view this chapter as the first step in the illumination process, helping you to move from the darkness of hopelessness into the light of hope. In the forthcoming chapters we will be suggesting ways that you can further brighten your prospects for mastery, attachment, and survival.

Hopelessness can be treated with a combination of cognitive therapy, a healing relationship, and a spiritual practice. Cognitive therapy is widely accepted as the most effective nonmedical approach to treating disorders of mood and emotion. It consists of unearthing, challenging, and replacing irrational beliefs and ways of thinking. The hopelessness that results from disordered thinking is attributable to three factors.

First, irrational thought processes can function automatically. According to psychologist Judith Beck, they are nondeliberative and difficult to turn off. Second, both the disordered contents and the processes are invariably driven by negative beliefs that were instilled at an early age, forming the center of an individual's sense of self, the world, and the future. Beck pointed out that such core beliefs tend to be global, rigid, and overgeneralized. Third, beliefs, whether they are rational or irrational, wield great power over an individual. Mahatma Gandhi noted, "Your beliefs become your thoughts. Your thoughts become your words. Your words become your actions. Your actions become your habits. Your habits become your values. Your values become your destiny."

There are certain distorted ways of thinking that are common among individuals who suffer from hopelessness. We are not suggesting that every individual who experiences a specific type of hopelessness is having the same thoughts. However, certain distortions are more apt to be associated with specific forms of hopelessness. In short, if you have been feeling hopeless, your first step toward recovery should be to become more aware of your thought processes.

A healing relationship is the second method of reestablishing hope. A liberating relationship is especially therapeutic for those who feel doomed, helpless, or captive. A supportive relationship is particularly beneficial for those who feel alienated, forsaken, or uninspired. An empowering relationship is most likely to aid those who feel powerless, oppressed, or limited.

A spiritual practice, the third way of reestablishing hope, ensures the inclusion of a faith factor, another indispensable ingredient of hope. Because hope and spirituality are so intertwined, it is possible for individuals to derive a sense of freedom, trust, or strength from virtually any spiritual belief system. Nevertheless, as we emphasized in Chapter 4, certain belief systems are particularly well-suited for addressing particular hope needs.

Table 5.1 lists nine cognitive distortions that tend to plague individuals who are prone to depression and hopelessness. This list has been compiled from several sources, but it is derived primarily from the works of psychiatrist Aaron Beck and psychologist David Burns.

Table 5.1. Cognitive Distortions in Hopelessness

Varieties of Hopelessness	Typical Cognitive Distortions
Doom	Jumping to Conclusions
Helplessness	Magnification
Captivity	Emotional Reasoning
Alienation	Mind Reading
Feeling Forsaken	Overgeneralization
Feeling Uninspired	All-or-Nothing Thinking
Powerlessness	Discounting the Positive
Oppression	Personalization
Limitation	Labeling

DEALING WITH FEELINGS OF DOOM

Doom, helplessness, and captivity
are the survival-based forms of hopelessness.

Cognitive Processes

Those who feel doomed as a result of a medical or psychological diagnosis tend to jump to conclusions. Sometimes called "fortune-telling," this distortion involves a presumption (i.e., without first checking the facts) that things will turn out badly. This distortion can be particularly devastating in the context of cancer, AIDS, and other serious maladies that have become metaphors for hopelessness.

Norman Cousins once shared an anecdote about a woman in a hospital bed who was lying awake with her eyes closed. A doctor came by with a group of medical students. Thinking that she was asleep, the doctor turned to his students and uttered, "TI." The woman mistakenly assumed that "TI" meant "terminal illness." Within a very short time she was dead. In fact, the doctor was referring to a far less serious condition.

The best antidote for jumping to conclusions is to examine the evidence. If you are diagnosed with a serious illness, do your homework and get the facts. For example, Harvard anthropologist Stephen Jay Gould was diagnosed with a rare abdominal cancer at the age of forty. When told that the median survival time for someone with this disease was only eight months, he did some research. In his essay "The Median Isn't the Message," Gould shared how his knowledge of statistics helped him to examine the evidence. He was able to tell himself, "Fine, half the people will live longer. Now what are my chances of being in that half?" After factoring in his age, his relatively healthy lifestyle, the early stage of diagnosis, and the quality of healthcare available to him, Gould arrived at a far more hopeful prognosis. In fact, he lived another twenty years before succumbing to an unrelated illness.

Those who feel *helpless* may unwittingly engage in magnification. According to David Burns, such individuals are experts at diminishing the value of their actual virtues while magnifying their perceived weaknesses. For example, a very bright but chronically depressed college student repeatedly had thoughts that he was stupid. Whenever he did well on an exam, he considered it either a fluke or the result of an easy exam from a professor who had low standards. At the same time, he believed that his girlfriend was a virtual genius who deserved every accolade.

One antidote for magnification is thinking in shades of gray. If you are feeling helpless, instead of holding on to artificial dichotomies such as good or bad and perfect or terrible, orient your thinking around variations and continuums. In other words, stop thinking in terms of extremes. Keep in mind that there is a tremendous amount of gray area between total helplessness and complete self-sufficiency.

Captive self-imprisonment, which arises from low self-esteem, repetition compulsion, or projective identification, is also amenable to a cognitive approach. A distortion of thinking called "emotional reasoning" frequently underlies this form of hopeless attachment. Strong emotions are unwittingly transformed into the reasons for staying in an unhealthy relationship. It is common for both women and men to stay in bad relationships because they have a distorted view of love and commitment. As children, they may have been exposed to family interactions in which domination was viewed as love or in which total self-sacrifice was defined as commitment. As adults, they find themselves trapped by their own confused feelings. Unaware of the flawed thought processes underlying their emotions, they feel utterly trapped.

Captive self-imprisonment is best dealt with by using a *survey method*. If you feel stuck in a dysfunctional relationship, begin by asking yourself how others might construe your situation. Next, survey as wide a sample of individuals as possible, looking for a pattern or a trend in their perceptions. In this manner, you may be able to arrive at a more freeing way of thinking about your relationship.

During her childhood, Celie, the protagonist in Alice Walker's *The Color Purple*, was repeatedly raped and beaten by a monstrous father. As a teenager, she was married off to another despicable violent man who abused her. Fortunately for Celie, she met two assertive women, Shug and Sofia, who provided her with a vastly different perspective on love and commitment. In addition, she drew strength from her younger sister, Nettie, a missionary in Africa. From Shug, Celie learned the sweetness of intimacy. Sofia taught her dignity and self-respect, whereas Nettie demonstrated the power of a lasting love sustained by a shared spiritual mission.

Liberating Relationships

The best attachments offer liberation as well as security. Remember, it is the roots of hope that give it wings. A liberating relationship is crucial for those who feel doomed, helpless, or captive—the survival-related forms of hopelessness.

The individual who feels doomed by a serious illness or advancing years needs a freedom guide, an indefatigable hope explorer who will keep looking for every imaginable degree of freedom.

Individuals who feel helpless need a catalyst to help them unleash their potential. In her interviews with resilient adults, Gina O'Connell Higgins found repeated references to surrogate caregivers who "encouraged the resilient to let their talents unfold." In reflecting on the importance of these "gifted givers," Higgins quoted from Herman Melville's

Moby Dick: "When fortunes' favorites sail close by us, we, though drooping before, catch somewhat of the rushing breeze, and joyfully feel our bagging sails fill out."

Captive self-imprisonment is a snare within the psyche that develops in the very first years of life, before the advent of speech and logic. As a result of early interactions with caregivers, a template is produced that repeatedly drives an individual toward certain kinds of romantic partners. Psychologist John Money called these templates *love maps*. Marriage therapist Harville Hendrix dubbed them *ghost partners*. Psychiatrist Thomas Lewis and his colleagues named them *limbic attracters*, emotional magnets created from the brain areas that are associated with highly charged memories and the most basic experiences of pleasure and pain.

Complete liberation from your limbic bond is neither possible nor desirable. What *is* possible and desirable is to shed the destructive elements within the template. For example, it is perfectly fine to be attracted to a mate who has the same hair color, body build, religious background, or hobbies as one or both of your parents. However, it is extremely problematic if your attraction is motivated by an unconscious need to shore up a heavy drinker, please a critical authority figure, or secure the love of an emotionally distant loner.

Experts are divided on whether you should extricate yourself from a partner who embodies negative aspects of your love map. Some believe that it is best to disengage, invest in critical self-awareness, and find a healthier mate. Others, such as Hendrix, believe it is possible to "keep the love you find." Given that individuals seem destined to connect with partners with "complementary character defenses" and "symmetrical wounds," Hendrix argues that couples should work with nature's gift in what might be called a process of co-liberation.

If you decide to follow Hendrix's advice, make sure that your mate supports rather than undermines the cause of liberation. Co-liberation is more likely to occur when a couple shares four hopes: to each be seen as an individual, to relate in an emotionally corrective fashion by diverging from destructive old scripts, to develop a revised love map that positively transforms the couple's mutual attraction, and to grow as individuals as well as a couple. In the words of Khalil Gibran's prophet, "Love one another but make not a bond of love . . . Fill each other's cup but drink not from one cup."

Those held captive by other-imprisonment can benefit from a transcendent presence. Dramatic examples of this form of liberation have been provided by concentration camp survivors. Viktor Frankl, during his imprisonment at Auschwitz, was able to transcend the prevailing death and darkness by continually reflecting on his beloved wife:

> My soul found its way back from the prisoner's existence to another world, and I resumed talk with my loved one: I asked her questions, and she answered; she questioned me in return, and I answered. . . . A thought crossed my mind: I didn't even know if she was still alive, and I had no means of finding out . . . but at that moment it ceased to matter. There was no need to know; nothing could touch the strength of my love, and the thoughts of my beloved.

Rollo May noted that human beings have the capacity to experience the "freedom of doing" as well as the "freedom of being." In all but the most extreme cases of entrapment, there are still options available to an individual. Someone with cancer can still choose love over fear and vitality over despair. An aging individual can still choose to be productive. A condemned prisoner can still choose to die with dignity.

Freedom of being is especially important for those dealing with other-imprisonment. Viktor Frankl found a hiding spot behind a pile of corpses where he could be alone with his thoughts for five minutes every day. Wrote Frankl, "Everything can be taken from a man but one thing: the last of his freedoms—to choose one's attitude in any given set of circumstances." American prisoners of war in Vietnam wandered far and wide with their minds. Some built their dream homes, and others revisited old friends and neighborhoods.

Spiritual Freedom

Buddhism offers a powerful set of practices for those who are overwhelmed by feelings of distress associated with doom, helplessness, or captivity. Samatha (calm) meditation is used to cultivate mental and physical relaxation. Vipassana (insight) meditation is used to bring greater awareness. In fact, one translation of the Sanskrit word *vipassana* is to "see through," in the sense of looking beyond the barriers and obstacles of ordinary reality.

Although each type of meditation can transform consciousness and facilitate freedom from distress, they work best when they are used together. Start with a simple Samatha breathing meditation to achieve an initial state of mental and physical relaxation. Sit comfortably, close your eyes, and focus on your breath. Inhale for a count of four, and exhale for a count of six. After five minutes, switch to insight meditation. Thich Nhat Hanh's *Looking Deeply* is an excellent example of a meditation that is designed to penetrate the illusions of permanent suffering, isolation, and nonbeing. Here is a shortened adaptation:

AWARE OF A WAVE ON THE OCEAN, I BREATHE IN.
SMILING TO THE WAVE, I BREATHE OUT.
AWARE OF THE WATER IN THE WAVE, I BREATHE IN.
SMILING TO THE WATER, I BREATHE OUT.

Seeing the birth of a wave, I breathe in.

Smiling to the birth of the wave, I breathe out.

Seeing the death of a wave, I breathe in.

Smiling to the death of the wave, I breathe out.

Seeing the birthless nature of water in the wave,
I breathe in.

Smiling to the birthless nature of the water,
I breathe out.

Seeing the deathless nature of water in the wave,
I breathe in.

Smiling to the deathless nature of the water,
I breathe out.

Seeing the birthless nature of my consciousness,
I breathe in.

Smiling to the birthless nature of my consciousness,
I breathe out.

Seeing the deathless nature of my consciousness,
I breathe in.

Smiling to the deathless nature of my consciousness,
I breathe out.

Dealing with Feelings of Alienation

*Alienation, feeling forsaken, and feeling uninspired
are the attachment-based forms of hopelessness.*

Cognitive Processes

The attachment-related forms of hopelessness are fueled by the cognitive distortions of "mind reading," "overgeneralization," and "all-or-nothing thinking."

Mind reading is a form of jumping to conclusions in which an individual presumes to know what others think of him or her. Many people who feel alienated assume (wrongly) that absolutely no one is or ever will be in their corner. The antidote for mind reading is to *examine the emotional evidence.* This requires courage, in the form of trust and openness, to survey how others experience you. For example, although Ron Kovic thought that the entire country was against him and his buddies who had fought in Vietnam, this was obviously not the case.

Those who feel forsaken often overgeneralize. They may have suffered rejection from a parent or a potential romantic partner. From a singular affront, some individuals generalize to all family members or all potential mates. In the worst-case scenario, a person can feel abandoned by the entire human race.

Those who overgeneralize need to *examine the external validity* of their beliefs. If you feel forsaken, it is important to get outside your head, to see if your inner reality is an accurate reflection of the outside world. In assessing external validity, laboratory scientists review the size and the representativeness of their sample. Most people who feel forsaken are overgeneralizing from a relatively small sample of experiences. With more extensive sampling, it is highly likely that they will encounter more hope-promoting responses from others.

Many who feel uninspired have unwittingly fallen prey to all-or-nothing thinking. They have become boxed in by artificial dichotomies that leave little room for human imperfection or personal growth. Some students believe that straight As are the mark of intelligence and that anything less is not worth pursuing. Others formulate important goals but show little persistence. They want to eat better, stop smoking, or increase their level of physical activity, but they lose heart after the most minor setback.

All-or-nothing thinking can blind individuals to the availability of more appropriate role models. For example, consider African American boys who believe that their only choice is to emulate sports stars such as Michael Jordan or Donovan McNabb. Consequently, they might ignore inspiring teachers, civic leaders, or parents who are in their immediate environment.

To combat all-or-nothing thinking, it is also advisable to *think in shades of gray*. Consider things from a continuum perspective rather than in terms of arbitrary cutoffs. Be more accepting of your own potential for self-inspiration through incremental improvements or successive approximations. At the same time, take a closer look at individuals, famous and not so famous, who might serve to inspire you in terms of the really important qualities that underlie success.

Supportive Relationships

Seeking out supportive relationships is a must for those who feel alienated, forsaken, or uninspired. One of the meanings of *support* is "to give hope to." *The Oxford English Dictionary* defines *support* as "supplying what is necessary for the maintenance of life" and providing "courage, confidence, and the power of endurance." Emotional support is as vital for survival as air, water, or food. If you feel alienated, forsaken, or uninspired, it is imperative that you seek out hope providers who can offer a consistent attitude of acceptance.

Follow the advice of Carl Rogers, the "guru" of unconditional, positive regard. Rogers specified three conditions for cultivating therapeutic relationships. Although he originally envisioned them as criteria for psychotherapy, he made it clear that these conditions apply to all relationships. According to Rogers, those who are most supportive are real or congruent, which means that they are completely honest in the way they relate to you. They are accepting and caring, but in a nonpossessive manner. Finally, they provide accurate empathy so that you feel truly known by them.

In its most elevated form, unconditional love has been described as a connection from one person's center of divinity to another person's center of divinity. In describing the loving reach of Mother Teresa, a Nobel Prize official noted how "the loneliest and the most wretched, the dying destitute, the abandoned lepers, have been received by her and her Sisters with warm compassion devoid of condescension, based on [the] reverence for Christ in Man."

Unity and Inspiration

Spiritual blessings can be powerful antidotes for those who feel alienated or forsaken. In most faith systems, a blessing is viewed as a gift of approval as well as a form of moral support, often received from God or a higher power but sometimes transmitted via an earthly representative such as a priest or shaman. In Christianity, blessings are recited on the people by the clergy. In Judaism, blessings are recited by everyone many times throughout the day, such as before and after eating, after going to the bathroom, and on seeing the wonders of nature; blessings are an expression of an appreciation of God's benevolence and a means of sanctifying life on earth.

In the Christian tradition, the writings of Thomas Merton have long been a source of comfort for those suffering from feelings of alienation. Merton was a Catholic mystic who rose above his early years as a reckless, undisciplined youth to become one of the most influential spiritual writers of the twentieth century. Merton's most famous prayer can be found in his book *Thoughts in Solitude*. We present part of this prayer below. This quasi-meditative tool can be particularly inspiring for those who seek a spiritual connection. As with any spiritual or meditative practice, it is important to find a quiet space and enough time for unhurried reflection.

I DO NOT SEE THE ROAD AHEAD OF ME.

I CANNOT KNOW FOR CERTAIN WHERE IT WILL END.

NOR DO I REALLY KNOW MYSELF, AND THE FACT THAT

I THINK THAT I AM FOLLOWING YOUR WILL

DOES NOT MEAN THAT I AM ACTUALLY DOING SO.

BUT I BELIEVE THAT THE DESIRE TO PLEASE

YOU DOES IN FACT PLEASE YOU.

AND I HOPE I HAVE THAT DESIRE IN ALL

THAT I AM DOING.

I HOPE THAT I WILL NEVER DO ANYTHING

APART FROM THAT DESIRE.

AND I KNOW THAT IF I DO THIS YOU WILL LEAD ME BY

THE RIGHT ROAD THOUGH I MAY KNOW NOTHING

ABOUT IT.

Some may want to consider a Native American blessing. A number of prayers and meditations in Native American traditions were specifically designed to inspire mastery while also conferring approval and moral support. Although Native American cultures have been primarily oriented toward attachment and survival, they have also recognized the need for mastery, particularly in the service of the hunt. Many Native American blessings encourage the individual to join forces with the power of nature, to soar like the eagle, stand strong like the buffalo, or be cunning like the fox. The following "Great Spirit Prayer" is attributed to Chief Yellow Lark, a Blackfoot Indian:

Oh, Great Spirit, whose voice I hear in the wind, whose breath gives life to all the world. Hear me; I need your strength and wisdom. . . . Make my hands respect the things you have made and my ears sharp to hear your voice. . . . Make me wise so that I may understand the things you have taught my people. Help me to remain calm and strong in the face of all that comes toward me. Let me learn the lessons you have hidden in every leaf and rock. . . . I seek strength, not to be greater than my brother, but to fight my greatest enemy, myself. Make me always ready to come to you with clean hands and straight eyes. So when life fades, as the fading sunset, my spirit may come to you without shame.

DEALING WITH FEELINGS OF POWERLESSNESS

*Powerlessness, oppression, and limitation
are the mastery-based forms of hopelessness.*

Cognitive Processes

Three cognitive distortions underlie feelings of powerlessness and the other mastery-related forms of hopelessness: "discounting the positive," "personalization," and "labeling." When individuals cannot appreciate their talents and gifts, they are prone to discount any evidence of personal success or effectiveness. If they do well in an academic setting, they will attribute it to an inferior instructor or luck. If they perform well in an athletic event, it must have been a fluke, or the competition was soft. If they get a promotion, it was because the boss overestimated their competency.

It is common for those who are oppressed to engage in personalization and self-blame. This is particularly apt to happen in more individualistic cultures and when the oppression has accumulated layer upon layer, generation after generation, within the subconscious. Author Jacob Holdt has suggested that self-blame is on the increase among African Americans:

People can survive oppression if they are able to clearly identify their oppressor and thus avoid self-blame. This understanding let blacks see light at the end of the tunnel in the past. However, for the first time in history blacks have difficulties identifying their oppressor and therefore without hesitation look for the cause of their growing pain within themselves.

A strategy for counteracting self-blame is *reattribution,* which involves considering all the likely causes of negative emotions. For example, in *The Color Purple,* Celie and her doubly oppressed friends achieved a measure of hope when they vented their frustrations at the "gray-bearded, white God" and stood up to their male oppressors, black as well as white.

When individuals feel limited because of a perceived physical or intellectual disability, they may fall prey to labeling. Sometimes this kind of stereotyping is done by others, but it can also be a self-inflicted wound. Labels such as *crippled, defective, dumb,* or *lazy* can obviously be quite damaging to the ego. However, even seemingly politically correct designations, such as *special* or *disabled,* can be disempowering.

By accepting any label, individuals internalize all the conditions and limitations associated with that diagnosis. In contrast, if you are not the disorder, then it is possible for you to do more than the label would presuppose. To attack harmful labels, *define your terms.* For example, if you feel or are labeled *stupid,* reflect on the actual definition of the term. Are you always making bad decisions? Are you always careless and unable to learn? Unless these descriptions, taken from the *American Heritage Dictionary,* apply to you, then you are not stupid!

Empowering Relationships

An empowering relationship is rooted in shared control, commitment, and challenge. These characteristics define the character trait of hardiness. According to psychologist Salvatore Maddi, hardiness is "a set of attitudes and beliefs that provide the courage and motivation to do the hard work of turning stressful changes . . . into opportunities." More recently, Maddi has dubbed hardiness a form of "existential courage."

Empowering relationships instill hardiness by helping to transform an individual's sense of self. Empowered individuals experience shared control, which lies at the core of hope-based mastery. Moreover, they are brought into the fold of a higher purpose that binds together hope recipients and their hope providers. Finally, empowering relationships challenge individuals to actualize their potential.

In overcoming oppression, great liberators such as Martin Luther King Jr. and Nelson Mandela offered powerful experiences of commitment and shared control. In his famous "Letter from a Birmingham Jail," Martin Luther King Jr. wrote, "We are caught in an inescapable network of mutuality, tied in a single garment of destiny." In leaving office as president of South Africa, Nelson Mandela assured his nation that "Though I shall not be seen as much as I have been, I shall be amongst you and with you as we enter the African century; working together to make a reality of our hopes for a better world."

Full release from oppression cannot occur if leaders ask just for mere obedience or concessions from the majority in power, they must challenge the oppressed to rise to their full height. Nelson Mandela once noted the following:

Playing small doesn't serve the world. There is nothing enlightened about shrinking so that other people won't feel insecure around you. We were born to make manifest the glory of God that is within us. It's not just in some of us; it's in everyone. And as we let our light shine, we unconsciously give other people permission to do the same.

In this same spirit, Martin Luther King Jr. made the following point:

If a man is called to be a street sweeper, he should sweep streets even as Michelangelo painted, or Beethoven played music, or Shakespeare wrote poetry. He should sweep streets so well that all the hosts of heaven and earth will pause to say, here lived a great street sweeper who did his job well.

Hardiness, in the form of commitment and shared control, is also important for those who feel economically, physically, or intellectually limited. In *Restoring Hope*, Cornel West interviewed the award-winning journalist Charlayne Hunter-Gault. He asked her how the waning hope of African Americans might be bolstered, and she replied that the intergenerational transmission of hope could be disseminated by instilling values, sharing confidence-building stories, and imparting the wisdom of the ages. In Hunter-Gault's view, these three ingredients could propel ambition while ensuring a virtual "suit of armor . . . that is where the hope is."

Louis Braille is an example of an individual who rose to greatness on the wings of shared control and mutual commitment. Braille, who became blind at the age of three when he accidentally injured himself with one of his father's tools, was only twelve when he began working on a system of dots and dashes that would come to bear his name. He took the military's "night writing," a system of twelve dots that he learned from a soldier named Charles Barbier who had visited his school, and modified it into six dots. Among the individuals whom Braille credited with helping him was Valentin Haüy, who founded the first school for the blind—the Paris school that Braille had attended. After meeting Haüy, Braille felt "as if some great force of energy, some inexplicable understanding was communicated in that brief exchange." Always humble, Haüy later suggested to Braille, "It is God who has done everything."

Being challenged is also important for individuals who are dealing with intellectual or physical limitations. Psychologist Albert Bandura suggested that individuals develop feelings of self-efficacy when they succeed in tasks that they value and find challenging. A great example is provided by the actor James Earl Jones. As a child, Jones was a self-conscious stutterer. It was not until high school that he developed the confidence to express himself in public. Jones had written a poem that he showed to his favorite teacher. Sensing that James needed to be challenged, the teacher suggested that the poem was plagiarized and asked Jones to do an oral presentation for the class to prove that it was his own work. Recalled Jones, "This had a tremendous effect on me . . . [from that day on] my confidence grew."

Bill Cosby has traveled across the United States, challenging his fellow African Americans to assume more personal responsibility in their struggle for economic security. In particular, Cosby chastised young blacks for not trying hard enough to succeed in school. Speaking at one gathering, he exhorted them to remember the sacrifices of previous generations of African Americans: "Dogs, water hoses that tear the bark off trees, Emmett Till [a black youth tortured and murdered in Mississippi]. And you're going to tell me you're going to drop out of school?"

Spiritual Force

He who meditates on hope as Brahman—all
his desires are fulfilled through hope, his prayers
are not in vain; he can, of his own free will,
reach as far as hope reaches.

—CHANDOGYA UPANISHAD

Empowerment is a common theme in spiritual literature. In the New Testament, the Gospel according to John (15:5) states, "I am the vine, you are the branches. He who abides in me, and I in him, he it is that bears much fruit." Hindus believe that with persistence and the right attitude, the individual can unleash the power of kundalini, a form of coiled-up spiritual energy that is derived from a bridge with the universal *atman*, or inner god. From Sufism comes this passage: "Truth, God, came and dwelt within my heart, and was my understanding, ear, eye, and speech."

The following meditation is taken from the Brihadarany Upanishad, considered one of the most profound chapters in Hindu scriptures. A sage is asked if he knows the Great Sutra, the verse that deals with the Inner Controller. Because "he who knows the Sutra knows the worlds, he knows the gods, he knows the Vedas, he knows the self." The sage obliges:

He who inhabits all beings, yet is within all beings, whose body all beings are, and who controls all beings from within—He is your Self, the Inner Controller.

He who inhabits water, yet is within water, whose body is water, and who controls water from within—He is your Self, the Inner Controller.

He who inhabits the sky, yet is within the sky, whose body is the sky, and who controls the sky from within—He is your Self, the Inner Controller.

He who inhabits the air, yet is within the air, whose body the air is, and who controls the air from within—He is your Self, the Inner Controller.

He who inhabits the sun, yet is within the sun, whose body the sun is, and who controls the sun from within—He is your Self, the Inner Controller.

He who inhabits the moon and stars, yet is within the moon and stars, whose body the moon and stars are, and who controls the moon and stars from within—He is your Self, the Inner Controller.

He who inhabits light, yet is within light, whose body light is, and who controls light from within—He is your Self, the Inner Controller.

CONFRONTING DEPRESSION

Depression has been portrayed as evil incarnate. Writer Andrew Solomon dubbed it the "noonday demon." He recalled his own bout of depression as the time when "hell came to pay a visit." Psychiatrist Jonathan Zuess likened it to "the darkness that covers God." William Styron, another depression sufferer, labeled it a "storm of murk." Elsewhere he compared it to a form of suffocation that causes "psychic energy to throttle back to zero." Styron added, "Never let it be doubted that depression, in its extreme forms, is madness."

A major depressive episode consists of a low mood and/or a loss of interest and pleasure. In addition, the clinically depressed suffer from four or more of the following: decreased or excessive motor activity, sleep disturbance, eating disturbance, fatigue, feelings of guilt or worthlessness, concentration problems, and morbid or suicidal thoughts. However, although these are the official diagnostic criteria, many experts believe that the description is too narrow and fails to take into account individual differences in the expression and experience of depression.

Depression is not synonymous with hopelessness. From a logical standpoint, you can have one without the other. There are some individuals who are depressed but who do not feel hopeless. Others feel hopeless but not depressed. Nevertheless, these two emotional states typically occur in tandem because both are associated with breakdowns in mastery, attachment, and survival.

Psychologists such as Martin Seligman and Lyn Abramson suggested that depression results from a perceived inability to either achieve a desired goal (mastery) or avoid an aversive stimulus (survival). Neuroscientist Richard Davidson highlighted possible mastery failures at the biological level. Specifically, he and his colleagues demonstrated that parts of the left frontal lobe, which is linked to various goal-seeking behaviors, tend to be undersized and/or underactivated in some depressed individuals.

Psychologist Thomas Joiner viewed depression from an interpersonal perspective, noting that depressed individuals frequently demonstrate social skills deficits. They often speak more slowly and quietly and with little intonation or eye contact. Depressed individuals also tend to be poor care recruiters; that is, they display a strong tendency to solicit negative rather than positive feedback. Other attachment-defeating behaviors of the depressed include excessive inhibition or shyness as well as clinging and dependency.

Depression can also result from survival-related disruptions. Children who lose a parent early in life are at a higher risk for depression. Illness is another potential culprit. A recent study showed that nearly 80 percent of individuals who were seeking the care of a physician were depressed. Trauma is a particularly pernicious factor in depression. For example, in 2005, after many Jews were forced to abandon their homes in the Gaza Strip, a significant number of them were treated for depression. When they were surveyed, nearly three-quarters reported a profound loss of control, and more than half admitted having recurring dreams and nightmares.

Prolonged feelings of hopelessness can lead to depression. With this in mind, psychologist Lyn Abramson and her colleagues proposed a hopelessness theory of depression. We go further and suggest that there are *nine subtypes of hopelessness depression* (e.g., helpless depression, alienated depression, oppressed depression, etc.) Each of these types shares a *depressive layer* of symptoms, such as low mood, lack of pleasure, and sleeping or appetite problems. In addition, each variety of hopelessness depression also contains a *suffering layer* that arises from a particular type of motive disruption.

Hopelessness depression is more easily treated in its mild to moderate forms. In most cases, both the hopeless suffering and any associated depressive symptoms can be effectively reduced by using the three methods outlined earlier: cognitive therapy, a healing relationship, and a spiritual practice. However, if the depressive aspects become too severe, you may want to supplement these strategies with more biologically based interventions, including the use of antidepressant medications.

Depression is far from a condition of permanent hopelessness. Within a year of onset, more than three-quarters of those diagnosed with depression have significantly improved. Approximately two-thirds respond favorably to antidepressant medications. If you have a family history of depression, this does not necessarily mean you are fated to a life of melancholy. The best research indicates that, for most individuals, the environment plays a far greater role than your genetic history. (It is estimated that the ratio of influence of environment to genes is two to one.) Moreover, you should understand that you inherited not a disease but rather a vulnerability, which can be offset by bolstering your mastery, attachment, and survival motives.

DIFFUSING SUICIDAL IMPULSES

Hope is the major weapon against the suicide impulse.

—KARL A. MENNINGER

Every forty seconds, someone commits suicide. In the past fifty years, the suicide rate in the United States has increased 60 percent. Suicide is now the third-leading cause of death for individuals between the ages of fifteen and forty-four. In the richest and potentially most hopeful of the world's nations, suicide is the eighth-leading cause of death overall. In fact, more Americans die from suicide than from homicide.

In all but the rarest of cases, suicide must be viewed as an unjustified waste of life. Most individuals who commit suicide did not wish to die, they just wanted to stop the pain. However, for a variety of reasons, these individuals believed that death was the only way to escape their anguish and frustration. Thus, the wish to die emanates from a profound sense of entrapment, a belief that there is no exit from an intolerable and unalterable state. Medical historian George Rosen, who reviewed case histories of suicides among the ancient Greeks, Jews, and Romans, found repeated references to feeling trapped in situations too painful to endure.

For loved ones, suicide inflicts a mortal wounding of the soul, a searing pain that promises to never go away. On one suicide prevention website (http://netti.nic.fi/~suicide/links.php), someone wrote, "The person who completes suicide dies once. Those left behind die a thousand deaths." Gail Griffith, whose son narrowly survived an overdose of antidepressants, called the experience a "cataclysmic descent." Singer Judy Collins, whose son committed suicide, tried to convey the depth of her sorrow in a song entitled "Wings of Angels." In the lyrics she alluded to the "tears of saints," futile "prayers and promises," and a city that smiled and slept while her son cried and died.

Hope is conspicuously absent among those who commit suicide. In fact, the research indicates that hopelessness outweighs depression as a risk factor. Chronic states of hopelessness appear to be far more lethal than intense but short-lived experiences of despair. For example, psychiatrist Aaron Beck and his colleagues found that ten of eleven hospitalized individuals who scored high on a measure of "trait hopelessness" eventually committed suicide.

Suicides can be divided into two broad categories: subjective entrapment and objective entrapment. Some individuals falsely believe that there is no hope for empowerment, connection, or salvation. Quite often such individuals are saddled with one or more mental health disorders and/or have experienced an inordinate amount of stress. To quote psychologist George Weinberg, hope has not abandoned them, they have abandoned it. In contrast, it is possible to imagine justifiable suicides that arise from objective rather than perceived cases of entrapment. For example, it is usually easier to forgive, if not condone, an act of suicide committed by an individual who is dying a slow and painful death because of an incurable illness. In the early part of the twentieth century, the existential psychiatrist Ludwig Binswanger defended the suicide of Ellen West, a young woman who had been deprived of an authentic life by her insensitive and controlling parents and then given no hope of a cure by those in charge of her medical treatment. Sensing an ongoing resistance to realizing her real needs for mastery, attachment, and survival, Ellen chose to take her life. Below is one of her poems:

> I'D LIKE TO DIE JUST AS THE BIRDLING DOES
> THAT SPLITS HIS THROAT IN HIGHEST JUBILATION;
> AND NOT TO LIVE AS THE WORM ON EARTH LIVES ON,
> BECOMING OLD AND UGLY, DULL AND DUMB!
> NO, FEEL FOR ONCE HOW FORCES IN ME KINDLE,
> AND WILDLY BE CONSUMED IN MY OWN FIRE.

Consistent with the view of Binswanger, the eighteenth-century German philosopher Immanuel Kant defended the use of suicide for the purpose of retaining one's dignity. From his perspective, nothing was more important than the need to prevent the "dishonoring" of one's humanity. Wrote Kant, "Life, in and for itself, is not the greatest of gifts." Kant described those who commit suicide as a result of subjective entrapment as "reduced to despair" or "wearied of life" by a "series of misfortunes."

The available U.S. health statistics indicate that approximately 90 percent of all completed suicides in 2006 were committed by people who were mired in reversible forms of entrapment. Some of these individuals suffered from depression, bipolar disorder, or an anxiety disorder. Others had a personality disturbance such as narcissism or dependent personality disorder. Additional contributing factors included a history of substance abuse, access to firearms, and direct exposure to models of suicide in the media, by a family member, or in one's peer group. What all these factors have in common is the disruption of the motives that underlie hope: mastery, attachment, and survival.

Psychologist Edwin Schneidman proposed that the wish to die involves intense psychological pain (a "psyche-ache") due to a frustrated or thwarted critical need. Death is viewed as the only means of escape or liberation. He labeled the emotional pain a "perturbation" and the associated sense of entrapment a form of "constriction," a metaphorical tightening of the mind's "diaphragm."

Schneidman described five classes of suicidal individuals. Each type reveals a disruption of one or more of the motives that underlie hope. Two of his categories involved blocked achievement or power needs (mastery); another two were related to significant interpersonal losses or unmet love and belonging needs (attachment); and the fifth type was associated with an assaulted or shamed self-image, a sense of having been defeated in life (attachment and mastery). To this typology we would add a sixth type: those suffering from intense fear or physical pain arising from a history of trauma or a serious illness (survival).

Whereas Schneidman offered a purely psychological view of suicide, the eminent French sociologist Émile Durkheim examined its social roots. More than a century ago, he provided evidence that either too little or too much social influence can lead to suicide. Specifically, he outlined four classes of social suicide. In the first, the problem is over-regulation, as in the case of oppressed minorities, the poor, and those who are enslaved. The second is inadequate social grounding. When larger cultural institutions such as the church or the monarchy fall away, individuals are stripped of the usual sources of meaning. His third class, altruistic suicide, refers to individuals who are so overidentified with their group that they are prepared to sacrifice themselves for what they believe is a greater good. Suicide bombers are a modern example of this phenomenon. The fourth class, egoistic suicide, consists of alienated individuals who lack any sense of belonging.

If you are struggling with suicidal thoughts and feelings, it is very likely that you are experiencing intense pain regarding a mastery, attachment, or survival issue. Seek help in dealing with your suicidal thoughts. Try to be honest with yourself and others about your degree of risk. If you can't manage to feel safe between weekly visits to a clinic or a therapist's office, you may need to be hospitalized. How often do you think about suicide? Can you control such thoughts, or do they constantly intrude, leaving you feeling totally helpless? Have you developed a specific plan? Do you have lethal means available to you, such as firearms, poisons, or prescription medications? If your suicidal thoughts are persistent, uncontrollable, and highly specific, and you have access to lethal objects or substances, you may require more than a weekly outpatient visit.

Develop a fivefold safety plan using the following suggestions:

- *Create a safer environment.* Remove all lethal objects and substances from your immediate environment. If you are taking powerful prescription medications, ask your physician to prescribe smaller quantities and to meet or talk with you *before* offering a refill. Avoid any contagion effects that might be caused by listening to morbid music, films, literature, or Internet postings.

- *Build up your support system.* Enlist the help of your network of family and friends. Find a therapist who engenders trust and a sense of genuine concern. Keep in mind the qualities of a good hope provider that were discussed in Chapter 8.

- *Create a safer internal cognitive environment.* Improve your problem-solving skills. Work at visualizing options while minimizing all-or-nothing thinking. Collaborate with your support network in developing viable options for addressing your mastery, attachment, and survival struggles.

- *Create a safer internal emotional environment.* Increase your distress tolerance while cultivating greater self-acceptance. Seek out a dialectical behavior therapy provider or group. Surround yourself with positive and caring family and friends. Before you join a support group, social club, or Internet chat room, make sure that the context is validating and life affirming.

- *Request a comprehensive treatment plan.* If you have been diagnosed with anxiety, depression, or bipolar disorder and you also struggle with a substance-abuse problem, your risk for self-destructive behavior is greatly intensified. A truly comprehensive safety plan should include treatment for these dually diagnosed disorders.

ADDRESSING HOPELESS RAGE

Hopelessness can engender rage and violence. When this happens, homicidal and suicidal impulses can become interwoven. Prior to maiming himself, Vincent van Gogh attacked his friend Paul Gauguin. Van Gogh was so mortified by his own senseless act of aggression that he later cut off part of his left ear and ran into the street shouting, "Gauguin,

thwarted by another individual or group, they may become enraged and
even contemplate getting even. With this in mind, if you are a parent, a
teacher, or a counselor who suspects that one of your children, students,
or clients is suffering from at least one of these varieties of hopelessness,
make sure that he or she does not "fall through the cracks." Do whatever
is most appropriate. Take those who are at risk (or refer them) to a profes-
chologist, psychiatrist, or social worker who is part of a multidisciplinary
network of healthcare providers. This safety net can help with medication

6

Hope for Inner Peace

Were it not for hope, the heart would break.

—OLD SCOTTISH PROVERB

Hope is calming and supportive as well as liberating and life affirming. When you are buffeted by chaos and upheaval, hope can be a powerful anchor that keeps you emotionally centered. When danger lurks, hope can lessen the frequency and intensity of debilitating anxiety. When burdens mount and you feel unable to go it alone, a hopeful attitude can yield a caring presence. When you feel trapped or mired in darkness, hope can point you toward the light. When you think that time, age, or illness is chipping away at your sense of self, hope can help you to restore a sense of wholeness. These might be considered valuable gifts in any era, but they are particularly prized in these uncertain times.

We live in a world that seems increasingly dominated by senseless acts of terrorism and ominous references to weapons of mass destruction. New and resistant diseases are spreading, and concerns about global warming and the safety of our food, water, and air are becoming more and more urgent.

War, disease, and aggression have been part of the human experience since the beginning of recorded time. However, things are different today. The weapons are more deadly, the spread of disease is more rapid, and our awareness of danger is more thorough. Moreover, these are only the more proximate or obvious sources of our unease. Though stressful, they are dwarfed by even more fundamental problems, such as diminished community, disengaged families, mistrust of large institutions, and widespread lack of faith in God or a higher power.

In *The Meaning of Anxiety*, psychiatrist Rollo May wrote about the profoundly disturbing consequences of living within a "disintegrating society" in which "the values and standards underlying modern culture are themselves threatened." He considered this a deep-level threat because it signified that the very "charter" of the culture was under siege. Given all these stresses and uncertainties, it is not surprising that anxiety disorders have become the world's most prevalent form of psychopathology, affecting roughly one in every nine individuals.

You may be wondering how fear and anxiety relate to each other. Traditionally, psychologists have used the term *fear* to describe an externally directed response to a specific threat. In contrast, the term *anxiety* has usually been reserved for an unfocused or objectless state that resides within a person. According to this view, fear is about something "out there," whereas anxiety is about something "in here."

Hope-based survival is a matter of transforming both fear and anxiety. Strengthening your survival system can help you to deal with generalized anxiety, but developing greater resiliency might not be enough to address major fears, such as those involving death, loss, or identity confusion. These are matters of mastery and attachment as well as survival.

This chapter deals with the building blocks of the resilient self, the part of your hopeful core that is critical for dealing with issues of survival. In the next chapter we will address the specific fears that are associated with the hope motives. To use a medical analogy, this chapter can help to boost your psychological and spiritual immunity, whereas Chapter 7 will provide antidotes for specific ailments related to mastery, attachment, and survival.

A Gift or a Burden?

All living things are built for survival. Green plants bend toward the light. An amoeba is capable of adapting to a variety of physical conditions. Spiders collapse into a ball when they sense an intruder. In *Winter World*, biologist Bernd Heinrich detailed the amazing survival strategies that are employed by animals in colder climates. Heinrich appeared to be particularly fascinated by the tent caterpillars and the kinglet (a bird). Caterpillars have the ability to create glycerol in their blood, a kind of natural antifreeze.

The kinglet may have been Heinrich's favorite. These tiny birds must consume three times their body weight on a daily basis. This provides just enough energy for them to continue shivering on even the coldest nights, ensuring their survival. In the kinglet, Heinrich sensed "a grand, boundless zest for life," a testament to optimism, and proof that "the fabulous is possible."

Some degree of fear and anxiety is necessary for survival as well as for personal growth. As Rollo May emphasized, anxiety is essential to the human condition. The experience of anxiety defines "the experience of being affirming itself against nonbeing." That is, if you are fully committed to realizing certain goals, to defending a particular way of life, or to upholding a cherished institution, then any perceived attack on these centers of value may be experienced as an assault on your innermost self.

In *The Gift of Fear*, psychiatrist Gavin de Becker stressed that the key to staying out of harm's way is to follow your "hardwired intuition." As he described it, "You have the gift of a brilliant internal guardian that stands ready to warn you of hazards and to guide you through risky situations." Unfortunately, an overabundance of fear can drive some individuals into a state of emotional paralysis or total withdrawal. They devote so much time and energy to the work of worry or anxiety management that they have few resources left for anything else. Too much fear is not a gift but a burden.

Some individuals are temperamentally more fearful than others. Families can transmit healthy or unhealthy ways of coping to their children. In some cases, an early encounter with trauma, illness, or loss instills a chronic state of generalized anxiety and a heightened sense of personal vulnerability. At the other end of the coping spectrum, there are children as well as adults who demonstrate an extraordinary degree of resiliency. Despite a myriad of encounters with the dark side of life, they seem relatively well-adjusted and have moved beyond surviving, into the realm of thriving.

In confronting any sort of terror, you should strive for a deep-rooted hope that will empower you to address the endless vicissitudes of life. This does not mean that you should learn to ignore or deny the presence of danger. Aristotle noted that even courage can be destroyed by excess. In his view, the person who fears nothing is not courageous but is instead foolish and rash. A hopeful approach to life is not about denial or an attempt to evade the sober realities of existence by retreating within a cocoon of blind optimism. True hopefulness is a way of being, a manner of experiencing yourself, the world, and the future.

Tony's Story:

As someone who experienced a great deal of loss early in life, you might have presumed that I was not a big proponent of "care recruitment." Nevertheless, much of my present-day resiliency can be directly related to the care I received as a child and adolescent. Moreover, I am convinced that my positive experiences with my mother, my aunt in Italy, and my adopted aunt in America provided a "good enough" experience of survival-oriented trust to jump-start my search for care, particularly with respect to male role models who could teach me something about resiliency. With my background, developing a greater sense of terror management or liberation were always a strong priority.

I learned early in life that it is impossible to find one person who can teach you everything. Resiliency is no exception. In addition, I was lucky enough to be one of those children who could extract a lot of help from a little care. From my father Felice, I learned about liberation beliefs. From my brother Nick, I learned about spiritual integrity. From my uncle Biaggio, I learned about personal terror management.

My father was thirty-five years old when he came to America. Unable to speak a word of English, he had to follow a fast learning curve to survive. He took a night class to prepare for the citizenship exam as well as a course in basic English. To improve his fluency, he watched the local and national news every night, as well as popular children's programs that featured lessons on learning the alphabet and using proper grammar. For a while he toiled in a chemical factory where they waterproofed fabrics. He then found employment in another factory where they made switches for cars and railroads. Both jobs were stressful and provided barely enough money to pay the bills. When he was laid off from the switch factory, he decided to use his livestock trading and selling skills to buy and restore apartment buildings. This finally gave him the freedom to walk away from the grind of factory work. I admired his ability to transfer the skills he brought from the old country to achieve economic liberation in his new country.

My brother Nick was twelve when he came to America. He struggled with the language, was forced to repeat a grade, and was told by his high school guidance counselor to forget about college. Undaunted, he knew his capabilities and remained steadfast in his belief that all he needed was a little more time and a little help. He worked hard to improve his mastery of the English language. He enrolled in a junior college where he excelled. He transferred to a state university and did well enough to gain acceptance into several graduate programs, eventually earning a master's degree in comparative literature. He found employment as a high school teacher and enjoyed a long and successful career. Along the way, what impressed me most was his strong sense of purpose, particularly in carving out a new legacy for himself and his family, beginning with being the first in our family to graduate from college. He never looked for a shortcut or the easy way out; he knew what he wanted, and he was willing to do the necessary hard work. Moreover, he thought it was important for his family, and particularly his children, to see integrity "close-up."

My uncle Biaggio was one of the gentlest, calmest men I knew. I found it amazing that this easygoing soul had fought in World War II, even spending time in a concentration camp. I remember one night, when I was about eight or nine years old, he was telling some of his war stories to my family. He recalled being in a tent and having an animated discussion with a fellow soldier, when a bullet ripped through the canvas, hitting his buddy in the side of the head and killing him instantly. As my uncle put it, "One second we were talking about our dreams, our families, and what we would do after the war, and the next instant he was dead.

Having survived that experience, and witnessing firsthand the fragile and sometimes capricious nature of human life, I vowed to never again be afraid." Whether he was so relaxed all the time, I will never know, but in his company I felt a tremendous sense of ease and personal comfort.

Henry's Story:

I have always felt a strong need to feel free, physically as well as intellectually; to make my own decisions; to feel responsible for my choices. As soon as I began to walk at about ten months of age, I started running. My family grew frustrated chasing after me. They decided to connect me to a clothesline when we were outdoors. However, I intensely disliked being restricted in any way and I soon found a way to free myself from the harness. I also felt confined sleeping in a large crib. Shortly after my first birthday, I managed to break some of the wooden slats so I could sleep just on the mattress, free to move about when I woke in the morning. And I previously mentioned my early hospital experience just before my fifth birthday when I was put into a restraint following surgery.

At least in part because of my early family turmoil and losses, many situations made me feel a sense of discomfort or entrapment. I needed to have contingency plans and viable alternatives. I latched on to the saying, "America is a free country," a frequent rallying cry during World War II. I personalized the phrase with the addition, "so don't tell me what to do," much to the chagrin of my elders. I was drawn to creating my own "life structures" rather than conforming to preset guidelines. On the other hand, I valued the freedom of others and often found myself sticking up for them. Even as an elementary school student, I would protest whenever I felt another boy or girl was being unfairly "strait-jacketed." To this day, I believe no one should intrude on the rights of others. At the same time, no one should tolerate any infringements on their own rights. For me, there has never been a one-size-fits-all life formula. Each of us has to be feel free to find our own way in the world.

What Is Resiliency?

According to *The Oxford English Dictionary*, resiliency consists of the following: a tendency to rebound, an ability to return to a natural physical state, and the power of recovery. Hopeful resiliency involves a capacity for sustaining hope in times of stress and uncertainty. An individual who is resilient has the ability to bounce back from a crisis as well as a tendency to maintain emotional equilibrium in the midst of chaos. To fully appreciate the nature of resiliency, it is necessary to take into account the role of each of the hope motives. In doing so, you will gain not only a fuller understanding of the resilient self but also a better appreciation of the complexities that underlie the human coping process.

There are many types of survival. Physical survival has been a preoccupation for most of human history. However, in this age of anxiety, you may be finding yourself far more focused on emotional survival. If you are older, have struggled with substance abuse, or have battled a mental illness, you may be most concerned with sustaining a sound mind (cognitive survival). Perhaps you are especially worried about maintaining a particular lifestyle (social or economic survival). Alternatively, your priorities might be more transcendent, aiming toward a legacy or a spiritually assured afterlife (ultimate survival). Understanding your particular needs is crucial.

Do your hopes revolve around changing your life? What are you trying to alter? Is it something internal or external? Are you hoping to modify some aspect of your personality? Do you want your loved ones to change in some way? Are you seeking greater stability in your own life? Are you striving to remain emotionally grounded, or is your attention more focused on preserving some aspect of your environment?

Do you like to attack problems head-on, or do you prefer indirect strategies, such as taking a different perspective or going with the flow? Maybe your disposition is to focus on the positive aspects of a situation. Are you someone who attempts to address every issue on your own, or do you feel more comfortable marshaling support from family and friends? How likely are you to rely on religious or spiritual beliefs when dealing with crises in your life?

Beyond individual needs and styles, there are significant coping differences that result from cultural factors. In the West, there is a greater focus on direct problem solving, or primary control processes. In the East, there is a preference for secondary control processes, which involve making subtle changes in behavior to indirectly impact the outcome of events. For many individuals, spiritual beliefs play a major role in daily confrontations with stressful events. Calvinists, for example, believe that grace from God is sufficient for salvation, whereas Catholics believe that their final destiny is determined by their moral behavior, participation in the sacraments, and good works.

There is a third coping style, one that is more consistent with our way of thinking about hope. Psychologist Kenneth Pargament refers to this as *collaborative coping*. He has found that many of the healthiest religious devotees see themselves as engaged in a joint effort with a spiritual force or presence. Although they are assisted by a higher power, they do not view themselves as passive souls who need explicit formulas to address life problems. They view their own strength and skill as an important part of the equation. In a similar vein, Paul's Letter to the Philippians includes the following assertion, "I can do all things through Christ, who gives me strength." The Hindu practice of activating the *atman* (or inner divinity) is another example of a style of coping that lies somewhere in the middle of the control spectrum, halfway between a purely internalized power and a totally externalized dependence.

The Resilient Self

The resilient self is one of the three elements of hopeful core, along with the attached self and the empowered self. The building blocks of hopeful resiliency include the following:

- Survival-based trust
- Care recruitment
- Personal terror management
- Spiritual terror management
- Liberation beliefs
- Spiritual integrity

When threats surface, hopeful individuals draw on a reservoir of trust in others, including family, friends, and valued institutions. A hopeful person has the capacity to solicit care and support. Those who are hopeful are able to manage their fears in order to keep their minds at ease and their bodies well regulated. In times of adversity, hopeful individuals can rely on spiritual beliefs to assure themselves of a benign universe and their ultimate liberation. Finally, the hopeful among us are likely to demonstrate spiritual integrity, an impenetrable core that is linked to a deep sense of purpose and a steadfast commitment to establishing a legacy.

Survival-Based Trust and Care Recruitment

Individuals who believe others can and will help them are more likely to solicit and receive comfort and support. Conversely, those who lack trust are unlikely to reach out for help. Survival-based trust and care recruitment are thus intertwined elements of the resilient self, with the former virtue greatly affecting the development of the latter. By survival-based trust, we mean a particular form of trust—a belief in the willingness and capacity of others to provide help during stressful times. The first five or six years of life can be critical for the development of survival-based trust. While the circle of trusted others is typically enlarged over the course of a lifetime, the biggest advances tend to occur prior to adolescence. However, with the right effort and support, survival-based trust can always be developed, increased, or regained, no matter where you are in the trajectory of the life cycle.

Personal Terror Management

Resiliency suggests elasticity, the ability to bounce back from pressure and stress. This characteristic can be applied to inanimate objects as well as human beings. In engineering, materials are rated in terms of their tensile strength and stress-strain ratios. These properties are the result of the object's constituent elements, the quality of the bond that holds them together, and the curing process that hardens or sets the material in place.

It is possible to draw an analogy between the factors that govern the strength of materials and the factors that determine the resiliency of individuals. Nature and nurture provide the raw materials. In early childhood, these gifts and endowments are developed in the context of a relationship with a primary caretaker. In most cases, this basic attachment is augmented by a sense of connection with a higher power or spiritual presence. In middle childhood, newly discovered ways of coping must undergo reality testing. Like steelmaking, life skills must be forged in the presence of challenge and adversity. The individual with hopeful resiliency is like a strong metal, held together by a quality bond, tempered by fire, and capable of handling the inevitable strains of life. In *A Farewell to Arms*, Ernest Hemingway put it well: "The world breaks everyone, and then some are strong in the broken places."

A secure attachment contributes to the development of inner

resources for self-soothing and self-assurance. Commonly referred to as *emotional self-regulation*, the ability to manage fear and stress is profoundly affected by our early relationships. This capacity for personal terror management derives from two attachment processes: empowerment and attunement.

An empathetic parent, caregiver, or friend is attuned to your emotional and physical state. Furthermore, sensitive caregivers are able to lend an air of hopefulness that can sustain feelings of joy and wonder. In addition, they provide a calming presence in times of doubt or fear. Attunement even seems to affect the development of your brain anatomy and physiology. "In sync" caretaking appears to be a critical factor in the growth and refinement of the right side of the brain. Sometimes referred to as the "emotional" side of the brain, the right hemisphere has been associated with many aspects of social intelligence, including the ability to read facial expressions and to decode the emotional tone embedded in speech.

There is a critical need for attunement and self-other empowerment in the early years. At birth, attachment is essential for physical survival, and it continues to be important for the emotional survival of the developing child. At six months, infants are capable of experiencing sadness, and by the end of the first year, they show signs of separation anxiety. At approximately ten to twelve months, infants begin to rely on social referencing: gauging their own responses to events by observing the emotional and physical reactions of their caretakers.

When toddlers begin to walk and talk, their ability to self-regulate is further enhanced. They can now exercise more control in approaching or avoiding particular people or situations while verbally expressing their fears and concerns. Nevertheless, a young child still retains a need to be close to a trusted caretaker. As children's sense of self develops, so does their capacity for imagination and forethought. Ironically, this ability to project more clearly into the future serves as a precursor of both fear as well as hope.

In middle childhood, self-regulation is enhanced by several spurts in emotional intelligence. This allows for a more active role in coping with various fears. Children begin to understand the role of thoughts in controlling emotions as well as the possibility of feeling one thing while expressing another. At this stage, most children benefit from an expanding social network that includes peers and adults in addition to the primary caretaker. These encounters provide exposure to role models for alternative ways of coping with stress.

Do not despair if you were not blessed with the greatest parenting. There is increasing evidence that sensitive, attuned others, in the form of friends, lovers, or therapists, can help adults to repair or rebuild a strong self-regulatory system. In fact, it has been suggested that even the critical right frontal area of the brain can be rewired in a manner that creates a more bonded sense of self, if you are provided with a continuous dosage of healthy social transactions. In time, your capacity for trust, openness, and intimacy can be greatly transformed, bolstering both your attachment and your survival skills.

Spiritual Terror Management

Spiritual resources can be used to manage immediate fears as well as the distant terror of anticipated losses. For many individuals, the formative years for the development of "spiritual terror management" are from early childhood through adolescence. However, it is not unusual to encounter spiritually transformed older adults who have found peace after decades of anxious unrest.

The first task of spiritual development is typically the establishment of a felt bond with a powerful other, There is ample research evidence that a positive caregiver experience in childhood can jump-start a healthy spiritual life. On the other hand, a negative or an insecure attachment can result in a superficial spiritual veneer, if not a fervent antireligious stance. Secure attachments can contribute to a spiritual resiliency that reduces psychological distress. For example, psychologists Lee Kirkpatrick and Phillip Shaver found that individuals who felt securely attached to God reported much greater life satisfaction as well as less anxiety, depression, and physical illness than did those with an anxious attachment to a higher power. In another study, Kirkpatrick discovered that those who were "God-avoidant" tended to have a weakened sense of "symbolic immortality."

In middle childhood and continuing into adolescence, spiritual terror management evolves through exposure to myths and rituals in particular religious or spiritual belief systems. Traditionally, the beginning of adolescence is when children are formally admitted into a spiritual community through a confirmation, a bar or bat mitzvah, a vision quest, or another religious ceremony. Unfortunately, in the West there has been much less emphasis on the adolescent's spiritual development. We believe that this may be one of the factors that underlie the increased incidence of distressed and alienated youths.

Lacking spiritually based resources as well as stable family and community bonds, many teens and young adults do not have the necessary buffers with which to deal with the vicissitudes of life. Some turn to drugs for a quick dose of self-soothing, and others seek to manage their sense of vulnerability within the fold of a street gang. Moreover, one has to wonder if the dramatic rise in the presumed cases of childhood attention problems and bipolar disorder is partly attributable to a diminished social investment in the spiritual needs of children.

Spiritual development can occur at any point in the life cycle. In fact, even though the early research on spiritual transformation cited adolescence as the time that most of the change takes place, the more recent literature suggests that it is just as likely to happen after the age of thirty. A Gallup poll found that nearly 40 percent of Americans had experienced at least one major spiritual turning point in their adult lives.

In the spirit of hope, you should also know that there is more than one form of transformation available to you. Some move through a tradition conversion, changing from one religion to another (e.g., Buddhist to Hindu). Others experience an institutional conversion, moving from one religious subgroup to another (e.g., Catholic to Protestant). There are those who undergo a within-faith transformation, whereby their devotion is significantly altered and deepened (e.g., a Reform Jew who becomes Conservative). Finally, some have an affiliation shift, joining a new movement rather than an established religion (e.g., a Muslim who becomes a devoted nature worshipper).

Liberation Beliefs

Hope is about options and possibilities. Hopeful individuals believe that there is a way out of every difficulty. One of the classic symbols of hope is a bridge. Psychologist C. R. Snyder's perspective on hope emphasized both a sense of personal power and a dedication to seeking different routes to goal attainment. His approach paid homage to the old saying, "Where there's a will, there's a way."

Chinese novelist-philosopher Lin Yutang wrote, "Hope is like a road in the country; there was never a road, but when many people walk on it, the road comes into existence." Writer Anne Lamott stated, "Hope begins in the dark, the stubborn hope that if you just show up and try to do the right thing, the dawn will come." In contrast, one of the hallmarks of hopelessness is a feeling of entrapment, a belief that there is no exit from pain or suffering.

For the sake of clarity, it is possible to distinguish liberation beliefs from problem-solving strategies. Liberation beliefs derive from the survival system and come into play when an individual feels trapped or endangered. Problem-solving strategies spring from the mastery system and are typically employed in achievement-related situations, such as school or work. In the course of human development, these initially separate mastery and survival elements may be fused together or blended with aspects of attachment.

Major gains in liberation beliefs occur during adolescence. There are compelling data that support this conclusion. For example, developmental psychologists have confirmed important shifts in reasoning that occur during puberty. These cognitive advances have been variously referred to as formal operational thought, hypothetical reasoning, or abstract problem solving. The defining feature of this new way of thinking is the ability to anticipate future problems while devising alternative solutions.

A study conducted by Tony went even further in establishing the impact of adolescence on liberation beliefs and hope. In this research, the coping strategies of children and teens were compared by age and degree of hopefulness. Each participant was told a story about a child who was lost in the woods. The participants were then asked, "How many ways of escaping or getting back home can you imagine?" On the average, the younger children were able to come up with two solutions, whereas the adolescents were able to think of three. When only the most hopeful participants were studied, an even more dramatic difference was noted: the adolescents averaged four solutions, and their younger counterparts averaged only two and a half solutions.

However, just because you are cognitively mature does not guarantee that you will capitalize on your ability to plan, imagine, and project into the future. Past trauma, a history of learned helplessness, and self-doubt are just some of the reasons that adults might not exercise their capacity for self-liberation. Psychiatrist and trauma expert Judith Herman recalls the case of a trauma survivor who "forgot" how to use a doorknob to open a door. Tony had a patient, a thirty-year-old graduate student with a very controlling mother, who dreamed of driving to her parents' house for Thanksgiving. As she approached the final part of her trip, her car swerved off the side of the road and became stuck in the mud, and the radio started to blare. In the dream she couldn't remember how to use the volume control knob to lower the sound.

Spiritual Integrity

In adulthood, individuals become increasingly aware of their personal limitations. There is a growing sense of mortality, a confrontation with the so-called portal of nothingness. This implies a need to further solidify the resilient self. The critical additive is spiritual integrity, a notion that is somewhat similar to Erik Erikson's ego integrity. Erikson was referring to a set of beliefs, values, and attitudes that can be found in those who successfully negotiate the final stages of the life span. These qualities include meaning and purpose in life, an absence of regret, and "a detached concern with life itself, in the face of death itself."

Our concept of spiritual integrity encompasses meaning and purpose as well as a heroic affirmation of life. However, we do not restrict the development of spiritual integrity to the final stage of the life cycle. From our perspective, spiritual integrity can emerge in the childhood years and even reach a high level of maturity well before middle age. Moreover, spiritual integrity more accurately describes an investment in the transcendent principles that characterize this facet of the hope foundation.

Integrity implies both moral strength and personal integration. These qualities are developed primarily in the second half of life. Granted, there are important changes in moral reasoning that begin in childhood and extend into young adulthood. However, the establishment of true character requires a fully matured ethical system that has been informed by a deep synthesis of life experiences. These personal qualities typically coalesce during middle and late adulthood. Here is listing of the qualities that are essential for the development of spiritual integrity:

- Meaning in life
- Purpose
- An incorruptible core
- Commitment to a legacy

Meaning in life includes both personal and cosmic meaning. Personal meaning suggests that your personal existence has been rendered sensible, that your life experiences have been integrated within a framework of values and principles. Cosmic meaning refers to belief in a larger plan, a vast design directed by a higher intelligence that is all-encompassing. Meaning is a prerequisite for purpose in life.

Whereas lower animals are driven by instincts, human actions can result from plans and ideas. Regardless of what happens in life, if experiences can be meaningfully assimilated, then an individual has a basis for continuing to persevere. Viktor Frankl, a psychiatrist who survived Auschwitz, was often called upon to give his fellow prisoners a reason for hope. After a particularly trying day in the camp, he beseeched his despairing friends to recall the words of Friedrich Nietzsche: "He who has a *why* to live for can bear almost any *how*."

Many hopeful individuals believe that they have been endowed with special gifts. Furthermore, they presume that their talents obligate them to play a role in upholding particularly cherished values, traditions, or institutions. An educational curriculum to foster this aspect of spiritual integrity was designed by the Center for Life Calling and Leadership at Indiana Wesleyan University. Its mission statement at http://www.career.indwes.edu reads as follows:

> A life calling is larger than a job or occupation, deeper than a profession or life's work. It is the confidence of an overriding purpose for your life, based on who you are, carried out in a connection to the universal community around you.

In the process of creating a meaningful life, it is often necessary to accept and forgive. This includes the realization that people usually do the best they can with the information that is available to them at the time. *This includes you.* Don't wallow in regret. Hindsight should be an ally, not a foe, in building hope for the future. It should strengthen and inspire rather than debilitate and demoralize. Erikson put it succinctly when he suggested that healthy adults accept that the life they have lived is the one they were meant to live.

Affirming life. Hopeful individuals understand that dealing with adversity is part of the process of affirming life. In the 1970s, psychologist Suzanne Kobasa conducted a large study of employees who were threatened by job loss or relocation. She found that some of the employees handled the stress better than others. The group of hardy individuals showed few, if any, signs of stress-related symptoms. The cluster of attitudes that constituted hardiness included a belief system in which change was viewed positively as a challenge that could engage one's capacity for mastery and survival.

Rather than defining themselves in terms of a setback, a handicap, or a disease, hopeful individuals retain an incorruptible core of attitudes, feelings, and beliefs. By *incorruptible* we mean morally as well as spiritually resistant to inner deformation or ruin. Hopeful individuals refuse to allow their sense of self to be compromised by life circumstances or physical decline. For example, they would repudiate such narrow and crippling labels as *failing student, cancer patient,* or *disabled veteran.*

One might think that the spiritual integrity of elderly people who suffer from memory loss would be subject to erosion. However, senility does not necessarily threaten this aspect of a hopeful core. First of all, most age-related changes involve only short-term memory. You might have noticed this in older friends or family members; they might not recall the details of a recent conversation, but they can accurately describe an event that happened thirty or forty years ago. Compared to short-term recall, long-term memory is more important for sustaining hope and spiritual integrity.

One's basic core of spiritual integrity runs deep, pervading one's entire being. Morrie Schwartz (of *Tuesdays with Morrie*) espoused this spirit of incorruptibility when he commented on his battle with Lou Gehrig's disease:

> It was very important for me to make clear to myself that my body is only part of who I am. We are much greater than the sum of our physical parts. The way we look at the world is fashioned by our values and our thoughts about good and evil, things that go into making us who we are.

Persisting through their triumphs and travails, ever hopeful individuals create a life story that can rise to the level of the heroic. The great nineteenth-century poet Alfred Lord Tennyson put it well:

> Come, my friends, 'tis not too late to seek a newer world. . . . It may be that the gulfs will wash us down: It may be we shall touch the Happy Isles, and see the great Achilles, whom we knew. Tho' much is taken, much abides; and tho' we are not now that strength which in old days moved earth and heaven; that which we are, we are.

Hopeful individuals create a powerful legacy of possibility that serves as an example for peers, friends, and loved ones. What they bequeath is a kind of hope script, a spiritual road map that can offer a unique approach to mastery, attachment, or survival. At the same time, these legacy makers are rewarded with a bounty of meaning, purpose, and hope. Their own joy comes from having helped to perpetuate a world and a way of life that is consistent with their values and sense of self. Erikson related this "grand generativity" to the sacred Hindu call for each of us to do our part for the maintenance of the world.

Precocious Integrity. Sometimes extraordinary circumstances accelerate the maturation of spiritual integrity. This precocity may occur in young adults, or even in children, who encounter tremendous adversity. Psychiatrist Robert Coles wrote a number of books about the experiences of poor and disenfranchised children. He believed that as a society, we greatly underestimate the spirit and determination of young people.

In *Children of Crisis*, Coles documented the struggles of African American children living in the South during the turbulent 1960s. Many of them, like six-year-old Ruby, were thrust into a firestorm that erupted after the Supreme Court decided to end school segregation:

> Ruby was six years old when it began. She came, by chance, to be the only Negro child entering one of the previously segregated schools in New Orleans. For weeks, angry whites mounted a boycott protesting her presence. Each day, accompanied to the door by her mother, Ruby walked past a threatening mob. . . . She heard obscenities, insults, and, from one white woman, the particularly fearful threat of death by poisoning. [Ruby told Coles,] "Maybe it'll have to be a race, and I hope we win. . . . Some people think we won't. . . . But I don't believe them for too long."

Ryan White was another inspiring example of a child who developed spiritual integrity at an early age. He was thirteen when he contracted AIDS from a blood transfusion. When word spread of his illness, Ryan was badly mistreated and initially barred from attending school. Journalist Taro Yamasaki wrote movingly of Ryan's plight:

> He would walk down a totally crowded hallway in the school and people would run and hug the opposite wall. He would have horrible things written on his locker. Kids would move their desks away from his. . . . He felt like he had been at the center of a freak show. On the other hand, he felt that it was important for people to start learning what AIDS was really about—how you got it and how you didn't.

Ryan White died of complications from AIDS on April 8, 1990, but his legacy has been enormous. Federal legislation has been passed in his name. Innumerable Ryan White HIV prevention and treatment programs have been created across the United States. Since 1993 there has been an annual Ryan White National Youth Conference. Teens from all over the country gather to help those who have been diagnosed with HIV and to disseminate information to help prevent the further spread of this disease.

More than a decade after Ryan died, Taro Yamasaki encountered a young teacher working in Croatia. When she was a teenager in Connecticut, this woman had read Yamasaki's stories about Ryan. "She had cut them out [and] put them in a book. She framed one of those pictures of Ryan [and noted] that it was Ryan's story that had inspired her to give more of herself to other people."

It is important to make a further point about the resilient self. If individuals are deprived of basic survival-related resources, such as cultural traditions or spiritual beliefs, they may come to rely even more on mastery or attachment to achieve a sense of security. For example, there are many disadvantaged children who pin all their hope on becoming professional athletes. In essence, they are banking on their physical mastery to help them escape the downward spiral of drugs, violence, and social oppression.

The documentary *Hoop Dreams* covered six years in the lives of

William Gates and Arthur Agee, poor kids from the streets of Chicago who shared the unwavering dream of playing professional basketball. Because of their talent, they were recruited to attend St. Joseph's High School, a perennial basketball powerhouse. However, this meant getting up every day before dawn to commute ninety minutes to a school that had very few African American students. Gates and Agee, as well as their families, were willing to sacrifice everything for their common dream.

Film critic Roger Ebert was particularly impressed with *Hoop Dreams*. He believed that the film transcended the topic of basketball, that it was essentially about "much larger subjects," including "a determination and resiliency that is a cause for hope." Retired basketball star Charles Barkley was invited to write the introduction for the book version of *Hoop Dreams*. Barkley grew up in poverty, nurturing his own dreams of playing professional basketball. Despite being undersized for his position, he became an all-star power forward who was selected as one of the fifty greatest National Basketball Association players of all time. Reflecting on the significance of hoop dreams, Barkley mused, "N-B-A; those three letters spell hope, escape, and promise."

BUILDING RESILIENCY

Perhaps you see yourself as lacking in hopeful resiliency. Maybe you felt abandoned or betrayed as a child and now find it difficult to trust others. Perhaps you were not blessed with a calm temperament. Maybe you just received little spiritual guidance as a child. Can you really go back and shore up your resiliency? Did not Freud imply that "the child was the father of the man"? Is it really possible to break free from the thoughts, feelings, and attitudes that were impressed upon you during the first five or six years of your life?

Using Mahatma Gandhi as an example, Erikson suggested that great individuals often rise above their early circumstances to become their own parents. In a sense they find a way to be reparented, resocialized, and respiritualized. Gandhi himself demonstrated a remarkable degree of personal transformation. As a child he was not a good student, he was very shy, and he often became tearful when he was doubted. However, by the time he was in his twenties, Gandhi was leading nonviolent protests for civil rights in South Africa. Returning to India, he focused his attention on the liberation of his country and on equal treatment for members of different castes, including the untouchables. Having been a sensitive and somewhat alienated youth, Gandhi had a special place in his heart for those treated as outcasts.

Throughout the next half century, Gandhi suffered numerous beatings and imprisonments. On many occasions he undertook long fasts that led him to the brink of death. He did this not only to inspire his people but also to win particular concessions from the British. In one instance, he even vowed to fast to death unless the untouchables were given the same basic rights as those from the upper castes.

Another model of transformed resiliency, on a level closer to most of us, is self-help guru Lucinda Bassett, the author of *Panic to Power*, a bestseller about coping with fear and anxiety. She is cofounder of the Midwest Center for Stress and Anxiety, and she herself is a recovering agoraphobic who recalls extended bouts of severe anxiety that date back to her early childhood. For decades Bassett suffered from constant worrying, panic attacks, and fears of dying. Nevertheless, she found the inner strength and the external resources to transform herself into a national expert on the treatment of anxiety.

Senator John McCain, who survived six years in a North Vietnamese POW camp, offered an analogy between the building of character and physical conditioning. He pointed out that if we exercise courage, it tends to grow, much like a muscle that undergoes repeated strength training. In fact, similar to the inheritance of a weak bodily constitution, the presence of a vulnerable psyche can actually spur some individuals to incredible acts of heroism. To quote an old English proverb, sometimes "fear lends wings."

TRUST LESSONS

If your resiliency is being hampered by trust issues, keep the following five *R*s in mind:

- Respect
- Research
- Risk
- Receptiveness
- Repetition

First, respect your individuality. Some people are genetically predisposed to be more outgoing and assertive than others. However, introverts as well as extroverts can profit from social support as long as it is tailored to their particular personality style. Extroverts may do better with a larger network of relationships that are moderate in emotional intensity. Introverts can make up for their typically smaller circle of friends by cultivating more intense bonds.

You will not look for something unless you believe in its existence. Those who have frequently been let down by others may cease to believe that there is still goodness in the world. If you have had disappointing relationships, do a little social experiment. Consider it your job to research and find examples of what writer Anne Herbert called "random kindness and senseless acts of beauty." Watch a "feel-good" movie or read a heartwarming tale from a compilation such as the *Chicken Soup for the Soul* books. Another great collection of inspiring personalities can be found in *Hope Dies Last* by Studs Terkel. If you have access to the Internet, visit the Random Acts of Kindness Foundation website at http://www.actsofkindness.org.

If you are religiously or spiritually inclined, consider doing some research on the lives of saints, prophets, or humanists. An excellent example of selfless giving was demonstrated by Eric Liddell, whose athletic prowess was featured in the film *Chariots of Fire*. Liddell was a Scottish track and field star who won an Olympic gold medal. A devout Christian, he once refused to compete in a high-profile race because it was held on a Sunday. Forgoing the opportunity for further fame and fortune, Liddell became a missionary. He traveled to China and risked his life to serve the poor and care for the wounded during World War II. He died in a Japanese POW camp when he was only forty-three, and accounts of his unwavering spiritual integrity have continued to serve as an inspiration for generations of children in both Europe and Asia.

Some risk might be necessary to lead a hopeful life. The philosopher Gabriel Marcel wrote that "openness allows hope to spread." Even in the most supportive environment, an individual who is emotionally withdrawn has little chance of securing hopeful input. Of course, individuals who have suffered from abuse or abandonment are likely to require some initial encouragement before opening up. However, those who are excessively cautious should not try to overcompensate by being indiscriminately open. Ultimately, the best way to secure lasting hope is through a measured receptiveness. Whether intuitively grasped or gained through experience, care recruitment demands some discretion. An old African proverb puts it simply: "No one tests the depth of a river with both feet."

How do you achieve an effective degree of openness? Think of your task in terms of boundary making. The invisible yet palpable emotional barriers that exist between individuals are often referred to as boundaries. A poor attachment history can engender boundaries that are either too rigid or too loose. Individuals who have what is called reactive attachment disorder are likely to be either emotionally disengaged or indiscriminately enmeshed.

Your goals in this area should revolve around the concepts of symmetry and degree of relatedness. To ensure symmetry, match your level of disclosure and commitment to others' capacities for sharing and intimacy. Meet them halfway, in other words. If you go less than halfway, the person who is more open might experience you as distant. However, if you go more than halfway, the person who is more reticent might view you as intrusive.

You must also consider the nature of your relationship with the other person. Are you trying to connect with a friend, a lover, a parent, or a child? Recall the advice of Confucius, who proposed guidelines for maintaining different kinds of relationships. Also consider the wisdom offered in Tolstoy's *War and Peace*, when Andrei tells his friend Pierre, "You can't everywhere and at all times say everything that is on your mind." An excellent contemporary resource for cultivating better boundaries is *Your Perfect Right* by Robert Alberti and Michael Emmons.

It is important to repeat the research and risk steps. Don't give up if you are disappointed at the outset. Keep on trying, and you will discover that there are kind and generous individuals in the world who are willing to listen and even provide direct assistance. There are sources of goodness in the world, and the more you look, the more you will find. Regaining trust takes time. We speak of *building* and *earning* trust for a reason: It doesn't happen overnight. You need patience and perseverance to build hope.

Many years ago, researcher Harry Harlow found that infant monkeys preferred a soft, cuddly surrogate mother to a wire alternative, even though the latter was equipped with a milk bottle. In a follow-up study, Harlow's focus shifted to helping some of the monkeys that had been raised in total isolation. He and his colleagues discovered that it was possible to rehabilitate the withdrawn youngsters by exposing them to well-functioning peers. However, the period of resocialization had to equal or exceed the duration of the initial deprivation.

TERROR-MANAGEMENT LESSONS

If you suffer from constant worry, consider an all-in-one treatment package for reducing distress. Two popular options are Lucinda Bassett's anxiety-management program and dialectical behavior therapy. Bassett's home-study course involves a blend of traditional cognitive and behavioral strategies. Such techniques have been found to be particularly effective in the treatment of mood disorders. For further information, you can visit Bassett's website (http://www.stresscenter.com).

University of Washington psychologist Marsha Linehan was the originator of dialectical behavior therapy (DBT). She combined cognitive and behavioral techniques with Buddhist principles such as mindfulness, detachment, and acceptance. Linehan's approach was designed to help individuals self-regulate their emotions and moods. DBT has been used primarily in the treatment of borderline personality disorder. Individuals with this condition find it very hard to control their reactions to daily stressors and are prone to severe bouts of anxiety, depression, and rage.

DBT offers hope for anyone who is struggling with destructive emotions, including those with severe anxiety, mood swings, or anger management issues. If you are interested in learning more about DBT, visit http://bipolar.about.com/od/dbt/Dialectical_Behavioral_Therapy.htm. This website includes links to DBT forums, overview articles, and contact information for locating a trained professional in your area. In addition, you may want to read psychologist Scott Spradlin's book, *Don't Let Your Emotions Run Your Life*.

As an alternative to DBT or Bassett's program, you might consider selecting from a menu of self-regulation techniques that target your particular issues. Do you need help with intrusive thoughts? Are you debilitated by beliefs that leave you feeling anxious or depressed? Are you tense? Do you feel constantly overaroused or "wired"?

If you want to explore the full range of possibilities for dealing with such problems, take a look at *The Relaxation and Stress Reduction Workbook*. This resource is a compilation of techniques prepared by psychologist Martha Davis and her colleagues. To create your own tailored self-help program, we recommend meditation for the control of obsessive thoughts and cognitive restructuring for reducing feelings of anxiety or depression. Progressive muscle relaxation can decrease tension, and biofeedback will help to stabilize an overly active nervous system. You can also seek out a professional to assist you in incorporating one or more of these techniques into your daily life. In either case, commit yourself to spending at least thirty minutes per day on this for a few months. Have faith in the process and do not despair if your desired results take some time to materialize.

Regular exercise offers an effective, if underrated, means of reducing tension and worry. In fact, research has indicated that exercise is far more beneficial and healthier for most individuals than standard medications for anxiety or depression. A good workout can increase the availability of phenylethylamine, a kind of natural antidepressant. Another by-product of exercise is the release of beta-endorphins. These are neurotransmitters that bind to the same receptors as morphine, resulting in lowered anxiety and increased pain tolerance.

Aerobic activities such as running, swimming, or cycling promote deep breathing. This helps to keep your vagus nerve toned, a critical factor in determining how well your heart and your autonomic nervous system react to stress. If you suffer from stress-related pain and muscular tension, also consider some weight training, yoga, or tai chi.

Techniques alone will not bring you inner peace. An element of faith is also required. Note that Marsha Linehan incorporated Buddhist principles in her DBT approach. Similarly, psychologist Jon Kabat-Zinn, an expert in pain management, included Buddhist and Hindu teachings in his mind-body program. Even Herbert Benson of Harvard Medical School, who spent decades promoting the benefits of his no-frills "relaxation response," later modified his technique to incorporate a "faith factor."

Each of the major spiritual traditions offers a particular set of lessons in terror management. For example, Buddhism might help you to achieve a deep level of meditative detachment. This can be of enormous benefit in controlling obsessive thinking and managing the suffering component that accompanies physical pain. Nevertheless, Buddhism may prove inadequate for more mastery- or attachment-oriented individuals because of its emphasis on letting go and the renunciation of desire. A mastery-oriented individual who hopes to reduce stress levels might be more drawn to Hindu practices such as yoga. Attachment-oriented Christians might turn to the Book of Proverbs for guidance or draw comfort from Psalm 23: "Although I walk through the valley of the shadow of death, I will fear no evil; for thou art with me."

Whether or not your belief system is religiously based, it must provide you with enough faith-based hope to persevere in this age of anxiety. We can't emphasize enough the limitations of a purely technique-driven approach to terror management. It is one thing to borrow a meditative principle here and an inspiring verse there, but it is quite another to craft an overarching philosophy of life. If this has eluded you, commit yourself to more fully incorporating the lessons in this section with those of Chapter 4 concerning spiritual intelligence. It is both a challenge and a privilege for you, as a human being with particular faith needs, to fashion a belief system that gives you a hope for all seasons.

LIBERATING THOUGHTS

Hope is about options and possibilities. A hopeful mind-set is liberating because it includes the belief that you can find a way out of any predicament. To be a genuinely hopeful person, you must be persistent and creative. To fully expand your degrees of freedom, you need to draw on all your resources: psychological, physical, and spiritual.

In the field of psychology, the development of alternative solutions is called *divergent thinking*. As with any life skill, you can strengthen your capacity for this method of problem solving. According to educator Edward de Bono, divergent thinking can be enhanced by adopting multiple perspectives. The following is a streamlined version of his "six-hat" approach to problem solving.

- White hat: Gather information, assemble facts and figures, and outline options.
- Red hat: Draw on your feelings and intuition to enhance your possibilities.
- Black hat: Critically evaluate the flaws or weaknesses inherent in each option.

- Yellow hat: Evaluate the strengths and opportunities associated with each option.
- Green hat: Assess the growth potential of each option.
- Blue hat: Stand back, look at the big picture, and organize your options.

Many mental health professionals rely on a short-term model of treatment called solution-focused therapy (SFT). This type of intervention bears some resemblance to de Bono's six hats approach by encouraging the development of alternative strategies for dealing with the seemingly irresolvable quandaries of life. Sometimes described as an approach based on hope and respect, SFT presumes that people possess adequate resources for solving their problems. The general principles of SFT can be readily applied to a wide range of life situations. These principles are as follows:

- Consider that your existing strategies may be part of the problem, not the solution.
- Learn something from every previous mistake or unsuccessful strategy.
- Start with your desired hope or end point in mind and work backward.
- Recall any past successes that may be related to your desired end point.
- Envision the simplest sign of progress toward a large and complex goal.
- Carefully track your progress on a daily or a weekly basis.

In your search for alternatives, don't neglect your body. You need to find ways to keep yourself calm and relaxed. Highly anxious individuals, regardless of their age, intelligence level, or educational background, do poorly on measures of creativity. In contrast, a limber body and a mind flowing with possibilities are two sides of the same coin.

The Taoist approach to mind-body health revolves around the concept of chi, or vital energy. To ensure the continued flow of chi throughout the body, millions of Chinese rely on tai chi or qigong. These are moving meditations that are designed to keep the body operating flexibly and to enable the mind to cultivate such qualities as creativity, openness, and responsiveness. You can derive similar benefits from regular exercise that includes stretching and running or walking. Make sure to balance your workouts with adequate rest and an occasional warm bath or massage to prevent "stiffening" of your mind and body.

Stimulate the right hemisphere of your brain, which is involved in creative and holistic approaches to problem solving, by listening to classical music. There is some evidence that just a few minutes of Mozart or Beethoven activates right-brain activity. In contrast, rock and pop music are more likely to trigger left-brain activity.

For many, spirituality provides the ultimate grounding for liberation beliefs. Creativity researcher David Perkins contrasted "plans deep down" with "plans up front." The former refers to underlying beliefs and blueprints for action, whereas the latter involves conscious thoughts and plans for the future. A religious or spiritual belief system can be likened to a plan deep down, because it provides individuals with a set of blueprints for hopefulness in coping with feelings of anxiety and terror. Although spiritual liberation runs deep, accessing it may require solitude, prayer, or meditation.

Muslims can draw on the Qur'an to learn that Allah "does not lay a burden on any soul except to the extent of its ability." The Rig Veda encourages Hindus to "let noble thoughts come from everywhere!" Christians have their own liberation mantra: "When God closes one door, He opens another." Buddhism offers the Eightfold Path to open the eyes, bestow understanding, and cultivate peace of mind.

A HOPE MISSION

The key to building spiritual integrity is to discover your mission in life. This will ensure a life of meaning and purpose while also establishing an incorruptible core, thus providing an enduring legacy of hope. Pastor Rick Warren's book, *The Purpose Driven Life*, is a testament to these building blocks of spiritual integrity. According to him, without a mission, "life has no significance or hope. . . . Hope is as essential to your life as air or water. . . . If you have felt hopeless, hold on! Wonderful changes are going to happen in your life as you begin to live it on purpose."

Although many of Warren's suggestions presume Christian beliefs, including the existence of God, most of what he says can be used by followers of other faiths as well as by humanistic atheists. In fact, his basic tenets are remarkably similar to Erikson's prescriptions for a successful negotiation of the adult stages of life. Both Erikson and Warren propose that human beings must commit themselves to a larger cause. For Warren, this higher purpose is God's will; for Erikson, it involves a "faithful participation" in one or more cultural institutions, such as religion, philosophy, politics, or economics. For Warren, the ultimate goal is glorifying God; for Erikson, it is perpetuating a valued way of life. It is in this broad, philosophical sense that Erikson sees a convergence between his call for a kind of "grand generativity" and the Hindu dedication to maintaining the world.

Why is having an enduring life mission so crucial? Warren believes that "we are made to last forever" and invokes "God's plan for our eternal place in Heaven." Erikson alludes to the more basic need for humanity to "transcend its mortal confinement in time and space." Alternatively, an evolutionary biologist might suggest that the quest for immortality is a by-product of the reproductive impulses embedded in our genes. Spiritual leaders may point to an underlying theme found in every major faith, suggesting that each human being is created in the image of a greater intelligence that seeks to manifest itself in the world.

We might also consider the thoughts of the German philosopher Georg Hegel. According to Hegel, there exists an absolute spirit, a universal force that seeks its own self-development as well as the integration and unity of everything in nature. The absolute may be conceived of as a form of potential energy that is realized in the creation of each individual. Every person is therefore a finite-infinite composite who incorporates a "unique mortal coil" along with the eternal elements of "a vast and infinite absolute." Inspired by a sense of the absolute, individuals are prompted to develop and maintain enduring values and institutions. In turn, these institutions function to push forward the spiritual development of each individual. Enlisted as spiritual codevelopers in the service of the absolute, people and institutions can be viewed as mutually reinforcing parts of a forward-moving cosmic chain of hope.

Even Ernest Becker, a skeptical humanist, concluded that there has to be a life force that bridges the individual will to live with the increasing expansion of the universe. Becker insisted that we must honor this unifying impulse as "knights of faith":

> Man must reach out for support to a dream, a metaphysic of hope that sustains him and makes his life worthwhile. . . . Who knows what form the forward momentum of life will take in the time ahead or what use it will make of our anguished searching? . . . We must fashion something, and drop it into the confusion, make an offering . . . to the life force . . . the person who prides himself in being a "hard-headed realist" and refrains from hopeful action is really abdicating the human task.

Both Erikson and Warren suggested that an individual's contribution to a larger purpose must include both unique and shared elements. The unique component consists of your particular talents and efforts. The shared aspect is your sense of fellowship and participation in a community of like-minded individuals. In short, a life mission unites the particular and the universal as well as the present and the future. Erikson preached of literally "giving yourself to the future" whereas Warren noted the importance of "contributing to one's generation." He insisted, "There is no greater epitaph . . . [than to] do the eternal and timeless in a contemporary and timely way . . . this is what the purpose driven life is all about."

A mission will become evident to you when you grasp the nature of your unique gifts and discover something larger, a cause beyond the self that is worthy of spiritual investment. Your faith can be entrusted in one or more centers of value, but these do not have to be religiously grounded. Recall from our earlier discussions of faith and spiritual intelligence that there are many potential centers of value, including science, technology, and the forces of nature. The only prerequisite for success is a lasting commitment to a center of value that reflects your passions and your worldview. If you are still searching for your particular life mission, try to answer the following questions:

- What are your core values and beliefs?
- What are your unique skills or talents?
- What is your spiritual type?
- Which particular faith options appeal to you (e.g., religion, politics, science)?
- How are you going to contribute to your chosen center(s) of value?

It is worth considering the complementary roles that Buddhism and Hinduism might play in helping you to become a more resilient human being. Remember that hope is about options. Pearls of wisdom can be extracted from any of the various spiritual traditions. With this in mind, you might want to think more like a Buddhist when you are focusing on the development of terror-management skills but adopt a Hindu perspective to craft a life mission by more fully appreciating existing institutions while developing a deeper understanding of your stake in their continued existence.

7

Hope, Not Fear

Never fear shadows. They simply mean
there's a light shining somewhere nearby.

—RUTH E. RENKEL, *AUTHOR*

Fears can multiply. This is particularly likely when threats fall upon the psyche too rapidly, like a sea of cascading waves pounding the shore. A newly divorced man or woman may have to deal with the fear of living alone, of being a single parent, of paying the bills, of the long-term impact on the children, of trusting a new partner, and of creating a new family. The recently unemployed may fear the next mortgage payment; the slightest rise in oil or gas prices; the loss of a pension; the inability to find a new job because of age, sex, or race discrimination; the possibility of having to move to a less preferred part of the country; and the ending of longtime friendships with coworkers. A child of an alcoholic parent may fear the next round of verbal or physical abuse, the next humiliating scene of drunkenness in front of family or friends, the next tuition check that bounces, and the next wisecrack from schoolmates or neighbors about his or her "boozed up" mom or dad.

FEAR OF HOPE

It has often been argued that fear is the opposite of hope. Thomas Aquinas wrote that "hope is contrary to fear" because the former involves an imagined "future good," whereas the latter is based on an envisioned "future evil." Although fear does not always lie on the other side of hope, it happens enough to merit our attention. If you are a runner who hopes to win a particular race, it would be natural for you to fear losing or coming in last. Parents may bring a cancer-stricken child for chemotherapy, hoping for a cure. At the same time, they may fear that the medication will not work or will even make matters worse. In such situations, we would be hard-pressed to argue with Benedict de Spinoza, who claimed that "there is no hope unmingled with fear, and no fear unmingled with hope."

The element of fear that invades hope cannot be totally vanquished. There are no guarantees in striving, loving, or living. Some individuals cope with life's uncertainties by crafting an illusion of total optimism. However, when obstacles and calamities appear, these people are often unable to move forward. Others are so afraid of any kind of risk that they turn away from the future or simply give up. They are defeated from the start. In short, neither blind optimists nor those paralyzed with fear demonstrate much hope. Hoping is based on faith and reason, trust and courage.

In this chapter, we provide strategies for dealing with a variety of debilitating fears. The key to overcoming fear does not lie in merely trying to reduce or eliminate it. The mind, like anything in nature, abhors a vacuum. Fear must be replaced with hope. The deepest fears of humanity involve unrealized hopes and dreams. If you truly want to be free of the most debilitating types of fear, think in terms of transformation rather than excision. A great fear must be supplanted by a great hope.

There is a time-honored method for handling problems of a manifold nature. In Sun Tzu's ancient classic, *The Art of War*, a military leader faced with a superior force is advised to take a divide-and-conquer strategy. Similarly, in higher mathematics, complex equations are disassembled into more manageable subsets using a divide-and-conquer algorithm. Likewise, a bundle of terror can be reduced by dealing with the fears one at a time. This philosophy of separation was exquisitely conveyed in an episode of the television drama, *Kung Fu*. Master Caine, the ever wise Shaolin priest, drew on his Zen Buddhist roots to reassure a frightened acquaintance: "I too have many fears. . . . Small, fragmented, tiny terrors can be examined. They can be held in the hand and broken. Only when all fears come together will they become overwhelming. "

FEAR STORIES

The examples below illustrate the kinds of inner fears that haunt many people on a daily basis, leaving them feeling helpless and hopeless. Moreover, each of these fears may obscure a deeper hope; antidotes for replacing each type of fear with a corresponding hope are described in the remainder of this chapter.

Fear of Being

A man plagued by mysterious foot and hand problems was referred to a psychotherapist. As a result of his intolerable foot pain, he rarely left his house. His hand condition was making it impossible for him to succeed as an architect. The therapist outlined the various modalities offered at her clinic, including biofeedback, cognitive therapy, and hypnosis. As each treatment option was mentioned, the client sarcastically interjected, "Been there, done that."

When the therapist asked the man about his hope for treatment, he angrily snapped back, "I don't believe in hope. I prefer the Buddhist approach to life. I don't think about hope." In essence, this man was afraid of being. His difficulty with leaving home was a metaphor for being unable to go forward in life. He lacked a sense of freedom and responsibility. He mistakenly sought refuge in Buddhism, believing (incorrectly) that it would eliminate the burden of hoping.

Fear of Harm

A survivor of sexual abuse told her therapist that she was grateful for two things: her nine-to-five job and her computer. "If I didn't have these things in my life, I don't know what I would do." She confided, "My current job is beneath my skill level, but it gives me a secure income and a solid retirement plan." She loved surfing the Web. "Thank God I have unlimited Internet access. It lets me see what's going on in the world from the comfort of my own home." Despite having some strengths, she complained of spiraling anxiety and chronic insomnia, adding, "I never feel rested or at peace with myself."

This woman was afraid of harm. As an abuse survivor, she experienced the world as unsafe and had lost her faith in other people as well as the future. She settled for a job that was beneath her because it guaranteed safety and symbolized something she could rely on. The Internet allowed her to connect with the world from a safe distance while distracting her from unsettling thoughts about the future. As psychiatrist Judith Herman has noted, trauma survivors may continue to live under a constant threat of annihilation, a cloud of vigilance that leads to a narrow and diminished existence.

Fear of Loss

A woman in her early forties was being treated for a long-standing hoarding problem. Never married, she occupied one floor of a large Victorian house owned by her sister and her brother-in-law. Most of her rooms were filled with faded newspapers, old notebooks, and outdated grocery store circulars. An excellent student throughout her life, she had earned an MBA from an elite business school, yet she seemed unable to hold on to even the most menial job. Everything about her, from her slow gait and tired speech to her drooping eyelids, suggested a profound sense of despair. Nevertheless, she was highly resistant to making changes, fearing that "I might lose my true self." She wanted to stop bringing more "useless things" into her home but had no intention of discarding what was already there.

This woman was afraid of loss. A highly sensitive individual, she had internalized the wounds and sorrows of her entire family. At an unconscious level, she was striving to offset her fear of loss (and theirs) by holding on to as many material things as possible. Newspapers and old magazines were especially prized because they represented written records of the past. Grocery circulars that highlighted comfort foods offered a semblance of the nurturance she sought but believed that she had never received. Her fierce hold on the past was also reflected in her unwillingness to shed unhealthy aspects of her personality.

Fear of Success

A first-year college student had battled with depression for most of his life. Despite having a high IQ, he struggled to complete his schoolwork. Frustrated and confused, he made an appointment at the university counseling center. He described a time-management problem as well as a personality conflict with a certain professor. He also revealed a very stormy relationship with his controlling father.

This young man was afraid of success. He engaged in various forms of self-sabotage, including procrastinating and battling with his professors. He unwittingly invited criticism and additional resistance from his father, who carried his own burden of abandoned dreams. The student's father had once had aspirations of being an airline pilot. However, he was forced to give up his plans when his own father became sick. At an unconscious level, the son had identified with his dad's fear of "moving up."

Fear of Death

A forty-four-year-old salesman tried to convince himself that everything in his life was just fine. He constantly touted his career achievements and wonderful family life. Actually, however, his marriage was falling apart and he had become completely alienated from his children. He sought out a therapist when he found himself unable to shake off his increasingly intrusive and debilitating thoughts.

His obsessive preoccupations began on a business trip when he found himself fixated on signs that indicated a speed limit of forty-five miles per hour. For days he was unable to get the thought out of his mind that he might die at the age of forty-five. While driving over a bridge, he was struck by the fear that he might never again cross it. This man was afraid of death. Paradoxically, when he attempted to suppress the fear, it seeped into every corner of his life. As his thoughts grew darker, he even felt anxious in the presence of an evening sunset. His therapist asked him, "Do you hate sunsets because they represent the 'death of the day,' a reminder of your own mortality?"

HOPE FOR AUTONOMY

The fear of being is rooted in avoiding choices and responsibilities. Many philosophers and humanists, such as Erich Fromm, have suggested that certain individuals harbor a fear of freedom. Endowed with an enormous capacity for planning and self-reflection, human beings are the only creatures that can actively participate in their own self-development. This is too frightening for some people, who view freedom as a curse rather than a blessing. They can't handle the responsibility that comes with committing themselves to a particular lifestyle, mate, or career. They can't find it within themselves to make choices, to say yes to one possibility and no to another.

The fear of being is typically more insidious and damaging than the fear of either success or failure. The fear of being represents a more thorough straitjacketing of the mastery motive. The developmental disruption is more extensive, often involving disturbed attachment experiences. Moreover, the damage typically occurs earlier in childhood, usually before the age of six. This is when virtues such as will and purpose, the prerequisites for truly being in the world, are acquired. In contrast, the fear of failure and the fear of success are more likely to spring from problems in later childhood, when a sense of competence must be developed from both within and outside the realm of family life.

The antidote for a fear of being is the hope for autonomy. According to psychologist James Averill, autonomy is the capacity for self-rule as well as "the ability to make choices and pursue divergent goals." These conditions can be met if individuals act on the basis of their own chosen principles rather than those imposed by others. Such principles should be broad enough to guide various types of behavior yet flexible enough to allow for growth and change.

The road to autonomy begins with self-awareness. You need to care-fully assess your values and priorities before you can arrive at a set of life principles. Are you really committed to autonomy? Are you ready to accept responsibility for creating your own life? What will you have to give up in the process? Are you willing to absorb those losses?

Some might argue that the task of establishing principles should be left solely to the individual. After all, isn't the whole point of autonomy to foster self-rule? However, for those who have tasted little freedom, a bit of inspiration can go a long way. Role models who have blazed an innovative path can inspire others to consider new and more productive courses of action. If you follow Averill's advice and think in general terms, it will be easier to incorporate strategies developed by others for your own purposes. For example, instead of limiting yourself to emulat-ing a famous athlete's swing or toss, pay attention to his self-discipline and drive for excellence. Rather than focusing on a world-class musi-cian's repertoire or manner of holding the instrument, you might try to duplicate her work ethic or commitment to the craft.

Create a list of well-known people whom you admire. Try to identify the qualities they embody. Maybe you can find a book about them in your local library or get more information from the Internet. Descriptions of courageous historical figures can also be inspiring, espe-cially if they chronicle the lives of individuals who displayed great integrity while challenging popular opinion. If you enjoy classic litera-ture, read one of Ralph Waldo Emerson's essays, such as "Self-Reliance" or "Character." The latter begins with the boldest of pronouncements: "The sun set; but set not his hope: Stars rose; his faith was already up."

If you are religiously or spiritually oriented, you may want to consult the biblical Book of Proverbs, the sayings of Confucius, or parts of the Qur'an. Many of the "suras" found in the Qur'an offer counsel for dealing with doubters and hypocrites. The first sura, entitled the "opening," includes the following passage, "Thee do we serve and Thee do we beseech for help. Keep us on the right path." The Upanishads is another excellent source for developing character and inner strength. A major source of Hindu wisdom, this collection consists of texts that deal specifically with the realization of one's *atman* (inner divinity). In particular, the Katha and Mundaka books contrast the more vulnerable socialized ego with the deeper *atman*, one's true source of power and autonomy.

If you want to balance these sober renderings with a more lighthearted approach, check out *All I Really Need to Know I Learned in Kindergarten* by Robert Fulghum. If your fear of being is deep-rooted, you might want to invest in an extended period of self-examination. Psychotherapy is a possibility. If you enjoy processing and assisted reflection, seek out a therapist who offers a client-centered approach or who stresses an existential perspective. If you are more skills oriented, seek out a cognitive-behavioral therapist or one who employs a solutions-focused approach. Both types of treatment options emphasize active coping and the development of specific behavioral strategies.

Ultimately, it is most important to feel fully involved in the process of choosing the principles that will guide your life. This truth is beautifully expressed in Khalil Gibran's *The Prophet*. Asked to discuss the nature of good and evil, the great sage replied, "You are good when you are one with yourself. . . . You are good when you are fully awake in your speech. . . . You are good when you walk to your goal firmly . . . with bold steps."

HOPE FOR SERENITY

The fear of harm is ubiquitous today. In a sense, we all live in a post-traumatic society, a world that is filled with new and troubling threats as well as an eroding spiritual foundation. The media barrages us with daily references to weapons of mass destruction and the fear that chemical and biological agents might get into the wrong hands. Consequently, many of us are apt to feel like trauma survivors, fated to a future of forced vigilance. If a sense of peace cannot be secured in the midst of these troubles, then the next public health crisis, the plague of the new millennium, might very well become the fear of fear.

Those who fear harm are desperately in need of serenity. Although they long to be free of worry and conflict, many have abandoned any hope for peace. Indeed, they are always prepared for the worst in matters of loving, striving, or long-term survival. For those who live in countries besieged by war or ravaged by disease, there are the added presumptions of oppression and an early death.

Post-traumatic stress disorder (PTSD) is the most dramatic example of a fear-driven adaptation to harm. Situations that can precipitate PTSD include war experiences, natural disasters, kidnapping, robbery, and physical or sexual abuse. Other debilitating fears include *panic attacks* and *phobias*. The underlying cause of such fears is typically a combination of predisposing factors, including individual temperament, family coping style, and a history of early loss or serious illness.

Effective interventions for most fears would include combine cognitive-behavioral therapy (CBT) and in some cases a limited use of medication. CBT involves retraining the way you think about yourself, the world, and the future. Moreover, CBT provides techniques for actively coping with anxiety-provoking situations. If you suffer from a phobia or panic attacks, seek out a mental health professional who can provide CBT. In some cases, a therapist may recommend a medication evaluation. If medication is suggested, you ought to think about it as a complement to CBT rather than as an alternative solution. By combining these two forms of intervention, you are more apt to effect long-term improvement rather than merely achieving a temporary state of relaxation. To boost your level of hopefulness, you must do more than simply recharge your brain chemistry. You must develop new ways of thinking about and responding to the inevitable stresses of life.

There has been tremendous progress in understanding and treating trauma. Drawing on the seminal work of psychiatrist Judith Herman, many trauma centers now employ a three-phase treatment program. These phases can be construed as sequential hope work, geared toward a systematic repair of the survival, attachment, and mastery systems.

In the first phase, the focus is on care recruitment and rebuilding survival-based trust. Herman described the relationship between the therapist and the survivor as a collaborative process involving a "working alliance." As part of their hope work, the clients must reestablish or learn new methods of terror management and self-care.

In the second phase of treatment, the survivors are encouraged to recall and repeat their stories to a therapist or other hope provider who offers moral solidarity. They also share their experiences with a sympathetic group that bears witness to each survivor's testimony. This process allows the survivor to integrate and make sense of the trauma experience. Equally important, the therapist and the group align themselves morally and spiritually with the survivor. By being available and fully present, the therapist and the group aim to establish a hopeful imprint upon the survivor's sense of self.

This second phase is often the longest and the most difficult to negotiate. Struggling to assimilate and incorporate the full meaning of the trauma, some survivors experience a profound sense of helplessness and hopelessness. To restore hope, talk therapy may need to be supplemented by other techniques. This is not surprising, since there is compelling evidence that highly traumatic memories might be stored differently from normal life events. Because of this, it may be necessary to include some form of mind-body therapy, such as calming hypnotic techniques, massage, exercise, or specially crafted breathing exercises.

In the third phase, there is a need for the survivor to reengage with the world and to establish bridges of intimacy. Similar to our hope-centered notion of shared or mediated control, this requires a convergence of mutual support and individual autonomy. Survivors must learn to forgive and to turn their attention to the future, including the performance of tasks for the care and protection of others.

For survivors, a capstone experience often involves the realization of spiritual integrity within the framework of a life mission. For example, Herman quoted a survivor of domestic abuse who made the decision to become a district attorney. Describing her passion for prosecuting cases of domestic violence, she stated, "I want women to have some sense of hope, because I can remember how terrifying it was to not have any hope—the days I felt there was no way out. I feel very much like that's part of my mission."

HOPE FOR REUNION

Loss is a painful but inevitable fact of life. There are physical losses, such as the death of a spouse, a parent, a child, or a friend. For many individuals, a separation or divorce may be just as unsettling as a death, or even more so. There are symbolic losses, including the loss of one's reputation or role in society. In addition, there are secondary losses that can accompany a physical or a symbolic loss. These include a financial setback after the death of a spouse or decreased social interaction due to the loss of a job. Here we focus on the death of a loved one and the hope for some form of reunion.

The fear of loss refers to the difficulties associated with anticipatory grief as well as the burden of coping that follows a loss. If a loss is anticipated, such as the imminent death of a friend or a family member, the individual may find it hard to concentrate on anything else. A person in this situation might experience nightmares, engage in self-blame, avoid others, and even begin to question his or her religious or spiritual beliefs. After a loss, the grieving person might fear that the pain will never subside, that life will never again be meaningful, or that the deceased will be permanently erased from memory.

Therese Rando, a psychologist and grief expert, has observed that even though death has always been part of the human experience, individuals are less prepared to deal with it today:

A hundred years ago you would not have needed to read [a self-help book]. . . . The typical American family had strong emotional ties. . . . They [family members] had deep roots in their community. . . they [watched] others cope with grief and mourning . . . there were strong religious beliefs that helped families cope. . . . Rituals and ceremonies provided support and gave the family direction.

For most of the twentieth century, the dominant approach to bereavement counseling was based on the notion of grief work. According to this perspective, grieving individuals had to directly confront their loss. They needed to feel the pain, then emotionally detach themselves from the deceased, and finally move on to establish a new life for themselves. In contrast, those who experienced relatively little distress or refused to let go were thought to be in denial and risking long-term harm. It was not until the early 1990s that some scientists and practitioners began to seriously challenge the grief-work hypothesis.

James Averill was one of the first psychologists to express concern that grief was increasingly being viewed as a disease to be overcome rather than as a natural human experience. Danish investigator Margaret Stroebe noted that venting, detaching, and moving on could be viewed primarily as a twentieth-century invention. Other investigators found striking differences in the way that men and women coped with loss. In general, men tended to focus on restoring normal functions, whereas women were more likely to dwell on their feelings of loss.

Central to the grief-work hypothesis is the task of letting go and moving on. How legitimate is this prescription? Writer Tom Crider lost his only child, Gretchen, in a fire. She was just twenty-one years old. In *Give Sorrow Words*, Crider made a powerful argument against letting go and moving on:

> What horrifies me is the suspicion that, like the uncaring world, I, too, might one day go on living as though nothing had happened . . . something very strong in me seems to not want to "recover" because as long as I stay aware of [her] absence, in a way I am keeping [her] alive in my inner being.

Fortunately, there *are* some basic bereavement guidelines that you can follow. Taken together, these strategies offer real hope. They can help you to transform your relationship with the deceased, solidifying a place of hope within your heart and your mind. They also provide a means for rebuilding your connections with surviving loved ones and other members of your community. Equally important, these guidelines will help you to restore your emotional and physical equilibrium. Instead of thinking about the suggestions as grief work, you might want to frame them as guidelines for hope work.

Give yourself options. Grieve in your own way. You are not obligated to go through prescribed stages of grief. You do not have to detach or move on. You are not even obligated to feel devastated. In fact, you might even discover a new source of hope and inspiration in the midst of your grief. Clearly, there are different meanings attached to various losses (e.g., the death of a spouse versus the loss of a child). Hope is akin to a "vehicle," capable of transporting one from a tunnel of darkness into the dawn of light. However, only you can fathom the destinations that can satisfy your need for reunion.

Denise, a young woman tortured by her own unresolved grief, was so moved by Tom Crider's story that she was prompted to write him a letter. Sensing a kindred spirit struggling with the darkness of loss, she began her letter with a Spanish proverb: "Traveler, there is no path. Paths are made by walking." Denise confessed to Crider that she had been unable to gain much solace from either traditional self-help books or her religious faith. Nevertheless, she was "open to that which may indeed put all this right some day . . . hopeful that some great and benevolent force that is beyond my comprehension will reveal itself upon my own death . . . maybe I do have a God after all . . . his name is HOPE."

Build two bridges. The bridge work of bereavement is a psychological balancing act, involving an alternating investment in experiencing and coping. First, there is a definite need for some emotion-focused grief work, including dealing with the pain in whatever manner is best for you (e.g., crying, solitude, or venting your anger). If you are struggling with pent-up feelings, an excellent resource is Mary Jane Moffat's book *In the Midst of Winter.* Designed to "serve as an axe for the frozen sea within," the book includes many of the greatest literary passages on grief, with selections from William Shakespeare, Emily Dickinson, Pearl Buck, and Walt Whitman.

Gradually try to reestablish some of your old routines. At the same time, it may be necessary for you to develop some new skills. For example, the deceased may have been the one responsible for home repairs or managing the finances. This is your second bridge to build. For inspiration you might read the chapter on work in Khalil Gibran's *The Prophet.* "To be idle is to become a stranger unto the seasons and to step out of life's procession."

Create an inner presence. Designate a certain time during the week, or a particular place in your home, to reflect on the meaning and impact of your relationship with the deceased. It might be comforting to invoke images of warm embraces, acts of expressed forgiveness, or moments of shared laughter. Maybe you will be able to more fully grasp what made your connection unique or special. It's natural to experience moments of longing and regret in the midst of your reflections, especially in the first six months after a loss. Typically, there is a shift toward increasingly positive memories by the end of the first year. However, this is by no means the end of the process.

Create an outer presence. Organize and restore photographs of the deceased. Arrange for a plaque to be made, honoring his or her contributions and unique characteristics. Consider fashioning a memorial quilt for display or even to wrap around yourself. Many readers are probably aware of the AIDS quilt, which by 2007 included more than 90,000 names and weighed more than fifty tons! You can get design ideas from Original Quilts (www.originalquilts.com) by reviewing dozens of handmade memorial quilts that individuals have fashioned from clothing and photographs of their loved ones.

Devise hope rituals. If you are religiously oriented, consider having an annual memorial service. Light a candle at home or in your place of worship. Provide flower arrangements, if that is appropriate. Marines honor their fallen comrades with designated place settings at a dinner ceremony. A red rose is set on each plate, the glasses are turned upside down, and the chairs are tilted in toward the table.

Perhaps you will reconnect with your loved one by traveling to a favorite vacation spot or a restaurant that the two of you frequented on special occasions. Try to integrate these preservation efforts into your life in a manner that will also give you the opportunity to maintain a daily exchange of hope with family and friends. In other words, balance your vertical bridge work across time with horizontal bridge work across clusters of the living.

Make a public offering. Consider supporting an organization that is devoted to preventing or curing the illness that claimed the life of your loved one. You may even be able to gather community support for your efforts. For example, many individuals recruit sponsors to support their participation in such events as the AIDS Walk, the Alzheimer's Association Memory Walk, or the Susan G. Komen Breast Cancer Foundation's Race for the Cure. In addition, you could offer support to any cause in the name of your loved one, regardless of whether it had anything to do with the circumstances of his or her death. Whether planting a tree, giving funds to restore a community landmark, or establishing a scholarship fund, try to capture the spirit of the deceased.

Pace yourself. It is important to take regular breaks as you grieve. Psychologist Margaret Stroebe gathered some impressive data suggesting that individuals process a loss much better if they "oscillate." This refers to moving back and forth between grieving and focusing on the resumption of normal life activities. You need to weave your mourning with breaks for work, socializing, and even play.

Cut yourself some slack in reaching particular goals. As with recovery from an operation or an illness, it is normal to feel better one day and worse the next. You can't rush the healing process. Keep in mind that there are typical tendencies associated with gender. Men frequently do not devote enough attention to the emotional side of grieving, whereas women are more apt to put off the tasks of daily living. In studies dealing with the temporal aspects of loss, psychologist James Pennebaker found that many individuals experience considerable relief after about six months. However, for most, it takes another year or so to integrate the loss and shift from grieving to fond remembrances.

Get support. Sharing your grief with others can be extremely helpful. Because loss is one of the few truly universal experiences, it is very likely that someone will pass on a bit of valuable coping wisdom. You may even derive invaluable technical or financial advice for settling an estate or getting back on your feet. However, the most important benefit of having social support may be in facilitating your search for meaning and providing assurance of your loved one's continuing presence in the world. British sociologist Tony Walter has written about the importance of reaching out to others in order to develop a stronger and fuller sense of the deceased. He recommends sharing stories about your loved one with friends and family, as well as contacting individuals who were well acquainted with the deceased in order to enlarge your understanding of their place in the lives of others.

Think globally. The funeral rites of the African practitioners of Ifa rival those of Native Americans in terms of organized family and community involvement. To express their gratitude for being brought into this world, the offspring of the deceased help to prepare the body for life in the next world. The family and friends provide the cloth with which to wrap the body, and the amount and the quality of the material are presumably linked to the degree of respect that is afforded to the deceased. After the burial, the family and friends make contributions for several days of feasting and celebration. Musicians are hired to play throughout the village. The songs and instruments are carefully chosen to reflect the personality and the tastes of the deceased.

If this kind of funerary support strikes a chord with you, make an effort to learn more about the practices of other attachment and survival-oriented cultures. For example, Orthodox Jews sit shiva at home for seven days after the burial. During this period, visitors come to pay their respects, share food, and often join in prayers. After a death, Quakers gather in their meeting house. They invite nonmembers as well as members to join in a spiritual retrospective, to rise and speak about the deceased individual when they are moved by the spirit.

HOPE FOR FULFILLMENT

The fear of success, when present, tends to be submerged in the unconscious. Public awareness of this phenomenon surfaced in the latter half of the twentieth century, during the struggle for equal rights by women and minorities. It was in this context that psychologist Matina Horner published her classic study indicating that a significant number of college women remained ambivalent about succeeding in higher education. Horner suggested that such women might be unwilling to risk alienating power-sensitive men or their more traditional female counterparts. Moreover, according to Horner, these conflicted achievers might intentionally underperform and sometimes even engage in unwitting acts of self-sabotage. Later research indicated that other factors such as parental values, sex-role identification, and self-presentation strategies were often more important than fear of success in determining a woman's level of aspiration. Nevertheless, Horner's research had a profound impact, raising the consciousness of an entire generation of women.

The fear of success is not always the product of gender stereotypes. It can result from any set of restrictive racial or class-based norms that impact the motives that underlie hope. For example, a young man from an economically impoverished neighborhood might deliberately under-achieve if he believes that breaking new ground will lead to ostracism from his peer group (attachment) or to physical violence against him or his loved ones (survival).

Sometimes the fear of success derives from not wanting to replace a valued family member who has occupied a special niche. This can hap-pen when a sibling dies, especially if he or she had a special talent or was somewhat precocious. In an unconscious effort to preserve the place of the deceased, there may be covert pressure against, and even the sabotage of, a surviving sibling's mastery efforts.

The antidote for a fear of success is the hope for fulfillment. By *ful-fillment* we mean the actualization of your potential in whatever manner or direction is right for you. No one can or should define success or ful-fillment for you. Transforming fear of success into hope for fulfillment is a multilayered process that involves self-awareness, detachment from inhibiting forces, supportive others, and decreased performance-related anxiety.

The fear of success is often associated with expectations and demands that have been imposed by parents or significant others. Try to separate what *you* really want from what others want *for* or *from* you. In terms of your life choices, you may ultimately decide that some types of indi-vidual success are not worth the interpersonal cost, but first clarify for yourself who wants what and why. To realize your hope for fulfillment, find a supporting cast. For example, there is evidence that a person from a minority group who has strongly achievement-oriented parents will be able to overcome broader social obstacles to accomplishment.

How do you overcome performance-related anxiety? This can arise when you have not clarified your fulfillment needs. Ask yourself what will make you feel genuinely happy, complete, or at peace. Is your heart or your sense of self at odds with success scripts imposed by others? Perhaps you already know the answers to these questions, but generalized anxiety is making it difficult for you to pursue what gives you a feeling of bliss. Go back to the terror-management suggestions in Chapter 6. Replace your worry with a calming and clearing routine that includes some aerobic exercise and a meditation practice to still the mind.

If you seek additional clarity of purpose and greater stillness of mind, consider incorporating Zen Buddhist principles into your daily routine. Zen can be particularly effective in helping those who are struggling with fear of success. Zen principles have been applied to nearly every human endeavor, from sports and martial arts to business and gardening. Proponents of this philosophy include Thich Nhat Hanh, the Vietnamese monk who helped spread the practice of mindfulness among Westerners, and NBA basketball coach Phil Jackson.

Zen can help in a variety of ways. Individuals who are plagued by the fear of success are often divided against themselves as a result of trying to meet conflicting family, social, or gender expectations. Zen facilitates a fusion of mind, body, and spirit. In aiming for satori, or enlightenment, one encounters *kensho*, or the experience of seeing into one's true nature. Many Westerners are impatient and narrowly focused on results, a mind-set that can seriously hamper the development of true mastery. In contrast, Zen is a philosophy of process and self-discipline.

In the West, there is a singular conception of practice that is reducible to repetition. In Zen there are half a dozen practice-related possibilities that embrace a full spectrum of intentions and attitudes, and these may either facilitate or detract from an individual's quest for fulfillment. The fear of success includes a constant flow of negative self-talk, which consists of inner-directed criticism and doubt. In contrast, Zen encourages a selfless approach. By removing the ego, one eliminates the object of distraction, freeing the mind and the body to perform at a much higher level.

Consider reading German philosopher Eugen Herrigel's spiritual classic *Zen in the Art of Archery*. Herrigel wrote this book while spending six years in Japan under the tutelage of a master archer. At one point he confessed, "When I have to draw the bow . . . unless the shot comes at once I can't endure the tension. . . . So I must let loose whether I want to or not." The master replied, "The right shot at the right moment does not come because you do not let go of yourself. You must wait for fulfillment."

HOPE FOR IMMORTALITY

What human beings fear most is their own death. Moreover, they will do just about anything to keep it at bay. The ancient Egyptians developed an entire culture around their quest for immortality, fashioning the great pyramids to serve as resurrection machines and orienting the pharaoh's burial chamber to face a constellation of stars known as the "indestructibles." *The Tibetan Book of the Dead*, first published in the eighth century, was preceded by a centuries-old oral tradition.

In the middle of the twentieth century, anthropologist Geoffrey Gorer complained of what he labeled the "pornography of death." In his view, death had become the new taboo, replacing Victorian sexual repression. Two decades later, Ernest Becker was awarded a Pulitzer prize for *The Denial of Death*, a psychological and social analysis of the many ways that individuals and groups attempt to cheat, defy, or ignore the reality of death. Becker summed it up best: "The idea of death, the fear of it, haunts the human animal like nothing else."

The United States remains a death-denying nation. More than 80 percent of Americans die without having made a will. Burial preparations

are usually handled by funeral directors, one of the many cultural practices that keep death "out of sight, out of mind." Loved ones refer to the
deceased as having "passed" or having "left this world" rather than as
having died. Psychologist Paul Wong has commented specifically on
those individuals who "wage an all-out war against death," including
extreme "calorie minimizers" who seek to lower their body metabolism
in a desperate race to "slow the progress of life."

The extent of an individual's preoccupation with death is a function of
many factors, including age and exposure to particular life events. The
death of a loved one, news of a tragedy, or a serious illness can all bring
about a more immediate sense of one's mortality. There are also moments
when each of us is so fully immersed in the realization of our finiteness
that it produces a terrifying shock, what existentialists call *ego chill*.

As long ago as 1896, G. Stanley Hall found that more religiously oriented individuals reported less fear of death. Perhaps demonstrating their
own death avoidance, few contemporary social scientists have followed up
on Hall's findings. Although the psychological literature on death-related
fears is limited, it does offer some guidance. Individuals with relatively low
death anxiety are more likely to share the following characteristics: purpose
in life, quality relationships, spiritual beliefs, and intrinsic faith.

Laboratory studies indicate that individuals who report having a purpose in life spontaneously produce imaginative stories about death and
dying that are less negative and foreboding, which suggests adjustment
in this regard is deeply anchored. Quality relationships provide a buffer
against death anxiety because they generate a sense that one has lived a
meaningful life and has touched others deeply, including members of
future generations.

Spiritual beliefs and religious faith provide benign interpretations of
death and the promise of an afterlife. Even individuals who have a deep

nonreligious intrinsic faith of some sort tend to demonstrate relatively low levels of death anxiety. In contrast, the sheer frequency of engagement in religious or spiritual rituals such as church attendance, meditation, or prayer does not seem to be predictive of an individual's level of death anxiety.

Tony has found in his own research that a more spiritually oriented hope is associated with less death-related depression and anxiety. For example, in one study, his research team showed young adults a ten-minute segment of the movie *Philadelphia*, starring Tom Hanks. The film is about a successful young lawyer who contracts AIDS, deteriorates, and ultimately dies. Prior to viewing the film, the study participants were given a hope scale. Before and after the film, the participants received a death-anxiety scale. The outcome that was measured was a difference score, which was calculated by subtracting the prefilm death-anxiety score from the postfilm death-anxiety score. A large score suggested a significant increase in death anxiety, whereas a zero or a negative number indicated no change or a reduction, respectively, in death anxiety. Higher scores on the spiritual dimensions of hope, and feelings of transcendent oneness with others, were associated with either a reduction or no change in death anxiety.

Countless immortality formulas have been proposed in an effort to quell death anxiety. *The Egyptian Book of the Dead*, for instance, provided the ancient Egyptians with a spiritual road map for the afterlife. Explicit guidelines for ensuring the immortality of the soul can also be found in the Bible, the Qur'an, and other sacred texts. (In 2009, Amazon.com listed more than 400,000 titles under the topic of *death*.)

The death commentaries of Buddha, St. Paul, and the poet-theologian John Donne have become classics of world literature. In a sutta (Buddhist discourse) entitled "Fearless," the Buddha outlined five hopeful escapes from the terror of death. Two focus on survival skills: cultivating deep faith and letting go of Earthly cravings. Another two derive from attachment: showing goodwill toward others and offering peace to the distressed. The fifth requires a commitment to mastery: dedication to skillful behavior.

In Paul's First Letter to the Corinthians, he assured his fellow Christians that "we will be changed in a flash; in the twinkling of an eye. . . . The perishable will be clothed with the imperishable [and] the mortal with immortality."

In *Death Be Not Proud*, John Donne created a salvation poem for the ages:

Although some have called thee mighty and dreadful, thou art not. . . . For those whom thou think'st thou dost overthrow, die not. . . . Thou art slave to fate, chance, kings, and desperate men, and dost with poison, war, and sickness dwell. . . . Why swell'st thou then? . . . One short sleep [and then] we wake eternally, and death shall be no more. Death, thou shalt die.

What do people fear most about death? It's actually not just one thing. What makes the prospect of death so overwhelming is its multifaceted nature. Death anxiety really encompasses a number of separate terrors rolled into one. Psychologist Ahmed Abdel-Khalek effectively summarized the fears of death as follows:

- Fear of pain and punishment
- Fear of religious or spiritual failings
- Fear of losing worldly involvements
- Fear of parting from loved ones

Abdel-Khalek's perspective coincides with our motive-based approach to hope. The fear of punishment and the fear of spiritual failings concern survival in the afterlife. The fear of losing worldly involvements is about goal interruption, or loss of mastery. The fear of parting from loved ones is a crisis of attachment. His analysis can also be compared to psychiatrist Robert Jay Lifton's concept of psychological death. According to Lifton, *psychological death* can be defined in terms of severed connections (attachment), a lack of will (mastery), and real or perceived disintegration (survival).

Another perspective on death and dying that dovetails with our approach to hope can be found in the literature on the end of life. The members of this interdisciplinary specialty include scientists as well as laypeople who are dedicated to a better understanding of the dying process. The picture of a "good death" that emerges from their interviews with the dying consists of manageable levels of distress (survival), maintenance of social connections (attachment), and clarity of mind (mastery).

In short, death is humanity's greatest fear because it threatens the most basic foundations of hope.

The Double-Life Prescription

How should you cope with the fear of death? We believe that the best prescription calls for leading a "double life." You must balance living in the here and now with a more long-range view that will provide an eternal perspective. That is, you should anchor your existence in the future as well as the present, relying on strategies that address each of the hope motives.

The Wisdom of the Here and Now

One half of the double-life prescription consists of living in the present moment. This means temporarily letting go of the past and suspending any thoughts about the future. It represents a mindful or nonjudgmental approach to every aspect of life, from mundane tasks to rare encounters with the sublime. Mihaly Csikszentmihalyi's concept of flow is a vivid metaphor for this way of being in the world. According to him, it is the moments you are actively involved, as if being carried away by a current, that confer the greatest amount of joy and life satisfaction.

Eckhart Tolle offered another rendition of this present-oriented philosophy in his book *The Power of Now*. He combined insights from a number of traditions, including Buddhist and existentialist. The following sums up his approach:

> Make it your practice to withdraw attention from past and future whenever they are not needed. . . . Things, people, or conditions . . . for [ensuring] your happiness now come to you with no struggle or effort on your part[, so] you are free to enjoy and appreciate them—while they last. . . . Life flows with ease.

The idea of living in the moment dates back to the ancient Greeks. Epicurus wrote that "the art of living well and the art of dying well are one." Hafiz, a fourteenth-century Persian poet, framed his message in verse: "Come, for the [future] is built on sand: bring wine, for the fabric of life is as weak as the wind." In the nineteenth century, Ralph Waldo Emerson offered this sage reflection: "Our fear of death is like our fear that summer will be short, but when we have had our swing of pleasure, our fill of fruit, and our swelter of heat, we say we have had our day."

The Wisdom of the There and Then

Respecting the power of the present is a necessary ingredient for crafting a full life. However, it is not enough to quell death anxiety. A philosophy of the present must be combined with both hindsight and foresight, a balanced temporal existence that honors the power of the past along with the power of the future. This time-extended approach underlies many of the qualities that make us uniquely human, including religion and spirituality as well as love, honor, and other transcendent virtues.

Consider that a large percentage of the human brain is dedicated to either recalling the past or anticipating the future. The frontal lobe, which is responsible for planning, takes up more than one-third of the cerebral cortex. Memory storage is also pervasive, spanning the upper, middle, and lower regions of the brain.

Rollo May argued that the dominant temporal orientation for humanity is toward the future rather than the past or the present. According to him, humanity is primarily oriented toward becoming rather than simply being. This does not imply escapism, it merely indicates an inherent human tendency toward growth and self-actualization. In fact, psychologist Herbert Rappaport found a connection between a future-oriented perspective and lower death anxiety. His research team surveyed a group of adults, asking them to report the number of significant thoughts and plans they associated with the past, the present, and the future. They found that a greater focus on the present was linked to higher scores on a measure of death anxiety. In contrast, a stronger investment in the future was related to having a greater purpose in life as well as lower death anxiety.

The wisdom of adopting an eternal perspective has its own ancient history. In the Book of Ecclesiastes, the author reflected on the futility of living exclusively in the present:

> Generations come and generations go, but the earth remains forever. . . . All streams flow into the sea, yet the sea is never full . . . there is nothing new under the sun. . . . I tried cheering myself with wine and embracing folly [yet] my mind still guided me with wisdom. I wanted to see what was worthwhile for humans to do under heaven during the few days of their lives. . . . Cast your bread upon the waters, for after many days you will find it again. . . . Sow your seed in the morning [so you may reap the harvest at day's end].

The German theologian Jürgen Moltmann went a step further. Grounding his ultimate hope in God and the prospect of a redemptive resurrection, Moltmann argued that the individual with faith did not have to choose between happiness in the present and a future satisfaction. According to Moltmann, "Does [such] hope cheat man of the happiness of the present?" How could it do so! For it is itself the happiness of the present." For Moltmann and others, a deeply centered happiness is preferable to fleeting moments of "excited pleasure."

The call for a more eternal perspective is not limited to the Bible or even to those with a purely religious orientation. The great pragmatist William James opined that "the greatest use of a life is to spend it on something that will outlast it." Former Czech president Vaclav Havel, who has described his beliefs as more spiritual than religious, had this to say about hope and time: "Hope is an orientation of the spirit, an orientation of the heart; it transcends the world that is immediately experienced, and is anchored somewhere beyond its horizons."

Symbolic Immortality

Death is not the last word. Human beings can extend their hope indefinitely through acts of symbolic immortality. Robert Jay Lifton developed this idea from his interviews with survivors of the Holocaust, Hiroshima, and the Vietnam War. Through his research, he was able to identify as many as five different ways of transcending death. You can achieve immortality through your progeny or by creating something of lasting value. You can follow the traditions of Native Americans or other Earth-centered cultures that link the transient life of the individual to the eternal cycles of nature. You can seek salvation in religious or spiritual beliefs. You can also realize moments of immortality through meditation practices that temporarily suspend your awareness of time and space.

Psychologist Mario Mikulincer called attention to the role of close relationships in fostering a sense of symbolic immortality and reducing death anxiety. He noted that social bonds often serve as critical buffers throughout the life span, helping individuals of all ages to cope with their greatest fears. For example, when infants and children are frightened, they seek out their caregivers. Similarly, adults look for the company of others when they are bracing themselves for a challenge or a painful encounter.

A powerful example of securing peace in troubled waters can be found in Tom Brokaw's book, *The Greatest Generation*. Brokaw traveled around the United States, interviewing World War II veterans about their most harrowing combat experiences. He also joined a group of them in France for the fiftieth anniversary of D-day. As they toured the beach at Normandy, an old solider recalled the following:

> That hillside was loaded with mines . . . a unit of sappers had gone first, to find out where the mines were. A number of these guys were lying on the hillside, their legs shattered by the explosions. They'd shot themselves up with morphine and [now] they were telling us where it was safe to step. . . . [Then I knew] I'd live another day.

Mikulincer argued that close relationships can also provide a shield against the deeper fear of losing one's social identity. He noted that all individuals fear that they will be forgotten. Having strong and lasting relationships instills a sense of having mattered to others and of having left a mark on humanity. "By forming and maintaining close relationships, people can feel more confident that their social identity will not be lost and [that] their friends, spouse, and children will remember them after their death."

The greatest assurance of symbolic immortality often comes from having children. As a parent, you come face-to-face with your past, your present, and your future. In the company of your offspring, you see life before and after you. If you cast your imagination into the distant future, you can almost see infinity in the progress of the coming generations. In the daily rituals of child care, you also wonder about the hopes and dreams that sustained your own parents when they embarked on the journey of raising a family.

Parenthood offers a concretized legacy. If you are a biological parent, half of your child's DNA comes from you. The child may inherit one or more distinct physical features, such as the shape of his or her nose, mouth, or ears. Indeed, there is a remarkable continuity in the chain of life. For example, a child's fingerprints, the most unique physical characteristic of the human body, are 98 percent inherited. For many other physical traits, the heritability quotients are also remarkably high (e.g., height, 87 percent; weight, 70 percent; and brain size, 94 percent).

If you are an adoptive parent or a stepparent, do not underestimate your influence. Much of the child's inner core, including approaches to problem solving, attitudes about life, and ways of relating to others, can be profoundly affected by your positive involvement. For example, approximately 40 percent of the variation in IQ scores is attributable to environmental factors and not genetics.

The data on attitudes is even more reassuring. Psychologists James Olson and his colleagues studied more than 300 pairs of identical twins, including those reared together and those raised in different environments. The researchers assessed a wide range of attitudes, from "abortion" and "the death penalty" to "reading books" and "playing sports." The findings indicated that approximately two-thirds of the variability in social values and interests was due to environmental factors. Clearly, both genetics and life experiences interact in complex ways to shape human behavior. All parents, biological or not, can have a tremendous impact on the development of their children.

The unconscious also appears to be deeply affected by family experiences. Evidence for a "family unconscious" comes from the work of Carl Jung. He administered a word-association test to twenty-four families, collecting more than 22,000 responses. When he compared the responses of various family members, Jung was amazed at the degree of similarity. For example, when the word *law* was presented to a young woman, her association was *Moses*. Her mother, though tested separately, replied, "God's commandments." To the word *strange*, both women independently responded, "Traveler."

We previously noted how the presence of effective and nurturing caretakers can facilitate the development of a hopeful core. Such emotional imprints also establish ways of relating to others, particularly in intimate relationships. Even the most casual observer of pop psychology is aware of the Freudian notion that individuals are "destined" to marry someone who reminds them of their mother or their father. Psychologist Harville Hendrix's concept of an imago is a more recent expression of this notion, the idea that individuals harbor a kind of prototype lover in the unconscious as a result of early child-parent interactions.

Try not to think of symbolic immortality as an inferior substitute for the real thing. Although planning and imagining may burden us with death anxiety, these particularly human qualities can also provide for our psychological salvation. Human beings inhabit two worlds: the physical and the symbolic. The latter consists of transcendent values and lasting memories as well as eternal hopes and dreams.

Transcendent Hope

To craft a transcendent hope, you must choose wisely when considering your options for achieving symbolic immortality. You will notice that each of the strategies we have outlined so far involves one or more of the motives that underlie hope. The use of meditation to override the normal limits of time and space derives from the survival motive. Establishing a legacy of creative accomplishments brings forth the mastery motive. Both attachment and survival concerns are reflected in sustaining close relationships, identifying with nature, or becoming a parent. A religious or spiritual belief system can involve one, two, or even all three of the hope motives.

To actualize a transcendent hope, you must keep two things in mind. First, it is important to address all three of the hope motives: mastery, attachment, and survival. For example, if you embrace many of the tenets of Buddhism and do regular meditation (survival), consider also doing something to fulfill your mastery and attachment strivings. Second, you must commit fully to your faith choices. Recall the earlier research that showed death anxiety is not lowered by merely going through the motions.

Below are some additional ideas for navigating this part of your hope journey. (In considering these suggestions, remember to choose the activities that are best suited to your spiritual type as well as your abilities and interests.)

- *Do your "blood work"* (attachment and survival). If you have children, be a consistently involved parent. Organize family reunions. Send photos and cards to loved ones. Create a calendar with pictures of family members, including birthdays and other important dates. Put together a scrapbook or produce your own family video. Do some research on your family tree. Write your memoirs and give a copy to younger family members.
- *Be creative* (mastery and survival). You don't have to be an artist to create something of lasting value. Build a tool shed or a playhouse for your children. Grow a garden, showing your children how to prepare the soil and harvest a crop. Get involved in a neighborhood project to establish or improve a playground or a ballpark. Spend a week with Habitat for Humanity, helping to provide housing for low-income families.
- *Commune with nature* (attachment and survival). Go camping. Learn more about the inner workings of nature. Do some bird or

whale watching. Spend a day walking in the woods or attend a science museum. Read about Jane Goodall's spiritual experiences in the wild or Rachel Carson's crusade against pesticides.

- *Strengthen your spiritual beliefs* (mastery, attachment, and survival). Consider attending a spiritual retreat, joining a Bible study group, or obtaining an annotated version of your favorite sacred text. Teach a religious class for children. Devote a half hour to prayer in the morning or the evening. Take a continuing education class on world religions or alternative spiritual traditions. Contribute to a charity sponsored by your particular faith group.

- *Meditate on a regular basis* (survival). There are many meditation traditions, including Japanese Buddhist, Chinese Taoist, and classic Hindu. If you seek pure detachment, then try the Zen or Tibetan Buddhist varieties. If you desire a more active process that will relax your body as well as still your mind, try tai chi or some form of yoga. Regardless of which technique you choose, make it a priority and commit yourself to a daily ritual.

- *Spread your love* (attachment and survival). Nurture your relationships. Look up old friends. Join Facebook.com, Classmates.com, or a similar Internet-based social network. Become a member of a community-based organization such as the Masons, the Chamber of Commerce, the Lions Club, or the Rotary Club. Heed Erik Erikson's sage advice to include institutions as well as other people in your circle of care. Donate your time to a local YMCA or YWCA, a favored political party, or helping the elderly. Sponsor a child from a third-world country or contribute some time to a youth sports league. Become a mentor to the younger generation, whether through teaching, coaching, or some other form of volunteering.

PART THREE:

THRIVING WITH HOPE

In Part Three we shift from coping to thriving, focusing on attachment, mastery, and health. Hope is part and parcel of the good life. Loving unions, a noble purpose, and sustained perseverance will yield a stronger, fuller hope. At the same time, a more hopeful disposition will go a long way toward building better relationships, increasing your prospects for success, and maximizing your potential for health and healing.

In Chapter 8 we revisit the importance of attachments in the development of hope. Along the way we highlight the importance of trust and openness, and outline the skills you should look for in a good hope provider. We also explore how lovers and friends can be sources of hope and ways that you can increase your chances of having a spiritual connection. In Chapter 9 we provide guidelines for achieving a sense of genuine success. We describe the four most important skills required for true mastery, the role of inspiration and dreams, and how to clarify your purpose in life. In Chapter 10 we cover both health and healing, examining the importance of a balanced approach to mastery, attachment, survival, and spirituality. We offer specific hope prescriptions as well as an overall philosophy for healthy living. We conclude with a look at hope-based fitness and hopeful aging.

8

Hope for Love

Humankind—of all ages and cultures—is confronted with one and the same question . . . how to achieve union. . . . The question is the same for primitive humans living in caves, for the nomadic herder taking care of his flock, for the peasant in Egypt, the Phoenician trader, the Roman soldier, the medieval monk, the Japanese Samurai, the modern clerk and the factory hand.

—Erich Fromm, *The Art of Loving*

Hope is not a private matter. A strong bond between an infant and his or her caregiver gives rise to basic trust and the first blush of empowerment. Parents' dreams for their sons and daughters will transform them into "hope providers" for life. The expectation of an ongoing love will sustain an open heart and forge a commitment to oneness. Faith in a higher power or a greater intelligence will frame a horizon of anticipated unity and harmony.

We begin this chapter with three vignettes that highlight attachments to people and places. To put these examples into a broader context, we rely on Erich Fromm's thoughts on the evolution of a separate consciousness and humanity's great hope for reconciliation. Next, we outline the qualities you should look for in an effective hope provider. Then we discuss strategies for building hope through your relationships with friends and lovers. The chapter concludes with a set of guidelines for creating hope-based spiritual connections.

THE BONDS OF HOPE

Among our daily references to hope are words and phrases that suggest it is a gift that can be provided, exchanged, or received. This makes perfect sense. As social creatures, we cannot live in isolation. Aristotle labeled those who seemed content to live by themselves "beasts or gods." The seventeenth-century poet John Donne echoed this sentiment when he wrote, "No man is an island." Centuries earlier, the Chinese sage Mengzi similarly noted, "It is [human] bonds that fill the space between heaven and earth."

The three following hope vignettes highlight the power of intimate relationships to engender hope. Moreover, they illustrate the frequent intertwining of the attachment motive with the drive toward mastery or the impulse for survival. Two are personal reflections; the third involves a group of Pennsylvania miners who narrowly escaped death.

Tony's Story:

For the first three years of my life, I was raised by my aunt Antoinette, a petite woman less than five feet tall. Due to a doctor's mistake when she was a child, her growth was permanently stunted and she was left with a badly curved spine. She co-owned our modest stucco house in the village of Cantalupo with my father and her other brother. When my parents and the other adults of the household went out to the fields, she stayed back to cook, clean, and take care of me. When both of her siblings left for America, my aunt became my sole caretaker. She also attended to my paternal grandmother, who was strong and sharp for an eighty-year-old but was legally blind as a result of diabetes.

My aunt never married nor had children. She rarely left the compound that she created for herself in that remote village of Italy. I came to America at the age of three and communicated with her by phone a few times a year, usually at Easter and Christmas. However, my mother spoke constantly of my aunt and kept her memory alive for me with tales of my early years, which my aunt had recounted to her.

More than two decades later, I planned a summer trip to visit my aunt. As fate would have it, she had been feeling ill and took a turn for the worse. Hearing this from other relatives in Italy, I rush-ordered a new passport and booked the first possible flight. Much to my dismay, I arrived five hours after she died, apparently from an undiagnosed bleeding ulcer that had progressed from medical neglect. When I reached our hometown, I was directed to the local hospital and brought to see my aunt lying dead on a cot. Instead of enjoying a nostalgic reunion over pasta and wine, I spiraled downward into shock. When the numbness wore off, it was replaced by a painful mixture of grief and regret that hung over me for many months.

Although I had spent only a few years with her and thousands of miles separated us, I always felt a strong connection with my aunt. Moreover, her life strongly affected not only my approach to hope (in terms of mastery, attachment, survival, and spirituality) but also my personal way of being in the world: the way I think, feel, and act to sustain my own sense of hope. She has been gone for more than two decades, but I still feel guided by her presence and her example.

My aunt had three passions that were the basis of all her mastery efforts: family, God, and cooking. With few educational opportunities open to her, she nevertheless sought and obtained certificates of training in religious education and the culinary arts. My aunt made pilgrimages to Lourdes and did volunteer work for the town parish. She exemplified a life committed to higher goals as well as the importance of spirituality and faith. Perhaps most important, she showed me that love transcends both time and distance.

It makes me sad that what I also took from my aunt were tragic lessons about coping, illness, and health. As a child she was irreparably harmed by the medical profession. As an adult, perhaps because of this life-altering trauma, she chose to "go it alone," with even more terrible consequences. I don't blame her, especially given her childhood experience, the limited medical resources available at the time, and her hard-won independence. At the same time, her physical problems only served to reinforce the larger lesson I drew from her life: the importance of collaboration in any life domain, whether it is self-care or the care of others, mastery efforts, or survival issues.

Henry's Story:

My parents were great sources of hope for me. Looking back after these many years, I still hold on to my father's sense of purpose and resourcefulness as well as my mother's acceptance and courage. Both my parents have long since passed away. It has been more than six decades since my father died; four since the passing of my mother. However, my relationship with them persists to this day; it is an enduring source of hope that has become a large part of my spiritual life.

My father was a furniture salesman and an air raid warden during World War II. As a child, I was impressed by the uniform, hat, and whistle that he wore while patroling for enemy planes. He often took me along, and although I was pretty naive about the nature of the conflict, it was obvious to me that he felt a solemn duty to be part of the war effort. My dad was also Mr. Fix-It around the home, repairing broken toys and utensils, always seeming to find a way around any obstacle or problem. He truly personified the philosophy of "Where there's a will, there's a way."

My mother was a "tough cookie." She lost her husband at a young age and worked full-time as a bookkeeper and secretary. At night she cooked our meals, and on weekends she baked special treats. I had a lot of energy as a child. Today I'm sure that I would be labeled hyperactive or that my restlessness and willfulness would be attributed to attention deficit disorder. My mother was routinely criticized for being too lax with me. She did express her disapproval when I was reprimanded by teachers, school principals, athletic coaches, or even the police, on a few occasions. However, my mother never failed to listen to my side of the story, taking me seriously even when she didn't feel entirely comfortable with my behavior.

In addition, whenever I asked her to trust me at a pivotal point in my life, she questioned me at length but ultimately, if grudgingly, always gave her support. For example, when I was in elementary school, all my classmates went home for lunch. Because my mother worked full-time, this was not an option for me. I convinced her that I could safely get to the local diner, eat lunch, and make it back to school.

Above all, my mother never wavered in her faith in my mastery and survival skills. Even when I was underachieving in high school, she conveyed her faith in my "street smarts." When I finally went to college and succeeded, it was a victory for both of us, a shared hope that had been realized, and a vindication for giving me the space to prosper in a meaningful way. When my clinical internship director wrote a glowing evaluation letter for me, my mother put it in her purse and kept it there until the day she died.

What did I learn about survival and spirituality? I lost my father a week before my sixth birthday, and I lost my mother when I was thirty. Nevertheless, I continue to have a relationship with both of my parents. I often reflect on how much they coped with and survived, given how much physical and emotional adversity fell in their paths. I'm sure that my father hoped someday to be a grandparent, but he never had a chance to realize this dream. In a way, I am realizing his dreams for him now. Because my parents (particularly my father) died at relatively young ages, I learned to appreciate each day. I never take tomorrow for granted. I learned early in life that you never know how much time you have, so it is important to live every day.

THE PENNSYLVANIA MINERS

All mankind is of one author, and is one volume . . .
therefore the bell that rings to a sermon calls not upon the
preacher only, but upon the congregation to come . . .
any man's death diminishes me, because I am involved
in mankind; and therefore never send to know
for whom the bell tolls; it tolls for thee.

—JOHN DONNE, MEDITATION XVII

One of the most memorable images of 2002 was the sight of nine miners as they were rescued from a collapsed shaft in rural Pennsylvania. They had endured seventy-seven hours in a cold, dark hole that was nearly 250 feet below the earth's surface. In terms of hope, what is most interesting are the relationships that sustained them during their ordeal. They huddled together for warmth, shared bites of one dry sandwich, and related stories of their lives and families.

The men alternated between thoughts of rescue and concerns about abandoning their loved ones. Blaine Mayhugh agonized over the fact that he had forgotten to kiss his wife before going to work. Once rescued, he fought back tears, explaining it was "the only day in my life I didn't kiss my wife before I went to work . . . that had to be the day." A number of his fellow workers stated they would never mine again, emphasizing not their own mortality fears but their reluctance to ever put their families or community through any future tribulations.

When they were trapped together, the miners quickly developed a profound sense of unity that soon encircled their families, the rescuers, and the entire nation. Randy Fogle recalled telling the others that they needed to put their faith in the rescuers: "I told them we have the resources of the whole world around us and they will have everything that we will need." When the miners were finally pulled to safety, the 150 rescuers danced and shouted the nicknames of each miner. Family and friends staying at a nearby firehouse erupted into celebration. Signs were erected at rest stops and gas stations, declaring *Nine Alive!* and *Prayers Answered*. Looking back, Blaine Mayhugh noted, "We vowed to live or die as a group . . . My father-in-law tied us all together with a rope so we wouldn't float away from each other."

Mystical Unions

Come, come again, whoever you are, come! Heathen, fire worshipper or idolatrous, come! Ours is the portal of hope.

—RUMI, *DISCOURSES*

Reports of mystical experiences come from all over the world. Among Hindus, Zen Buddhists, and Muslim Sufists, transcendence and union is the daily spiritual goal of every follower. Although vivid examples of mystical transformation are not as common in the West, they are hardly rare. Among others, William Shakespeare, Johann von Goethe, Henry Wadsworth Longfellow, Emily Brontë, and Pope John Paul II have provided detailed descriptions of their encounters with the numinous. Albert Einstein referred to such mystical states as the "center of true religion," adding that anyone "who can no longer wonder and stand rapt in awe is as good as dead." William James viewed mystical experiences as unsolicited and ineffable streams of timeless illumination, whereas writer Annie Dillard prefers the imagery of light and fire.

Sometimes a mystical experience is described as corporeal, filled with perceptions of images and objects such as a godlike figure, a pool of water, or a rainbow. Alternately, a mystical state may consist entirely of an inner experience, in which one is aware of a presence or feels engulfed by strong positive emotions.

The anthropologist Jane Goodall provided one of the most far-ranging discussions of spiritual awakening. In *Reason for Hope*, this world-renowned scientist recounted two stirring mystical experiences, the first at Notre Dame Cathedral in Paris and the second in an African jungle:

Many years ago I visited the cathedral of Notre Dame in Paris. I gazed in silent awe at the great Rose Window, glowing in the morning sun. All at once the cathedral was filled with a huge volume of sound . . . Bach's Tocata and Fugue in D Minor . . . it seemed to enter and possess my whole self. . . . That moment, a suddenly captured moment of eternity, was perhaps the closest I have ever come to experiencing ecstasy.

Lost in the awe at the beauty around me, I must have slipped into a state of heightened awareness. It is hard—impossible, really—to put into words the moment of truth that suddenly came upon me then. . . . It seemed to me, as I struggled afterward to recall the experience, that self was utterly absent: I and the chimpanzees, the earth and trees and air, seemed to merge, to become one with the spirit power of life itself.

THE ATTACHED CORE

Relationships are fundamental to hope. It is hardly surprising that those who have thought most deeply about hope have emphasized the role of trust, attachment, presence, and mutuality. The New Testament places faith and hope alongside love. The Qur'an scolds those who do not "embrace" Allah. The hope of those who practice Ifa, as well as of the Australian Aborigines, is to forge a link with the spirit world, including deceased ancestors.

In other chapters elsewhere in this book, we consider the role of relationships in strengthening the mastery and survival aspects of hope. In this chapter, the focus is on the attachment system itself and how it serves as a primary source of hope as well as the basis for our most compelling desires. The establishment of an attached core in the first years of life is one of the greatest blessings that can be bestowed on an individual. The attached core is an amalgam of hopeful imprints, relational trust, and openness.

Human beings rely on relationships with others to forge a stable, cohesive, and continuous sense of self. Such interactions create something far more profound than simply a self-concept. These emotional mergers impact how we experience ourselves, the world, and the future. From a hope perspective, the emotions that are engendered through our relationships with others can reverberate for a lifetime, impacting how connected, empowered, or safe we feel in the world.

Psychoanalyst Heinz Kohut described two kinds of bonds that develop between parents and their children. A *mirroring transference* takes place when parents confirm and admire a child's "strength and specialness." An *idealizing transference* occurs when parents encourage an older child to "merge with their own strength and power." Both experiences lead to the development of an enhanced sense of self, what Kohut called an internalized "self-object." Such internalized bonds can be either positive or negative, depending on the qualities that have been transferred from the parents. We prefer the term *hopeful imprints* to describe these core experiences of positive bonding with a strong and caring presence.

The stable presence of a caregiver, a friend, or a lover aids in the formation of *relational trust*. This form of trust can be distinguished from goal-related or survival-based types of trust. Goal-related trust is placed in someone because you believe that he or she has the ability to help you achieve a valued mastery-related outcome. For example, you might have complete confidence in a teacher, a coach, or a manager to create a blueprint for success. Survival-based trust relates to your prospects for continued well-being. For example, you might have total confidence in a primary-care physician to monitor and manage your health.

Relational trust is based on the assurance of a continued presence. You are confident that someone or something will stay by your side. The importance of having this feeling cannot be stressed enough. We benefit greatly from a stable parental figure in childhood, a steadfast friend in adolescence, a committed lover in adulthood, and even a trusted spiritual ally to support our quest for ultimate meaning and purpose.

Trust and *openness* are intertwined. Some amount of basic trust is hardwired, or present at birth. If an infant's caregiver provides a reliable presence, this initial trust and openness will be rewarded with a growing sense that the world is benign and receptive. Encouraged by attentive caregivers, it is natural for infants to reach out, to make social contacts, and to explore their surroundings. In *Fathers and Families*, Henry reviewed the vast amount of data showing that infants who are blessed with a positive maternal and paternal presence demonstrate a "two-parent advantage," which includes an increased capacity for dealing with unfamiliar individuals as well as other novel and complex situations.

THE GREAT HOPE

In *The Art of Loving*, Erich Fromm argued that the experience of being apart is the most painful aspect of the human condition. According to him, the disquieting feeling of being totally alone has preyed on the consciousness of men and women throughout human history. Fromm believed that humans had been "torn from nature" by virtue of their "self-awareness," making them the only species of "life aware of itself." No longer enveloped in an "Eden of oneness," a human being suffers the vulnerability of conscious self-reflection. Fromm writes as follows:

> This separate, disunited existence could be an unbearable prison . . . humanity would become insane if they could not liberate themselves from this prison and reach out, uniting itself in some form with others and the world outside. . . . [Humankind] can only go forward, finding a new harmony to replace the pre-human harmony that has been lost forever.

A sense of separateness can breed overwhelming anxiety, triggering maladaptive attempts to dissolve the pain of isolation. Fromm alluded to the use of drugs and sex as powerful but transitory antidotes. He noted that conformity and group membership provide more lasting possibilities but that these are too mild to allay intense feelings of isolation. For Fromm, the only adequate solution is to master "the art of loving." Love "is the most powerful striving force . . . it keeps the human race together."

It is hard to minimize the power of love and its essential place in human life. Jews and Christians may recall that in the Book of Genesis, the first human need addressed by the Creator is Adam's aloneness: "And the Lord God said, 'It is not good that the human should be alone. . . . For this reason a man will leave his father and his mother and be united to his wife, and they will become one flesh.'"

Fromm's brilliant insights suggest an even deeper need than love. Although mastering the art of loving may go a long way toward offsetting feelings of separateness, it alone might not quell the soul's unrest. A more pressing need derives from the hope for restored harmony and intimacy. Being torn from nature, humans seek an enduring physical, emotional, and spiritual connection. They hope for continuing contact and comfort. They hope for a common purpose as well as shared values and ideals.

One could devote an entire library to the expressions of attachment-focused hope. Moreover, these various expressions often cross-fertilize. The experience of greater physical or emotional intimacy may bring an individual closer to God, nature, or some other higher power. Alternatively, a transcendent or mystical encounter can sometimes spark a more intimate bond with one's community, family, or friends (Figure 8.1).

Figure 8.1 The Basic Expressions of Attachment-Related Hope

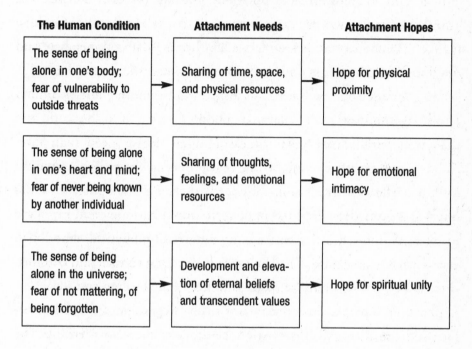

The Human Condition	Attachment Needs	Attachment Hopes
The sense of being alone in one's body; fear of vulnerability to outside threats	Sharing of time, space, and physical resources	Hope for physical proximity
The sense of being alone in one's heart and mind; fear of never being known by another individual	Sharing of thoughts, feelings, and emotional resources	Hope for emotional intimacy
The sense of being alone in the universe; fear of not mattering, of being forgotten	Development and elevation of eternal beliefs and transcendent values	Hope for spiritual unity

HOPE PROVIDERS

When you are searching for a good doctor, therapist, coach, business leader, or mentor, look for a genuine hope provider. A hope provider will offer availability, presence, and contact. If these are given in the right way, at the right time, and in the right amount, such gifts can inspire greater trust and openness. Moreover, availability, presence, and contact can lead to the development of hopeful imprints that will sustain you for years to come.

Availability and Trust

The *vail* in the word *availability* conveys that something of value has been placed within your reach. It is noteworthy that every major religion stresses the availability of spiritual blessings. In the New Testament, Matthew quoted Jesus: "Ask and it will be given to you; seek and you will find; knock and it will be open to you." In the Pali Canon, the Buddha listed the benefits of a contemplative life that are visible in the here and now, including inner assurance, tranquillity, and rapture.

True hope providers are available. By providing access, consistency, and sensitivity, they foster the belief that goodness is present in the world and the universe can be trusted. In contrast, if they are routinely absent, unreliable, or indifferent, they stymie the development of hope. Research indicates that adults with a history of unsatisfying relationships nevertheless often reveal an adequate number of social contacts. However, compared to those with a well-nurtured past, hope-starved individuals cite a shortage of trustworthy allies. With regard to the importance of availability, there is a convergence of the sacred and the scientific literature.

Access. A hope provider makes time, shares space, and remains flexible. In the Qur'an, Allah is situated "closer than the vein of your neck." The Rig Veda assures all Hindus that the fire god Agni is "knower of all that lives" and "stands in the presence of all beings." Surveys indicate that patients seek physicians and therapists who are interpersonaly as well as technically skilled. A need for trust is repeatedly emphasized, along with responsiveness, availability for appointments, and sufficient consultation time. Research on effective mentoring in business and education highlights the importance of one-to-one time and the development of sufficient trust between the mentor and the protégé.

Consistency. The hope provider exhibits consistency by remaining dependably nearby. The Navajo legend "The Dreamer" assures humanity that the Creator can be heard in the crack of thunder, felt in a steady rain, and seen in the rising cornfields. Similarly, psychological studies indicate that regular family visits reduce the stress levels of patients who have had a myocardial infarction and speed the recovery of elderly patients who have undergone major surgery.

Sensitivity. The hope provider is sensitive enough to be able to anticipate your needs. The Qur'an states, "You need not raise your voice, for He [Allah] knows the secret whisper and what is yet more hidden." Humans are programmed to look for such signs of attunement. Infants constantly monitor the facial expressions of their caregivers and show contentment when there is synchronicity between their own actions and those of the care provider. Conversely, if the adult is disengaged or insensitive to emotional cues, the baby becomes distressed. Moreover, if the caregiver is chronically depressed, the child is at risk for developing a more enduring sense of helplessness.

Presence and Openness

Presence literally means "to be in front of." Your potential hope provider must have a full-bodied presence, not one that is ghostlike or feigned. A hopeful presence is focused, safe, and authentic.

Focus. Hope is built on the experience of an adequate presence. One meaning of the Hindu word *guru* is "weight," or "heavy." Hope providers weigh in with their full presence. They do not hover in the periphery or shadows of everyday life. Focus is undoubtedly one of the major factors in the demonstrated effectiveness of quality time as a predictor of adaptive family functioning.

Safety. Your hope provider should offer a safe haven. Family therapist Virginia Satir has cautioned parents to avoid "interrogating" their children. Parents who press and probe like paranoid detectives will cause their children to retreat into further secrecy. Trauma expert Judith Herman wrote that the first and central task of the therapist is to provide a safe context. According to a Nigerian proverb, "one does not love if one does not accept."

Authenticity. Humanistic psychologist Carl Rogers believed that the best counselors were those who maintained a high level of congruity between their inner truth and their outward demeanor. Hope providers, to paraphrase the Moody Blues, "must mean what they say and say what they mean." Likewise, the Buddhist Eightfold Path encourages the use of right speech as a means of shedding all pretenses. Your hope provider should be authentic.

Contact: Leaving a Hopeful Imprint

We began this chapter with references to imparting and instilling the gift of hope. How can potential hope providers—be they parents, lovers, or friends—transfer their hopefulness to another? How can they help others to incorporate positive and sustaining images that penetrate to the core of their existence? Ultimately, hope providers must reach the center of another if they wish to become part of his or her inner essence. Their involvement should filter into another's thoughts and feelings, positively impacting an individual's sense of self. Making hopeful contact requires involvement, clarity, and repetition. When a hope provider approaches another in this manner, there is a far greater chance of instilling a hopeful imprint.

Involvement. A hopeful imprint results from a potent presence that is deeply infused into the thoughts, feelings, and actions of another. In the West, many individuals tend to live fractionated lives. Their impact on others is limited by a myriad of muted involvements. Invariably, this produces diluted empowerment, a watered-down presence, or halfhearted compassion. In contrast, consider the total involvement of the Australian Aborigines, who routinely devote an entire night to the Dreaming ceremony. Similarly, Orthodox Jews engage in a complex series of spiritual rituals every Sabbath, sanctifying a cup of wine and eating special meals while prohibiting themselves from nearly forty categories of weekday activities.

Clarity. Love comes in many forms. However, the most hope is transmitted by providing the appropriate sentiment at the time it is most needed. Hindus who practice Bhakti yoga recognize four ways of loving. Similarly, Rollo May identified care, lust, romantic love, and friendship as forms of love. Confucius delineated nearly a dozen types of kin and community relationships. A hope provider responds to your true needs.

Repetition. A hopeful imprint is more likely to take hold when there is repeated involvement. The internalization of hope takes time. Many Westerners reserve a mere hour every Sunday to receive their spiritual directions. In sharp contrast, Buddhists and Hindus may spend consecutive months, if not years, in the presence of their gurus, receiving the same instruction over and over. In the New Testament, Jesus keeps drumming home the same messages of prayer, love, and forgiveness through various anecdotes and parables. A good hope provider will be more than happy to reiterate and reinforce mastery, attachment, survival, or survival lessons.

Exercise 9: Are You a Hope Provider?

Rate each of the following statements as they relate to your typical thoughts, feelings, and behaviors. Use the scoring system that is provided below to quantify your rating. For example, if a particular statement describes a thought, feeling, or behavior that you would *never* think, feel, or do, place a zero (never true) at the end of the statement. On the other hand, if the statement captures *exactly* how you think, feel or act, place a 3 (always true) at the beginning of the sentence.

Never True	Rarely True	Often True	Always True
0	1	2	3

____ 1. I let friends and loved ones know where and when they can reach me (time, place, etc.).

____ 2. I stay focused when people tell me their stories.

____ 3. I make time for one-to-one conversations.

____ 4. I'm honest with others and myself about my willingness to be available.

____ 5. I am a good listener.

____ 6. I like to remind friends and loved ones of experiences we have shared together.

____ 7. I make an effort to understand the needs of others.

____ 8. When spending time with others, I take into consideration their fears and worries.

____ 9. In dealing with others, I try not to overstep their boundaries.

____ 10. My first impressions about a person usually prove to be right on the mark.

____ 11. I make an effort to help people feel comfortable in my presence.

____ 12. I keep things from my friends and loved ones that might upset, hurt, or embarrass them.

____ 13. I feel bad when I can't follow through on a commitment.

____ 14. I do not hide my feelings from others.

____ 15. I like to share rituals with friends and loved ones.

____ 16. I will stop in the middle of a project to make sure that I meet someone on time.

____ 17. I'm direct with others and can tell them what is really on my mind.

____ 18. I make a strong effort to preserve family and cultural traditions.

Computing Your Scores

Fill in your scores for each of the questions and add across the rows to compute your levels of availability, presence, and contact.

Availability: 1____ 4____ 7____ 10____ 13____ 16____ Total = ____

Presence: 2____ 5____ 8____ 11____ 14____ 17____ Total = ____

Contact: 3____ 6____ 9____ 12____ 15____ 18____ Total = ____

Interpreting Your Scores

Low: 0 – 6   Medium: 7 – 11   High: 12 – 18

If you scored in the low or medium range on one or more of the scales, consider reviewing the corresponding sections of this chapter. You may also want to examine more closely your scores on the specific components of availability, presence, or contact (access = 1, 4; sensitivity = 7, 10; consistency = 13, 16; focus = 2, 5; safety = 8, 11; authenticity = 14, 17; involvement = 3, 6; clarity = 9, 12; repetition = 15, 18).

LOVERS AND FRIENDS

For many individuals, relationships with lovers and friends engender a tremendous amount of hope. By *love*, we do not mean unhealthy relationships fueled by an unbridled ego, excessive dependency, or some other addictive weakness. In contrast to these desperate pairings, the deeper expressions of human love offer a true and lasting hope. Such a distinction appears in scriptures as well as in great art, literature, and film. For example, consider the New Testament passage from Paul's First Letter to the Corinthians, probably the most popular reading at

Christian weddings: "Love is patient, love is kind. . . . It always protects, always trusts, always hopes."

Literary classics also blend love and hope. A good example is Charles Dickens's *Great Expectations*. Many hopes are reflected in this tale of mystery, heartache, and redemption. Dickens introduced a number of unforgettable characters, each with their own particular set of love-begotten hopes. After a false suitor abandons Miss Havisham on her wedding day, she adopts three-year-old Estella in the hope of experiencing the love that was denied her at the altar.

An otherwise dour accountant named Jaggers manages to have Estella adopted by the wealthy Havisham in the hope of saving "one pretty little child from the heap of . . . children being imprisoned, whipped, transported, neglected." Unable to reverse mounting bitterness, Havisham negatively transforms her hope into grooming Estella to break the hearts of unsuspecting men, including young Pip. At the end of her life, Havisham finds that her cruelty has been nothing but a spiritual poison. Throwing herself before Pip, she repeatedly cries out, "What have I done?" thus expressing her hope for forgiveness and redemption.

Although Pip's "great expectations" include the promise of a large inheritance, the most compelling hope of his youth is to have Estella's hand in marriage. As his capacity for love is enlarged, so is his manner of hoping. For example, sensing that he might never possess the coldhearted beauty, he nevertheless hopes that Estella will save herself from the clutches of Havisham. In the hope of taking care of his kind but simple friend Herbert, Pip beseeches Havisham to arrange a secret allowance for him.

An escaped convict named Magwich becomes Pip's secret benefactor. He tells Pip that his abysmal "low life" in Australia was sustained by "one fixed idea": the hope of elevating Pip to the status of an English gentleman. Later, hoping to assure the dying Magwich of a good and peaceful death, Pip visits him every day, prompting in the convict a "placid look and brightened eyes," putting some distance "between his soul and the constant dark clouds."

Regretful of abandoning his adoptive parents, Pip tells them, "I hope you will have children to love . . . and some little fellow . . . who may remind you of another little fellow." In the last lines of the novel, Estella realizes that her heart has been "bent and broke, but—I hope into a better shape," whereas Pip is comforted by the "broad expanse of a tranquil light" and the hope of "no [further] parting from her."

John Steinbeck's *East of Eden* is another great literary tribute to hope. This was Steinbeck's favorite creation, the masterpiece he called his one "true book." It was released to the public in the summer of 1952. By November it was the nation's bestseller. A noted literary critic called it a tale with an optimistic ending. The novel is actually filled with sadness and heartache, repeated acts of pathological cruelty, unfulfilled longings, and unnecessary losses. It is not at all blindly optimistic book, but it *is* a saga of transcendent hope.

Among the many hope lessons in *East of Eden*, four stand out. The first lesson is that an especially gifted hope provider can stimulate all three of the hope motives: mastery, attachment, and survival. Samuel, the patriarch of the Hamilton family, is the most powerful of the hope providers. Samuel is a jack-of-all-trades and a first-class inventor. He is supremely kind and intuitive, one of the very few characters in the novel who finds his way into the center of another's soul. He meets the evil Cathy only once but immediately senses her cruel intentions and cold heart. Deeply attuned to Adam's suffering, he offers him the best antidote for a soul sickened by (Cathy's) false hope. After Samuel's death, Adam reflects on the life of his good friend, noting, "Somehow he made a man better than he was."

The second lesson is that those who offer false hope perpetrate a great evil. Cathy (aka Kate) is the clearest embodiment of counterfeit hope. Her mastery consists of egotistical pursuits. She never shares her power and wouldn't dream of asking for help. Her achievements are always rooted in deception, manipulation, and lies. Her attachments are superficial. She is unable to see, hear, or feel love. Even as a child, she used her body to lure young men into her evil snare. She killed her parents. She allows Adam to fall in love with her but keeps him at a distance while sleeping with his brother, Charles. She abandons her children.

Cathy's survival skills are also quite limited. She can't control her rage. She trusts no one and never feels safe. There is nothing eternal about her. She denies Adam the certainty of a legacy and mockingly insinuates that Charles may actually be the biological father of her children. As her outer beauty fades, her inner chaos takes over. Her growing helplessness is symbolized by the arthritic condition of her hands. She is literally and figuratively "losing her grip." Shortly before killing herself, she acknowledges her utter hopelessness.

The third lesson is that repeated abuse can push an individual beyond fear and rage into a state of complete indifference about his or her fate. As a child, Adam tries his best to earn the love of his family. Toward his brother, Adam is loyal, trusting, and kind, but Charles is cruel and takes every opportunity to torture him emotionally as well as physically. Cyrus, their father, is less vicious, but his actions prove equally destructive. Insensitive to Adam's needs, he forces him into the army, selfishly trading his son's life for his own twisted agenda of gain and glory. By forcing his reluctant son into the army, Cyrus effectively ends Adam's chance for a hopeful life.

Having lost his will to hope, Adam goes through the motions of being a soldier. Having forgotten his own dreams and desires, he keeps reenlisting, preferring extra duty to a fated and barren future. When he is finally cut loose from the army, Adam wanders about, lost and confused. To add insult to injury, Adam is arrested for vagrancy and assigned to a road gang. Through this he learns firsthand what captivity and abuse can do to the soul.

> He learned how men can consider other men as beasts . . . a clean face, an open face, an eye raised to meet an eye . . . these drew attention and attention drawn brought punishment . . . the savage whippings for the least stir of will, for the smallest shred of dignity or resistance. . . . Adam, like anyone in the world, feared what whipping would do to his body and his spirit. . . . He drew a curtain around himself. . . . He removed expression from his face, light from his eyes, and silenced his speech. . . . It was much more horrible afterward than when it was happening. . . . Adam reduced his personality to minus. He caused no stir, put out no vibration, became as invisible as it is possible to be.

The fourth lesson is that an abiding sense of hope comes from believing in a future that is filled with possibility. Some of the most hopeful words in the novel are uttered by Lee, Adam's Chinese servant. Lee adores the biblical story of Cain and Abel, especially the sixteen magical lines that revolve around the Hebrew concept of "timshal," often translated as "thou shall" or "thou mayest." (The actual passage in Genesis 4:7 reads, "If you do not do good, sin is crouching by the entrance. Its longing is toward you, and you shall rule it.") Timshal suggests that humanity's fate is far from sealed. The intimation of possibility, openness, and renewal fills Lee with hope. In the final pages of the book, Lee declares his faith in the future:

> When Samuel Hamilton died the world went out like a candle. . . . I relighted it to see his lovely creations, and I saw his children tossed and torn and destroyed as though

some vengefulness was at work. . . . I thought the good are destroyed while the evil survive and prosper . . . I thought that once an angry and disgusted God poured molten fire
from the crucible to destroy or purify his little handiwork of mud. . . . Maybe you'll come
to know that every man in every generation is refired. . . . . All impurities burned out and
ready for a glorious flux, and for that more fire. . . . Can you ever think that whatever
made us—would stop trying?

The love-hope connection has also been dramatically preserved in
great romantic films. Table 8.1 includes our analysis of the American
Film Institute's top ten romantic films. Unlike cliché-filled, boy-meets-
girl B movies, these films are filled with heartache and loss as well as
physical suffering and terminal illness. In eight of the ten films there is
a bittersweet ending. In seven of them, the lovers are separated by death
or forced apart by complex circumstances. What made these films great
is the dramatization of the most profound hope that human beings can
express within the context of an intimate relationship, culminating in a
desire for the life of another to be transformed for the better. Although
the typical romantic film supplies a dose of fleeting optimism, a great
one delivers an enduring sense of hope.

Table 8.1. The Ten Greatest Romantic Films

Rank	Title of Film	Primary Hope Theme
1	*Casablanca* (1942)	The hope of upholding what is most valued by another human being
2	*Gone with the Wind* (1939)	The hope for a love that can quiet a troubled mind and soothe a restless soul
3	*West Side Story* (1961)	The hope to be seen as one truly is rather than as a stereotype
4	*Roman Holiday* (1953)	The hope for the preservation of dignity in all human relationships
5	*An Affair to Remember* (1957)	The hope for redemption at "the place closest to heaven" (aka the Empire State Building)
6	*The Way We Were* (1973)	The hope of bringing out the best in another human being
7	*Doctor Zhivago* (1965)	An unflinching hope that supports all that is beautiful in the world
8	*It's A Wonderful Life* (1946)	The hope of friendship within a loving community
9	*Love Story* (1970)	The hope for a great love that transcends even death
10	*City Lights* (1931)	The hope for a generous love that brings healing to another person

Hope and love share a hint of uncertainty as well as a touch of euphoria. Whenever individuals love deeply, they risk a heightened sense of vulnerability. They are simultaneously confronted by the possibility of achieving or not achieving their greatest dreams. What could be more thrilling or terrifying?

Few other aspects of the human condition evoke as much passion. This is why love and hope are blended in the dramas of Shakespeare, the poetry of Dante, the music of Mozart, and the lyrics of Lennon and McCartney. This is why the hope of a healing love excited Plato, Confucius, and Carl Jung. This is why the hope for love moved even the atheistic Bertrand Russell to place it first in his pantheon of dreams.

Our investment in love is actually based on a myriad of great and small hopes. Psychologist Nathaniel Branden (the former protégé of Ayn Rand) listed several types of romantic needs. We prefer to conceptualize these desires as expressions of converging hopes. They include the hope to be nurtured and valued, the hope for a companion with whom to share your joys and your sorrows, the hope to realize yourself sexually, the hope to fully express your love, the hope to be seen as you truly are, and the hope to fulfill your true potential.

Considering all the hope that goes into a love relationship, it is no wonder that human beings invest so much time and energy trying to get it right. Love "makes the world go around," as they say, because it keeps hope alive. Indeed, the spiral of hope that is generated by giving and getting in romantic love is enormously powerful. The nineteenth-century French writer Stendhal wrote, "Love is the only passion which pays itself in a coin which it mints itself."

The Nature of Love

Love is about closeness. In *Too Good to Leave, Too Bad to Stay*, Mira Kirshenbaum highlighted the willingness of partners to make themselves available for each other. She viewed openness to the other as a vital regenerative property in healthy relationships. In contrast, an intimacy killer is "off-the-table-itis." This occurs when one or both partners block the other's attempt to discuss issues of importance to their relationship.

Love is trusting. Kirshenbaum noted the fundamental need for trust in love relationships. You must be able to feel that promises and agreements will be kept and that commitments will be honored. She puts it bluntly: "When you're married to a liar, your marriage is a lie."

Love is wise. Partners who are deeply in love refer to "being on the same wavelength." They easily "read each other" and have a strong sense of being "in sync." In one study, psychologist Dan McAdams asked couples to write imaginative stories. The couples who were greatly in love more often used words like *harmony* and *true understanding* than did couples who were not.

Love is expressive. Psychologist John Gottman has spent his career studying the foundations of successful marriages, including both verbal and nonverbal communication patterns. From his perspective, partners should familiarize themselves with each other's facial expressions, voice inflections, and body language as well as paying close attention to spoken words.

Love is fully present. Relationship expert Harville Hendrix has encouraged his clients to move toward a "conscious marriage." He espouses acting with a purpose rather than reacting out of habit or on the basis of old attachment wounds. Hendrix also implores his clients to look below the surface to seek the truth of the partner's inner life.

Love is safe. St. Paul's love is "patient." Shakespeare's love "is not love which alters when it alteration finds." Kirshenbaum, as well as the myth scholar Joseph Campbell, emphasized that your primary relationship should feel like a home within a home.

Love is honest. According to Hendrix, a conscious marriage includes a commitment to close all "relationship exits." These unstated forms of "invisible divorce" may range from rather subtle emotional manipulations to not-so-hidden affairs. One must have both feet in a love relationship to ensure a hopeful connection that is based on emotional as well as physical presence.

Love is about chemistry. Your unconscious can operate much like a gyroscope, pointing you in the direction of a particular person. Hendrix has written a great deal about the imago, the love template that is derived from your early attachment experiences. Part of the healing power of love comes from confronting old attachment wounds.

Love is about dreams. According to Gottman, "people form much more positive emotional connections when they encourage one another's dreams and aspirations." He encouraged lovers to become "dream detectors." Gottman added that the source of conflict within a relationship is often the failure to acknowledge the individualized hopes and dreams of each partner.

Love is about meaning. Gottman believed that "rituals of emotional connection" are the secret to increasing a sense of shared meaning. These rituals can be as simple as a weekend breakfast buffet, sitting down to watch a favorite television show, going to the movies on a regular basis, or arranging for a weekly card game. They might also involve sharing religious, cultural, or sporting activities. The magic and meaning of rituals is complex, but from a hope perspective, a key factor is experiencing something together that is both positive and predictable.

The Nature of Friendship

Friends are a prime source of hope. They can nourish our lofty dreams while providing a secure base of Earthly support. Friends also provide comfort and assurance in times of stress. Writing about the value of friendship, Cicero opined that "nothing better than this has been given to human beings by the immortal gods." Emerson referred to friendship as "nature's masterpiece" and "a possession for all time."

Scientists have generated some interesting statistics about friendships, including mounds of demographic data on factors such as the respective age, sex, and income of friendship pairs. However, there is little research on the inner workings of friendships. What is the essence of a good friendship? What should you seek in a good friend? Conversely, if you wish to be a true friend, what are the rules of comportment? Fortunately, there are innumerable nuggets of wisdom in classic literature. Inspiration and guidance can be obtained from Aristotle and Cicero, Francis Bacon and Michel Montaigne, Ralph Waldo Emerson and Henry David Thoreau, Khalil Gibran and Antoine de Saint-Exupéry.

A true friend, like a good parent or a good lover, will inspire trust, foster openness, and contribute to the formation of a hopeful inner life. Cicero observed that friendship "holds out good hope and does not permit souls to either fade or fall from view." Bacon suggested that friends "double joy and cut grief in half" and "maketh daylight in the understanding out of darkness." Emerson declared that "in the company of friends there is no winter and no night." Gibran unearthed the magic of friendship in shared rituals, noting how "in the dew of little things the heart finds it morning and is refreshed."

Friends are accessible. In *The Little Prince* by de Saint-Exupéry, the fox explained that a friend must "sit a little closer to me, every day." When asked who is a friend, a preschooler is apt to say, "Someone who will play with you." However, among adults, availability does not necessarily mean face-to-face contact. Perceived intimacy is far more important than physical proximity.

Friends are reliable and dependable. The fox told the little prince that his visits should "always be at the same hour." When adults are asked to complete the sentence "A friend is _____, their most common response is "someone I can trust." In a frequently cited *Psychology Today* survey, it was found that "keeping confidences" and "loyalty" were most often selected as the key ingredients of a lasting friendship. Centuries ago,

Epicurus wrote, "It is not so much our friends' help that helps us as the confident knowledge that they will help us."

Friends anticipate needs. According to Gibran, "Your friend is your needs answered." Lasting friendships endure between people who are attuned to each other's degree of desire for closeness, change, and personal growth. Aristotle believed that true friendship grew out of respect for the virtues embodied by the other. That is, our friends find our center and honor us by validating our dreams and our values.

Friends are fully present. Emerson's standards for friendship included a level of invested spontaneity. In his words, a meeting of friends "should never fall into something usual and settled but should be alert and inventive." A friend provides a full-bodied embrace rather than a halfhearted handshake. According to a Nigerian proverb, "A friend must be held with both hands."

Friends offer a safe haven. One of the classic metaphors of hope is a safe haven. How often is it said of a good friend, "I can be myself; I can let my hair down; I can drop all my pretensions." Preschoolers say that friends "don't hit you." Emerson said that in the company of a friend "I can think aloud." An Arab proverb states, "A friend is one to whom one may pour out all the contents of one's heart." Bacon likened the safety of friends to a family doctor who knows which medicine is best suited to your particular constitution.

Friends are honest. Feminist writer Letty Cottin Pogrebin found that duplicity was one of the few irreversible and fatal transgressions that could end a long-standing friendship. In the *Psychology Today* survey, "frankness" was ranked among the top five ingredients of true friendship. Cicero warned that "nothing at all artificial or simulated" may be tolerated among friends. Emerson declared, "Let me be alone to the end of the world rather than that my friend should overstep, by a word or deed, his real sympathy."

Friends respect boundaries. Cicero wrote, "Great fallings-out arise when something is demanded from friends which is not honorable." He advised "would-be friends" to hold the reins loosely on the heart of another and not to burden them with shameful demands, lest they wish to incur "eternal hatred." According to him, the best friendships demonstrate a total absence of any power differential. Friends, he noted, are able to "give counsel as well as take it."

Friends have regular contact. National surveys have revealed that more than half of all Americans call their best friend at least once a week. Sociologist Claude Fischer found that the frequency of intimate exchanges, rather than the type of communication, was the key to sustaining close friendships.

Friends are deeply intertwined. Among *Psychology Today* readers, "intimacy" was rated as the most important component of a good friendship. Preschoolers will tell you that a friend is "someone who shares toys." An increasingly broader range of similar interests and activities cements the lives of older children and adolescents. Among adults, the focus shifts to shared values and meanings. Adult friendships are sustained and enriched by a common history as well as mutual joys and sorrows. One-to-one time with a friend seems to be particularly important. Emerson wisely observed, "Three cannot take part in conversations of the most sincere and searching sort."

SPIRITUAL BONDS

The deepest romantic and platonic relationships can rise to the level of a spiritual connection. Lovers may refer to each other as soul mates, and a best friend might be called a kindred spirit. Beyond love relationships and friendships lies the realization of hope through a more encompassing spiritual union. We are able to differentiate at least two types of spiritual experiences. One is the more secular "brotherly love," which appeals to scientists and humanists, and the other involves the experience of a divine presence or higher power. Although varying in content and meaning, the basic requirements for connecting with these sources of hope are similar.

A Shared Humanity

At first glance the world's religions might seem to be at odds with one another. Some are founded on the notion of a single God, whereas others presume a multitude of deities. Many Buddhists do not even believe in a higher power. Religious rituals vary enormously, as do beliefs about the existence of an afterlife. Furthermore, members of a particular faith may view themselves as having a corner on the truth and insist that there is no one more powerful than their God.

Nevertheless, there is a broader sense of humanity that underlies all the major faiths. We are all mortal. We all share certain fears and anxieties as well as hopes and dreams. An appeal to these overarching existential realities is plainly evident in the New Testament as well as in the teachings of Buddha, Gandhi, and Confucius.

According to Erich Fromm, a sense of shared humanity is the most fundamental of all the experiences of love. This oceanic state encompasses feelings of care and respect along with the wish to enhance another's life. Above all, "brotherly" love requires knowledge of, and identification with, another person. This is the basis for compassion and the impetus for a full recognition of one's shared humanity.

The experience of a shared humanity can be overwhelming and life altering. It may develop over time or emerge suddenly. The trigger for one person might be observing a newborn child in the arms of a parent;

for another it could be encountering an elderly couple lovingly holding hands. For a third, the inspiration may come from reading a letter written by a soldier who is longing for his wife and his children. For a fourth, the catalyst may be participating in a funeral ceremony.

A feeling of a shared humanity can even stem from exposure to a great piece of literature, a fine play, or a film masterpiece. In fact, psychologist Michael Wallach proposed that the greatness of a work of art can be measured in terms of the extent to which it evokes certain universal emotions. A good example is Vincent van Gogh's famous painting *Fishing Boats on the Beach.* This work was completed in the summer of 1888 during one of the more positive periods in his tumultuous life.

Van Gogh's masterpiece consists of a simple but reassuring array of four colorful boats sitting on the margins of a beach and nearly touching the sea. If you look closely, you will see that there is a rope tied to each bow that extends all the way to the left edge of the painting. Rather than being held in place by an anchor or a dock post, the boats are attached to an inland moor. Subconsciously, this imagery evokes a powerful sense of attached hope, on the part of both the sailors and their loved ones left on shore. They may be separated for months, or even years, by miles of ocean, but they are nevertheless bound by love and unfailing devotion.

Thornton Wilder's *Our Town* is another great work that evokes a powerful response of love and hope. To strike a universal chord, Wilder fashioned a play with "little action, hardly any scenery, and dialogue based on philosophical ideas." A good deal of the play's setting is a cemetery, where a young woman who has died in childbirth must commune with other dead souls to learn about life. It is understandable that the producers of the play fretted that it was far too sad a production for the general public, but they were wrong. Audiences and critics loved it, and Wilder was awarded the Pulitzer Prize.

On the surface, *Our Town* is about daily life in a small New Hampshire village, Grover's Corners, around the turn of the twentieth century. At a deeper level, it touches on issues of universal importance and eternal relevance. Most notably, Wilder alluded to the brevity of life and the paradox of human existence. The characters poignantly demonstrate the inability of the living to savor what they have and the inability of the dead to care beyond the grave.

At one point in the play, the dead warn Emily not to revisit her life in Grover's Corners. They caution her that it will be too painful to watch as she and her loved ones fritter away precious moments with petty concerns. But this is exactly what Wilder intended: to have both Emily and the audience simultaneously straddle the domains of the living and the dead. Only in this difficult space does humanity realize the need for a transcendent hope that can override the limits of human finitude through a love of life and the love of all that is mortal.

Spiritual Bonding Guidelines

Many people find hope while communing with nature or a higher power. For example, Jane Goodall considered herself blessed because she had had a powerful mystical experience in both a cathedral and an African jungle. Countless others have reported feeling the presence of God, or an ineffable spirit, while standing on a mountaintop, exploring a dark cave, lying in a hospital bed, or sitting quietly by the ocean.

There are several keys to achieving a sense of common humanity, or a feeling of intimacy, with a larger spiritual force. Although the content may differ, both experiences derive from the same basic set of psychological processes: trust, humility, focus, openness, involvement, repetition, and ritual. To forge a spiritual connection, it is also important to develop an attitude of humility. The guidelines below are based on our integrative approach to hopeful encounters, including research on individuals who have reported recurring mystical experiences.

Trust. Both the humanistic and divine forms of spiritual connection begin with a trusting attitude. If you have been fortunate to have a positive early attachment experience, then you probably have sufficient basic trust to jump-start the spiritual bonding process. However, if your early caregivers were unreliable or otherwise inadequate, you might find yourself prone to an anxious or avoidant attachment style that can greatly interfere with spiritual bonding. If this is the case, it is important to come to grips with the extent of your anger, bitterness, and mistrust. It is also crucial for you to seek out corrective emotional experiences by surrounding yourself with relatively healthy and caring adults.

Humility. Spiritually prepared individuals are self-accepting but also aware of their shortcomings. They take pleasure in their talents while also appreciating the need for external support and guidance. In contrast, illusions of being unusually special or exceptional could preclude having a sense of "common ground." Moreover, those who view themselves as superior to others may find it more difficult to enter the midst of a higher power.

Focus. Pay attention to those around you. Do not let your prejudices or stereotypes get in the way of seeing the inner person when you interact with others. Erich Fromm wrote that "brotherly" love is dependent on connecting from the center of one's being to the center of another's being. How often do we succeed in achieving this spiritual bridge? If you are seeking the presence of a higher power, it may require even more focus and energy on your part. For example, you might find it helpful to adjust your time of meditation to coincide with your personal rhythms. One woman reported an "infusion of spiritual presence" into her life after she decided to get out of bed an hour earlier each morning to engage in prayer.

Openness. Make an effort to put yourself in the company of others who appear to be quite different from you. Travel to a new location. Visit an ethnic neighborhood. Sample a new cuisine. Read a *National Geographic* article or watch the Discovery Channel. Spend some quiet time in a place of worship, by a waterfall, by a babbling brook, or in a canopied forest with sunlight filtering down on you. Experiences of divinity are more often reported in the context of such sacred spaces.

Involvement. You are more likely to feel the stir of a common humanity if you get to know different people at different levels. An ancient proverb suggests that faith must involve the head, the heart, and the hands. You cannot simply will experiences of oneness. Try to open your heart, and consider participating in some form of spiritual routine. Those who report experiences of a higher power tend to read scripture, engage in regular prayer, chant, or meditate in a systematic fashion. They are apt to participate in retreats, study the Bible, or make pilgrimages to revered sites.

Repetition. Repeated images and sounds can aid in the alteration of consciousness. Sustained exposure to drumbeats, music, or dance tends to suppress the parts of the brain that divide the self from the external world and stimulate the regions that contribute to a feeling of oneness. Perhaps this is why Muslims pray several times a day or why Hindus utter the name of God thousands of times in one sitting.

Ritual. Consider cultivating a ritual that is comforting and consistent with your beliefs and lifestyle. It can be either a personal or a group activity as long as it is deeply engrossing and performed on a regular basis. It can range from an established religious practice to daily exercise or playing a musical instrument. According to some researchers, you may derive the most benefit by including a spiritual component. For example, if you select exercise or music as your ritual, try to coordinate it with an accompanying focus on the principles, beliefs, and values that define your journey of hope.

9

Hope for Success

The earth seemed to move with me. I found a new source of power and beauty, a source I never knew existed.

—ROGER BANNISTER, *TRACK AND FIELD LEGEND*

In this chapter we provide a set of transcendent principles for achieving lasting success, a dream plan that is sustained by clarity and purpose in life. To achieve genuine success, an individual must have a will for hope, a feeling of mediated power, and one or more guiding aspirations. In our discussion of these and other mastery-related skills, we take into consideration some of the advice provided by self-help gurus as well as the scientific literature on motivation and goal attainment. In addition, you will find mastery-related insights culled from different philosophical perspectives and spiritual belief systems.

Total mastery can take years, if not an entire lifetime, to achieve. Beyond having plans and strategies, you must also have a sense of purpose that is continually guided and nurtured. This labor of love cannot be achieved without inspiration. With this in mind, we devote the second part of this chapter to strategies for drawing inspiration from outside sources as well as from within yourself. We discuss how to make the best use of role models as well as learning from your previous successes or failures. We conclude with suggestions for deriving inspiration from hidden dreams.

PORTRAITS OF MASTERY

Our discussion of hopeful mastery begins with three profiles. Each of these individuals possessed a determined will for hope as well as higher aspirations that were privately nurtured yet widespread in their impact on humanity. While hope sustained these individuals, they in turn became pillars of inspiration for future generations.

Rosalind Franklin: Time and Self-Mastery

Rosalind Franklin was born July 25, 1920, in the Bayswater section of London. From an early age she demonstrated a deep interest in the inner workings of nature. Rosalind showed great promise in the classroom and was encouraged to compete for admission to the highly selective Newnham College of Cambridge University. While taking her entrance exams, Rosalind struggled with considerable test anxiety. She felt handicapped by what she believed was a subpar scientific background from an all-girls' school. Rosalind was convinced that women received mediocre training in the natural sciences because they were not viewed as serious contenders for future jobs in biology, chemistry, or physics.

Rosalind succeeded in gaining admission to Newnham and eventually earned a doctoral degree from Cambridge. Along the way, she compensated for her perceived training deficits by enrolling in extra courses and spending many of her nights, weekends, and holidays in the lab. As a Jew and a woman, Rosalind always believed that she had to fight and scrape for every bit of success and respect that she gained as a professional scientist.

Not long after getting her doctorate, Rosalind became one of the world's foremost crystallographers, able to capture the structure of irregular crystals with the use of x-ray beams. Within just ten years she made major contributions to the study of coal chemistry, human biology, and plant viruses. However, Rosalind would ultimately be remembered for a finding that was not credited to her until years after her death. For it was Rosalind's fate to become known as the "dark lady of DNA," the unsung heroine who took the famous "photo 51" that first revealed the double helix structure. John Bernal, another eminent twentieth-century scientist, described Rosalind's photo as "among the most beautiful x-ray photos of any substance ever taken."

Rosalind's achievements highlight the importance of time and self-mastery in the realization of true success. It was her lifelong belief that one should never report findings until all the data had been collected, analyzed, and verified, even if this meant opting out of the race to discover the origin of life. While James Watson and Francis Crick, her Oxford colleagues, were frantically rushing around, trying to beat everyone (including Rosalind) to the punch, she refused to alter her meticulous approach. For example, to get the best possible photos of the fickle DNA molecule, she managed to achieve the ideal temperature, humidity, and exposure time that was required. In fact, it was generally agreed that no other physical chemist in the world was as deliberate and precise as Rosalind Franklin. (She would sometimes devote as much as 100 hours to taking a single exposure of a DNA fiber.)

Rosalind's hard work was stolen and usurped by her male colleagues.

Watson and Crick, along with one of her coworkers, Maurice Wilkins, took her photos and her notebooks from her lab without her permission and made a mad dash to publish the structure of DNA. Frustrated with this betrayal and the lack of financial support at Cambridge, Rosalind left to pursue research on tobacco viruses. A few years later she was stricken with ovarian cancer.

In April 1958 she died, still convinced that Watson and Crick had rushed to judgment about DNA. Four years later, Watson, Crick, and Wilkins were awarded the Nobel Prize, and Rosalind was relegated to a minor footnote. Subsequent historical research suggests that Rosalind suspected that DNA was a double helix but that she wanted to be absolutely sure before reporting her findings. It was not in her character to do otherwise.

Roger Bannister: Mediated Power

In the 1950s every middle distance runner was obsessed with one goal: to run a mile in less than four minutes. However, many experts considered it an unbreakable barrier. Doctors warned that maintaining the necessary pace could be fatal for even the best-conditioned athlete. Some scientists went further, suggesting that such a feat would constitute a violation of certain immutable laws of nature.

On May 6, 1954, Roger Bannister of England achieved the "impossible" at the Iffley Road Track in Oxford. Two human pacesetters helped him to achieve his goal. In a well-executed three-man assault on the record, Chris Brasher took the initial lead, maintaining a fast but controlled pace. After three minutes he tired, and Chris Chataway took over, leading the group until the final 200 yards. At that point Bannister sprinted past him toward the finish line, completing the race in the heretofore unbelievable time of 3:59. 4.

After the race Bannister made several very poignant comments. He felt "propelled by some unknown force." He had found "a new unity with nature" and a "new source of power and beauty, a source I never dreamed existed." Bannister reflected that such an achievement can occur only when there is "the ability to take more out of yourself than you've got."

However, it is unlikely that Bannister would have been the first to conquer the four-minute mile without the help of his two pacesetting friends and their added supply of "legs, hearts, and lungs." From our perspective, his experiences of power, unity, and beauty were probably subconsciously mediated by the collaboration with his two running mates. His feat highlights the importance of support and empowerment in the achievement of mastery. For in addition to taking "more out of [him]self," Bannister was able to draw on the power of his alliance with Brasher and Chataway.

Oprah Winfrey: Values

Oprah Winfrey was born in January 1954, just a few months before Bannister's record-breaking performance. The child of unmarried parents, she was placed in the care of her grandmother. Oprah endured many heartaches, including ostracism by other children, battles with her fragmented family, and repeated acts of sexual abuse. Growing up in abject poverty, she vividly recalled watching the adults around her boil their clothes in makeshift washers constructed from discarded barrels. It was during one such moment that Oprah resolved to set her sights on a more hopeful horizon.

A lonely child, Oprah sought solace in books. Her grandmother soon realized that Oprah was a gifted reader and precocious in her oratory skills. When Oprah was only three years old, she was able to read out loud from the Bible, and by the time she was seven, she had memorized the epic poem "Invictus" by William Ernest Henley. Although she couldn't fully grasp the meaning of all the words in the poem, she sensed a message of personal relevance. In an interview more than a quarter of a century later, Oprah could still recall the opening lines: "Out of the night that covers . . . I thank whatever gods there may be for my unconquerable soul."

During college, Oprah began to work as a news reporter. However, she found it difficult to keep a professional distance while chronicling various horrific and tragic events. Instead, she wanted to connect, to make a difference in the lives of others, to help them see the light. She found her true calling as a television talk-show host. As a result of her own painful odyssey, she found herself especially drawn to serious social issues. Week after week she used her platform to raise awareness of such problems as homelessness, child abuse, poverty, and hunger.

Within a few years, *The Oprah Winfrey Show* was the number one program of its kind in the United States. In 2003 she became the first black woman, and only the second African American, to be listed on the Forbes list of billionaires. Her life story highlights the need for self-awareness and the importance of being true to oneself and one's values in the pursuit of mastery. She has repeatedly insisted it was never about the money, and that she would do her show if she never got a dime. Speaking at the Wellesley College Commencement Address in 1997, she noted, "Your true passion should feel like breathing. It's that natural."

THE WILL FOR HOPE

Willpower derives from the frontal lobe of the brain. Without this infrastructure, a human being is as good as dead. In the film *One Flew over the Cuckoo's Nest*, R. P. McMurphy (Jack Nicholson) brought an emboldened brand of hope to a ward of psychiatric patients who were more powerless than crazy. Unable to subdue his fighting spirit, the hospital administrators finally drugged him and then surgically deactivated his frontal lobe by performing a lobotomy. His Native American friend, "Chief" (Will Sampson), snuck into the recovery room to find that his friend had been reduced to a vegetable.

Chief was aware that the patients on the ward continued to draw inspiration from McMurphy's example. As their once free-spirited friend lay in an eternal stupor, they continued to trade fantasies, speculating on the daring acts of resistance that McMurphy might have engineered. To preserve hope for the other patients, Chief decided that he must end McMurphy's life. He smothered him, then hurled a heavy sink through a window and ran to freedom as his ward companions cheered him on. With these acts of affirmation, the formerly mute and passive Chief found the strength to speak and the will to live as a free agent.

For more than a century, there has been much speculation regarding the importance of certain motives. Friedrich Nietzsche argued that the will for power was paramount. Sigmund Freud suggested that humans were guided primarily by the will for pleasure. After enduring the Nazi death camps, Viktor Frankl deduced that the most important motive was the will for meaning. From our perspective, the central motive is the will for hope.

The will for hope incorporates a number of ideas put forth by existential and humanistic psychologists. It encompasses the idea of self-actualization described by Abraham Maslow as well as Erik Erikson's notions of "I am what I will" and "I am what I can imagine to be." It covers the growth-centered attitude emphasized by Carl Rogers as well as Robert White's notion of competence. The will for hope also borrows from Gabriel Marcel's philosophy of hope-based readiness, openness, and availability. Having the will for hope is not only about the realization of inner potential. It can also trigger an impulse to expand your circle of influence, to heed Ralph Waldo Emerson's call that "the universe is the property of every individual in it."

MEDIATED POWER

After willpower, a sense of hopeful effectiveness is the next mastery virtue to unfold. We prefer to call it mediated power because of the important role that is played by caregivers, other supportive people, and cultural institutions in facilitating and maintaining mastery strivings. The roots of mediated power lie in the early fusions of the self with more powerful parents or other caregivers.

Individuals with mediated power feel resourceful in meeting the demands of life. To paraphrase the words of Paul in his Letter to the Philippians (4:13), "They can do all things through their experiences with other people who have helped to strengthen them." In contrast, hopeless individuals feel constantly overwhelmed, as if external demands or even their own internal needs exceed their available resources.

When one addresses the goal expectations that fuel a hopeful mindset, it is more fitting to speak of aspirations than needs or drives. The word *aspiration* carries three meanings that link it with hope. In one sense it refers to cherished dreams; in another, it implies the pursuit of high ideals; and in the third, it refers to the act of inhaling or drawing in air. Like the definition of *spirituality*, this third connotation suggests that one has been infused with the breath of something vital and powerful.

Similar to Aristotle's golden mean, hopeful aspirations derive from a balance of power. Truly hopeful individuals are not passive or resigned.

At the same time, their actions are neither forced nor strained—quite the contrary. Hopeful mastery imparts a flow state that may be compared to the peaceful mastery cultivated by the followers of feng shui or the principle-centered philosophy of Stephen Covey.

THE KEYS TO SUCCESSFUL MASTERY

There are four keys to successful mastery: self-mastery, values, support, and time. These are the same factors that are discussed by experts in human motivation as well as by various spiritual leaders and many self-help gurus (Table 9.1).

True success begins with self-mastery. This is the most difficult of the four keys, but it is the necessary first step, the foundation for the other three. You should think of self-mastery in terms of creating a centered presence of self-awareness and self-discipline.

In the West, an increasing emphasis is being placed on developing self-awareness, particularly with respect to emotions. For example, in the past, many mental health professionals and self-help gurus emphasized the importance of "expressing one's feelings." However, there is now an increasing realization that self-regulation and emotional intelligence may be even more important than the mere ability to vent your feelings. In addition, there is a growing awareness of the need to be more "mindful" of the negative, self-defeating thoughts that give rise to handicapping emotional states.

In the domain of action, however, self-awareness has received relatively little attention in the West. The focus is completely reversed within the great Earth-centered religions, such as Ifa, the religion of the Australian Aborigines, and the various Native American belief systems. In such cultures, individuals are taught to be perpetually cognizant of the potential impact of their actions upon the family, the community, the land, and the spiritual world. Nevertheless, self-awareness without self-discipline may lead to behavioral paralysis or wasted effort.

Table 9.1. The Four Keys to Successful Mastery as Found in the Self-Help Literature

Self-Mastery	Values
1. Stephen Covey: Have a personal mission	1. Stephen Covey: Stay principle-centered
2. Napoleon Hill: Submit to a major purpose	2. Napoleon Hill: Live by the Golden Rule
3. Norman Vincent Peale: Practice positive thinking	3. Norman Vincent Peale: Cultivate moral strength
4. Cheryl Richardson: Build your courage muscles	4. Cheryl Richardson: Establish spiritual standards
5. Tony Robbins: Exercise decision power	5. Tony Robbins: Have a personal compass
Support	**Time**
1. Stephen Covey: Seek win-win relationships	1. Stephen Covey: Put first things first
2. Napoleon Hill: Study the work of others	2. Napoleon Hill: Budget your time
3. Norman Vincent Peale: Unlock the power of prayer	3. Norman Vincent Peale: Visualize success daily
4. Cheryl Richardson: Create circles of support	4. Cheryl Richardson: Prepare for change
5. Tony Robbins: Master relationships	5. Tony Robbins: Refocus your time frame

Conversely, in Eastern societies there is a great premium placed on self-discipline. Buddhists are encouraged to follow the Eightfold Path. Hindus readily assume the karmic consequences of their actions, and Confucians honor the principles of *jen*, the rules of appropriate social conduct. Throughout the East, the practice of martial arts serves as a prototypical example of intense self-discipline in the pursuit of mastery. Self-discipline without self-awareness can lead to a life of superficial and meaningless ritual.

Thus, you should strive to develop both self-awareness and self-discipline. Pay attention to your thoughts, your feelings, and your actions. Confident thoughts are a true source of power, whereas self-defeating thoughts will undermine your potential for mastery. Feelings as well as actions can serve as windows into your life calling or higher purpose.

Cultivate a greater awareness of the various influences on your behavior. The humanist Rollo May noted that each individual's behavior is simultaneously free and constrained. You should be aware of the limitations that are imposed by the time and place of your birth (cosmic destiny), the limits of your genetic makeup (genetic destiny), your ethnic and religious background (cultural destiny), and the reality of random accidents and coincidences (circumstantial destiny). These factors define the outer limits of what you can accomplish, but your range of available options is, in fact, quite extraordinary.

If you want to explore self-mastery in a more intensive fashion, the suggestions below may help. They include three Eastern formulas for developing self-discipline and three Western recipes for greater self-awareness.

Disciplined thinking. Buddhist forms of meditation offer an excellent way of focusing an easily distracted mind that tends to obsess without end. Buddha observed, "As the craftsman whittles and makes straight his arrows, so the master directs his straying thoughts."

Disciplined feeling. Confucianism and Taoism are considered the two opposite poles of Chinese philosophy. Together they provide a broad perspective for dealing with emotions that are harmful to oneself or others. By focusing on boundaries and appropriateness, Confucianism teaches the art of showing the right emotion at the right time to the right person. Taoism encourages a calm and less desperate reaction to the whims of the world and may be particularly helpful to those who are plagued by intense worry, impatience, or hostile feelings.

Disciplined action. Hinduism is an excellent model for disciplined action because it highlights the vital role of a guiding belief system. The Hindus believe in karma—that for every action there is a like consequence—they equate destiny to a seed that cannot grow without the soil of exertion and the practice of holy living. The words *discipline* and *disciple* both suggest a moral or philosophical aim as well as a practical agenda. You must practice what you preach and vice versa. This is true whether your commitment is to a religious faith, a career, or a particular program of exercise.

Awareness of thoughts. Cognitive therapy involves changing the destructive beliefs that can destroy your mind, your body, and your soul. It is based on the idea that negative thought patterns can be analyzed, challenged, and replaced with healthier alternatives. The Roman Stoic philosophers argued that we are troubled not by events but by our perception of them. In Milton's *Paradise Lost*, the angel cast into hell defiantly proclaimed that "the mind is its own place and can make a hell out of heaven or a heaven out of hell."

Awareness of feelings. Carl Rogers provided a simple but powerful formula for personal growth. In emphasizing the human need for unconditional positive regard, he realized that many adults pass on their fear of feelings to their children. Raised in such an atmosphere, individuals may find themselves in a no-win situation, whereby emotional authenticity is pitted against self-worth and social acceptance. If you have a problem expressing your emotions, seek out nonjudgmental and supportive individuals who are comfortable with their own feelings.

Awareness of actions. Reflect on the possible implications of your actions as well as your full intentions. If necessary, seek feedback from a trusted friend or a supportive group. Many people with the right intentions fail because they ignore the results of their actions. Native Americans, as well as the practitioners of Ifa and the Australian Aborigines, seek harmony with nature because they realize the interconnectedness of all living things. Herman Melville wrote that "a thousand fibers connect us with others . . . our actions run as causes and come back to us as effects."

Values

It is more than a coincidence that the most enduring books tend to deal with values in one form or another. In fact, if you think about it, you will realize that the greatest self-help books of all time are the sacred texts: the Bible, the Qur'an, the Talmud, the Pali Canon, and so on. In the so-called secular self-help category, two of the biggest blockbusters have been Napoleon Hill's *Think and Grow Rich* and Norman Vincent Peale's *The Power of Positive Thinking.* (As of 2010, more than 20 million copies of each book had been sold.) It is noteworthy that both authors placed mastery within a larger ethical and religious framework. Hill's ten rules for success included an adherence to the Golden Rule and sublimating one's energy to a major purpose. Peale emphasized prayer power and moral strength.

Among the classics of the ancient world, *The Art of War* by Sun Tzu is probably the quintessential values-oriented mastery text. He listed the various moral factors that a wise general should contemplate while preparing for battle. Included in his discussion were the following spiritual considerations: Is my side imbued with moral law? Do I hold the advantages derived from heaven and earth? Is my army animated by the heavenly spirits?

Attending to values is a primary factor in the success of Stephen Covey's book, *The 7 Habits of Highly Effective People*. Covey correctly identified resiliency as one of the three key elements underlying a valued-centered approach to mastery. To be successful in any endeavor, you must persevere. Specifically, Covey noted how a values-based perspective can serve as a buffer against the inevitable obstacles and disappointments that will come your way.

Values can advance your mastery pursuits in two other important ways: they ensure self-consistency and increase the amount of support that you are likely to receive. Be clear about your values and put them at the center of your life. This will make it less likely that you will end up disoriented or disillusioned. You may recall the old adage about misguided efforts: the second greatest disappointment in life is to not achieve their dreams. However, for some, the worst outcome is realized when they do achieve their "dreams."

If others sense your commitment to a calling, they are more likely to offer their support. Richard Simmons, the guru of weight loss, once worked as a restaurant host in Los Angeles. His break came when he told a wealthy patron of his dream to establish a fitness center for the average housewife. Pleased to contribute to such a worthwhile cause, the man gave Simmons a check for $25,000.

Support

Many great achievements are the result of a team of individuals working toward a common goal. Roger Bannister needed "three pairs of legs" to break the four-minute mile. Gertrude Ederle, the first woman to swim the English Channel, was spurred on by a floating fan club of supporters who rowed alongside, as well as by onshore crowds of onlookers who built huge bonfires to guide her home. The pyramids required about 20,000 workers. One account of the Great Wall of China suggested that more than 800,000 laborers were necessary to erect just the initial portion. Many of the Renaissance artists relied on a team of apprentices to prepare frescoes, outline figures, and paint the trunks of the bodies in each scene. The master would paint only the eyes, the hands, and other delicate features. Below are some more recent examples.

Hollywood filmmakers promote one or two leading actors, yet these individuals are typically surrounded by half a dozen supporting actors, a sizable cast of extras, and more than fifty behind-the-scenes professionals, including producers, directors, and technicians. Writers put words in their mouths. Makeup artists mask their physical imperfections and enhance their plainer features.

An author gets the credit for writing a book. In reality, the development, production, and distribution of just one book is typically a collaborative effort, requiring the resources of an agent, editor, and scores of staff at a publishing company. At the beginning of his bestseller, *Awaken the Giant Within*, Tony Robbins acknowledged the help of more than forty individuals. Some self-help gurus merely dictate or draft outlines, then ghostwriters do the actual writing. This is particularly ironic when the "author" is advocating a simplistic do-it-yourself approach to mastery and success.

The president of the United States is the chief executive. Yet he has a massive White House staff. There are twenty-one high-profile cabinet-level members. Behind the scenes, another several thousand staff members are busy handling mail, making travel arrangements, planning state dinners, and maintaining the grounds.

Martha Stewart, the guru of domestic life, is viewed as a master decorator, a culinary wizard, and a consummate landscape designer. Actually, Martha Stewart Omnimedia is a large company with more than 600 employees, including numerous artists and designers, cooks, crafters, and gardeners.

The above are examples of supported success; they highlight the power of a shared effort in very concrete terms. With a team, more can be accomplished, because others are helping to do the "heavy lifting." However, the consistent support or presence of others can run even deeper, affecting the very core of an individual's sense of self. It is no coincidence that we often speak of hopes or dreams in terms of aspirations, which implies the notion of breathing in a vital substance.

In hope-based strivings, the marriage of collaborative power and perceived support can lead to experiences of mediated success, the realization of aspirations that have been made possible by a hopeful inner core aided by the emotional support of others. The outcome is the result of several mastery-related benefits that are bestowed on the hope-filled individual. These blessings include flow experiences as well as feelings of interdependent mastery and spiritual justification.

Psychologist Mihaly Csikszentmihalyi was the first to highlight flow experiences. These are states of undivided attention and total absorption. Time pressures disappear; the clock no longer matters as individuals experience their performance rising to peak levels. The person may feel as if nothing can go wrong. Athletes refer to these moments as "being in the zone." Flow states have been reported by successful individuals from all walks of life, including musicians, painters, dancers, rock climbers, and surgeons.

Researchers have found that youngsters experience more flow when they are challenged to perform at higher levels while given sufficient emotional support. Such observations dovetail with the findings that link early child-rearing patterns with subsequent achievement strivings. Adults with strong achievement motivation are more likely to have had parents who set high standards while also providing a warm and accepting environment.

Growing up in a context of challenge and acceptance can also foster an interdependent spirit. The individuals who are best prepared for mastery pursuits are those who can marshal a variety of resources. They are neither limited by a rigid sense of individualism nor weakened by an extreme feeling of dependency. Given a hopeful core, an individual with high aspirations can balance autonomy with appropriate help-seeking. In this respect, we see things a bit differently from Stephen Covey, who focuses more narrowly on a move from dependence to independence, followed by another shift to interdependence. From our perspective, a hopeful core is more likely to be built on a sense of ingrained interdependence, beginning in infancy and continuing throughout the life span.

When individuals realize that at least one other person supports their dreams, they experience a sense of integrated mastery. They do not feel alone in their pursuits. Their goals are nested within the larger aims of a dyad, a family, a community, a world of values, or a perceived religious or spiritual presence. When they find that their goals converge with some exterior presence, they have a sense of destiny or positive fate, a belief that "I am meant to do this."

Hank Aaron's pursuit of Babe Ruth's home run record is a great example of spiritual justification. On April 14, 1974, Aaron surpassed Ruth's record of 714 home runs. Leading up to that night, Aaron had to endure tremendous pressure from hoards of reporters who barraged him with questions. Far worse were the hateful and threatening letters sent by racists across the country, vowing to murder him or members of his family if he did not stop chasing the Babe's hallowed mark. The following three letters are disgustingly typical of those sent to Aaron:

> Dear Nigger Henry,
> It has come to my attention that you are going to break Babe Ruth's record. I don't think you are going to break this record if I can help it . . . if you hit one more home run it will be your last. My gun is watching your every black move. This is no joke.

> Dear Nigger,
> You black animal, I hope you never live long enough to hit more home runs than the great Babe Ruth.

> Dear Hank Aaron,
> I hate you! You're such a little creep! I hate you and your family. I'D LIKE TO KILL YOU! BANG, BANG, YOU'RE DEAD. P.S. It might happen.

What allowed Aaron to persevere? When interviewed on this topic, he always cited the support of his wife, Billye, several close friends, and his mother, who ran to his side that historic night. (When she heard the popping sounds of celebratory cannons, his mother feared that assassins were shooting at him.) Aaron was also grateful for the thousands of encouraging letters he received from fans of all colors. Superimposed on these layers of support, he believed, was an additional benefactor:

> I didn't feel like I had to deal with it alone. Whatever forces seemed to be working against me in my career—whether it was bigotry or neglect or whatever—I always felt that a higher power was working for me. I might not have known what my destiny was, but I knew I had one, and something was helping me to attain it.

To increase your own sense of mediated power, consider adopting the following four strategies:

- *Absorb.* You can't use what you don't retain. Some of the most successful people will tell you how they "picked the brain" of a mentor, a coach, or a highly valued colleague. Pay attention to every aspect of your role models, including how they approach problems and situations, how they feel about their craft, what they have learned, and what they would do differently if they were starting over.

- *Evaluate.* As successful as your mentors or colleagues may be, you are a unique individual. You may have similar but not identical interests, as well as a different set of talents. As you absorb all that you can from others, run a parallel process of evaluating what is or is not relevant for you.

- *Integrate.* As you absorb and evaluate the lessons from your role models, think about how you can modify their principles, specific behaviors, and strategies to fit your skills, interests, and values.

- *Call forth.* Stay alert for opportunities to exercise your mediated power. This can help you to prepare for specific situations. As part of your mastery preparation, visualize what you have learned from your role models.

Time

Talent develops in quiet places. Character is formed in the full current of human life.

—Goethe

Time is a critical factor in achieving mastery. The very concept of mastery suggests that an individual's behavior has changed or evolved in some meaningful way over the course of time. To achieve true success, there are four aspects of temporal experience that you must master: time as a substance, time as a cause, time as a medium, and time as a direction.

Time as a substance. Time management belongs to this first aspect of temporal experience. This approach is based on a management philosophy of control, organization, and distribution of products, including time itself. Time management is an important part of the mastery process. The problem is that time management has been treated as if it were the *only* important aspect of time mastery. We would argue that management probably ranks last among the four aspects of time that must be mastered for an individual to experience true success.

Time as a cause. Time can be understood as a cause that has the power to create or destroy as well as to heal or harm. Viewed from this perspective, time can be seen as either a friend or a foe. Unfortunately, we live in an era that has adopted a restrictive philosophy of time. This view is based on the idea that taking less time is superior to devoting more time, and moving faster is better than traveling more slowly.

The entertainment industry contributes to this warped view of time by casting fresh-faced, twentysomething actors in the roles of seasoned lawyers, wise physicians, and hardened law enforcement personnel. In this context, it is difficult to experience time as anything but an enemy that must be controlled, limited, or managed. Part of the driving force behind this ethos of impatience is the rapidly increasing barrage of information that must be processed.

Ironically, whenever we confront a true masterpiece, we experience the force of time in a very different manner. As you gaze at a classic portrait or at a marvel of architectural design, you can appreciate the creator's enormous time investment. Perhaps you feel a sense of timelessness when you read a great work of literature or reflect on a classic poem. You may also experience time differently as you slowly savor a finely aged wine or a sixteen-year-old single-malt scotch. You might attend a sporting event and sit mesmerized while watching the athletes perform their magic.

The Great Pyramid of Giza and the Taj Mahal each required more than twenty years to complete. The construction of China's Great Wall began in the sixth or seventh century BCE and was finished between the fourteenth and seventeenth centuries CE. On a more individual basis, Michelangelo spent ten years lying on his back, painting the roof of the Sistine Chapel, and Dante devoted twenty-one years to perfecting *The Divine Comedy*. Rod Laver, who is considered one of the greatest male tennis players of all time, sometimes practiced for six hours *after* a tournament match.

How do you work with, rather than against, time? Try to adopt the mentality of a craftsperson. Think of time as an ally, helping you to hone your craft while allowing your creation to reach its full potential. Picture the two sections of an hourglass. The amount of time you invest is equal to the time it takes for the sand in the top section to run into the bottom section. The extent of your impact, measured in hours, days, or years, will be no more and no less than your input—just as the time it takes to fill the bottom section of the hourglass.

Take pride in your experience and be assured that there are no shortcuts on the road to true mastery. Trust that time will bring you to your highest level of meaningful accomplishment. Do your part and have faith in the power of time to do the rest. Realize that even the most gifted may need a decade or more of dedicated practice to produce a world-class performance in art, music, science, or sports. Moreover, research by psychologist Dean Keith Simonton and others suggests that the age of peak performance varies greatly from field to field. Here are some examples:

• Swimmers and gymnasts, ages fourteen to twenty-five

- Marathon runners, ages thirty to thirty-seven
- Musicians, ages twenty to thirty
- Mathematicians, ages twenty to forty
- Social scientists, ages forty to fifty
- Philosophers, ages sixty to eighty

Time as a medium. Time can conjure up the image of a conveyor belt that transports people and events at various rates. This dimension of time is perceived to move more quickly as an individual advances in age. This is because we take stock of each passing year against the backdrop of our past life experiences. Mastering this aspect of time requires paying attention to your four "clocks": the biological, the social, the emotional, and age.

Individuals vary greatly in terms of their metabolic rates and biological rhythms. For example, people idle at different rates at different times of the day; some are early risers, whereas others are night owls.

Your social clock is the pace of life that has been developed through a combination of geographical, cultural, personality, religious, and spiritual factors. For example, a Buddhist who is meditating on the shore of the Ganges River experiences the passage of time in a very different manner than a Methodist commuting in New York City during rush hour.

The way you perceive time can also be affected by your emotions. Both mood and arousal level impact the perceived duration of events. Positive experiences seem to pass by more quickly, especially if you are highly excited. Perhaps you recall a spirited wedding or a party that you attended years ago as just a "blur" (and you were sober!). In contrast, accidents, assaults, and even just incredibly boring activities may make time seem to unfold in apparent slow motion.

Regardless of your age, you always have time to enhance your sense of mastery. If you are older, it only *seems* as if time is passing more quickly. If you are still relatively young, realize that there is not an infinite amount of time in which to procrastinate.

In any case, do not shy away from making an investment in mastery that may take five to ten years. If you are prone to worrying or to having frequent bouts of agitation, opportunities for mastery may pass you by while you languish in protracted experiences of failure. To relax your body, engage in regular exercise or a favorite relaxation technique, preferably in pleasant surroundings. Consider meditation or yoga to soothe your mind and your spirit.

Time as a direction. Many Western cultures have constructed a linear view of time. In contrast, many Eastern cultures presume a cyclical view of time. There are advantages and disadvantages to each perspective. A linear view holds the promise of progress and putting the past behind you. A cyclical approach offers greater opportunities for redemption and healing old wounds.

You can combine the concepts of linear and circular time to create a spiral of hope. The concept of a forward-moving or ascending spiral combines the promise of progress with the opportunity to rework the past. As you spiral toward greater levels of mastery, you can revisit the same territory without fear of stagnation, realizing that each iteration is bringing you closer to your ultimate destination.

Not only is the hope spiral a more encouraging metaphor, it also rings true. Change is an undeniable fact of life. As the Greek philosopher Heraclitus wrote, "One cannot stand in the same river twice." However, you can also bear witness to the seemingly endless cycles of nature while resonating to the words of Ecclesiastes, "To everything there is a season." If life teaches us anything, it is that we *can* revisit the past and make repairs. This merger of past, present, and future was beautifully captured by T. S. Eliot: "Time present and time past are both perhaps present in time future, and time future contained in time past. . . . What might have been and what has been point to one end, which is always present."

FINDING INSPIRATION

Hope and inspiration form a natural pair. They are the twin virtues sought by every individual who is facing a difficult life challenge, and they are the spiritual currency of support groups and community organizations. Corporate leaders invest great amounts of money, time, and other resources to obtain hope and inspiration for themselves as well as for as their employees.

Without inspiration, musicians struggle to compose, writers are blocked, painters languish before an empty canvas, and actors betray their characters. Lacking a muse, politicians hesitate before crowds, and corporate leaders flounder in the boardroom. Aware of the great need for inspiration, Emerson observed how creative individuals will pursue it at any cost, "by virtue or vice, by friend or by fiend, by prayer or by wine."

The word *inspiration* suggests that something has been "taken inside" the individual. Plato believed that inspiration was a piece of divinity that came bursting into the soul. Philosopher Ignacio Götz called it "one of the most mysterious moments in anyone's life, the instant when things 'click' and fall neatly in place, or a new idea flashes in the dark." He explained it as follows:

> The mysterious instant goes by many names: inspiration, enlightenment, illumination, intuition, insight, vision, revelation, and discovery. . . . Religious mystics speak of ecstasy and satori; poets, painters, musicians, dancers, and historians invoke their Muses; while scientists and mathematicians, parsimonious and prosaic, claim only hunches and intuitions.

Hope can be viewed as a precondition for the experience of inspiration. The open and trusting attitude of hopeful individuals makes it more likely that they will be receptive to the voices of inspiration. In turn, inspiration can deepen hope. For example, psychologist Tobin Hart notes that inspiration can improve mood, increase self-worth, and enhance motivation. Translated into the language of our hope-centered perspective, inspiration strengthens the mastery motive.

Individuals find inspiration in many ways. For example, when psychologist Robert Ornstein tried to research this topic, he found that there were nearly as many sources of inspiration as people in his study. Australian health researchers Debbie Kralik and Kerry Telford asked individuals who were suffering from various chronic illnesses where they turned for inspiration. The responses were diverse, encompassing religion and loving relationships as well as the sound of birds in the morning, friends, and one's own endurance. In addition, a number of people cited an inspiring role model who had shown great courage in similar or even worse circumstances.

All sources of inspiration can be captured in two basic strategies: inside out or outside in. You can try an inside-out approach to discover inspiration from within, or you can adopt an outside-in technique to draw inspiration from the external world. If you seek inspiration from within, you can begin by using a simple but powerful technique recommended by many self-help gurus, including the late Dale Carnegie. Challenge yourself with empowering questions. For example, you might try the following: "I work hard. I have skills and talent. Why can't I be just as successful as my coworker (or neighbor, etc.)?"

If you are interested in finding inspiration from the external world, read widely, make contact with nature, visit new places, or watch inspirational films. Researchers have found that music can be a powerful source of inspiration. You can select songs to fit your particular mastery needs. If you are looking for general inspiration as well as a boost in attention and concentration, some studies suggest that classical music is especially effective, particularly the works of Bach and Mozart.

If you are facing a difficult challenge, try to reframe it as a growth opportunity, or part of a larger life lesson. Committing oneself to some form or action can unleash previously dormant, powerful inner forces. You may benefit from a combination of approaches. Many of those who have persevered, despite years of pain and adversity, have been able to combine a will to act with the belief that they are pursuing a higher calling.

Regardless of your chosen path toward inspiration, maintaining an attitude of trust and openness to new experiences is crucial. Abandon your need for complete control or perfect knowledge. You might begin by slowing down your mind and your body at least once or twice a day with the help of meditation, a quiet walk, or a form of exercise that you enjoy. A more tranquil mind is a more receptive mind, primed to receive inspiration from wherever it may come.

Role Models

There is a wealth of evidence about the power of heroes and role models to transform lives. For example, consider the influence of the Siddhartha legend on millions of Buddhists, or imagine the empowerment felt by Native Americans at the mere mention of Sitting Bull. How many American children have gained inspiration from Abraham Lincoln while reciting the Gettysburg Address? How many Hindus were lifted out of despair by the vision of Gandhi defying the British? A vivid description of the impact of a great hero, Martin Luther King Jr., was provided by Felicia, a senior high school student from Mystic, Connecticut:

When I see pictures of Dr. Martin Luther King . . . I dream of the privilege to be able to listen to such a great speaker. . . . He must have given so many people hope. . . . [I would have told him] Please never give up. . . . I love you and what you are doing for our people. You are truly an angel sent down from the heavens to preach your dreams. . . . Many things that I am able to do today I attribute to the contributions of Dr. King.

You may want to purchase or rent a DVD or CD of inspiring speeches. In 1991 Rhino Records came out with a CD boxed set called *Greatest Speeches of the Twentieth Century*, which included selections from political leaders and sports icons as well as aviation and science heroes. In 2004 Soundworks International released *The Greatest Speeches of All Time*, a DVD featuring fifteen renowned world leaders. You can find detailed descriptions of these and similar products at Amazon.com.

A hero does not have to be a famous political figure, movie star, or athlete. For example, best friends, parents, and teachers have served as inspirational figures for many individuals. In fact, the heroism of the average person is often more compelling because it is more immediate and real. For example, you may know a child who battled cancer or an individual who suffered abuse or neglect as a child but nevertheless grew into a healthy and loving adult. At the My Hero Project (http://www.myhero.com) you can find inspiring books and films as well as thousands of stories of unsung heroes who have made a difference in the life of a child or an adult.

If you do seek to be inspired by celebrities, then do your homework. Get to know them a little better by reading books or feature articles about them. For the truly motivated, there are fan clubs and websites. You may even be able to submit questions or chat live with your particular hero or heroine. The Classic Sports Network, the E Channel, MTV, and A&E have put together some great one-hour biographies. In the realm of sports, one of the most inspiring collections of hope profiles is *More Than a Game* by A. Lawrance Holmes.

Parental Inspiration

For many individuals, their feelings of mastery and awe are strongly connected to the success of their children. In *Top of the Class*, Soo Kim Abboud and Jane Kim outlined some of the values and principles shared by Asian parents in fostering their children's excellence in school and at work. In the realm of commitment, they noted "a love and need for learning and education" as well as a "respect and desire for delayed gratification and sacrifice." With respect to challenge, the parents emphasized professions offering both "intellectual fulfillment" and "healthy competition" as well as "financial security." Shared control was demonstrated in a variety of ways, including "parental acceptance of responsibility for school failures" and the practice of "surrounding children with similarly-minded friends and role models."

In *The Measure of Our Success*, Marian Wright Edelman shared her "25 lessons for life." She recalled, as an African American, the "ugly external voices" emanating from her small, segregated town in South Carolina. Still, she wrote, "We always knew who we were and that the measure of our worth was inside our heads and hearts and not outside in our possessions or on our backs." Applicable to all young people, but geared particularly to minority youth, Wright Edelman's lessons also reflect the need for commitment (set goals and work quietly and systematically toward them), challenge (don't feel entitled to anything you don't sweat and struggle for), and shared control (always remember that you are never alone). For Wright Edelman, the single greatest need is to move forward with a sense of integrity, purpose, and meaning, to "sell the shadow for substance," to "listen for the sound of the genuine" within oneself, and to "be confident that you can make a difference."

In a similar vein, Rabbi Shmuley Boteach advocates "lighting up the family with passion and inspiration." In *Parenting with Fire*, he encouraged both mothers and fathers to take stock of their own passions, and to work toward effectively sharing with their children their enthusiasm and commitment for these pursuits. If you can generate a reasonably broad menu of alternative passions, there are bound to be one or more that will attract the interest of your child. In *Fathers and Families*, Henry emphasizes how both parents can play a vital role in stimulating their child's initiative and achievement motivation while increasing his or her range of perceived domains for success.

Parents who wish to empower their children should strive for a hope-building middle ground. Ideally, your standards for mastery should be aimed just beyond your child's current ability level. Russian developmental psychologist Lev Vygotsky referred to this area between a child's current level of development and his or her soon unfolding potential as the "zone of proximal development." From this notion, educators developed the concept of scaffolding—erecting a temporary framework that allows the child to move up to the next level. A fitting analogy is the multistage rocket booster used to launch the Space Shuttle. Several rocket boosters provide over more than 80 percent of the initial lift; however, once the shuttle reaches a certain height, the boosters separate, leaving the ship to be guided from within.

It is helpful for parents to introduce a variety of mastery alternatives to their children. Psychologist Robert Brooks referred to these as potential "islands of competencies." He noted that a wise parent can provide repeated "success samplings" via careful "environmental engineering." For example, if your child is not athletically gifted, you might put more emphasis on music, art, or nature. On the other hand, psychologist Rick Snyder suggested that parents provide mastery opportunities that span the academic, social, and athletic domains. With respect to potential challenges, Snyder advised parents to normalize "barriers" and "roadblocks" by providing children with plenty of examples of *alternative strategies for goal attainment*. Keep in mind that you and your child may have quite different mastery preferences. Make sure that you are not pressuring them to fulfill your unrealized dreams. Snyder also recommended that parents tell their children about their own past experiences in overcoming obstacles.

HIDDEN DREAMS

The mastery guidelines provided in this chapter are broadly framed, applicable to just about any foreseeable endeavor. Although these open blueprints presume that one has a specific goal or direction in mind, we recognize that many people will reevaluate and perhaps even revise their goals as they move through life. We are also aware that sometimes the greatest obstacle to mastery is clarifying the nature of one's dreams.

Sustained by trust and openness, an individual can confidently enter the process of self-discovery with a sense of joy and wonder, eventually finding his or her voice or mission in life. Perhaps this is what Aristotle meant when he referred to hope as a "waking dream." Sometimes the process of self-discovery goes slowly. Individuals sense that something is not quite right in their lives and make plans to find themselves. They may switch jobs or careers, start a new relationship, or relocate to another city. Alternatively, an individual may have an epiphany, a sudden realization of a higher purpose.

A full commitment to self-discovery requires a courageous leap of faith. Unlike a planned trip or scheduled vacation, your final destination is unknown. This is undoubtedly why many of the great epic writers conjured up heroes engaged in arduous, soul-searching journeys. Both

Homer's Odysseus and Virgil's Aeneas had to battle demons on foreign soil before they could achieve inner peace. Siddhartha wandered all over India searching for the meaning of life. After forty-four years of tortuous asceticism, he finally learned that his truth lay within.

Is there a way out of this spiritual conundrum? Is it really necessary to travel far and wide or to suffer through decades of wanderlust before deciphering your calling in life? Is there a way to cut a more direct path? Fortunately, the answer is a qualified yes. Although there is no substitute for acquired wisdom or hard-won life experience, there *are* strategies that you can use to accelerate your self-understanding.

You might want to begin with a simple values clarification exercise, such as the one developed by psychologist Milton Rokeach. His list of values includes eighteen terminal values (desired ends) and eighteen instrumental values (desired means). Each list is present in alphabetical order. Individuals are asked to rank the values from 1 to 18, with 1 being most important and 18 being least important. Try it for yourself:

Terminal Values	Instrumental Values
Comfortable life	Ambitious
Equality	Broad-minded
Exciting life	Capable
Family security	Clean
Freedom	Courageous
Health	Forgiving
Inner harmony	Helpful
Mature love	Honest
National security	Imaginative
Pleasure	Independent
Salvation	Intellectual

Terminal Values (cont'd)	**Instrumental Values** (cont'd)
Self-respect	Logical
Sense of accomplishment	Loving
Social recognition	Loyal
True friendship	Obedient
Wisdom	Polite
World at peace	Responsible
World of beauty	Self-controlled

Learning from the Past

Sometimes, deeper needs and feelings as well as hidden talents can be uncovered only by pondering your past rather than worrying about the future. In fact, more than one philosopher has suggested that life can be understood only by looking backward. Metaphorically as well as literally, if you are lost in a crowded city or the middle of a forest, retracing your steps might help you to get your bearings. In *Four Quartets*, T. S. Eliot suggested that "in my end is my beginning" and "the end of all our exploring will be to arrive where we started and know the place for the first time."

Your ability to learn from the past dictates how much you can profit from experience. Some quick learners need only a few weeks to settle into a new position, whereas others take months, if not years, to feel comfortable. When the lessons extend to your life as a whole, the art of reflection becomes a bit more complex. Here are some suggestions for looking back:

- *Success review*: What have you already mastered because it was a labor of love?
- *Failure autopsy*: What have you failed because your heart wasn't in the task?

- *Perceived effort*: What kinds of tasks or activities have come easy for you?
- *Happy times*: What endeavors have brought you joy?
- *Miserable times*: What tasks or activities have brought you misery?
- *Pride experience*: What have you accomplished that is a source of pride?
- *Anger or resentment*: What activities have left you feeling angry or resentful?

Inspiring Dreams

An uninterpreted dream is like an unread letter.

—The Talmud, *Brakhot 55a*

Dreams have long been a source of inspiration. Some of the earliest "bestsellers" were dream books prepared by Egyptian scribes or Roman philosophers. In the Book of Genesis, Joseph won the favor of the Egyptian pharaoh through his uncanny knack for interpreting dreams. The grand master of the collective unconscious, Carl Jung, devoted his life to analyzing more than 80,000 dreams. Freud considered *The Interpretation of Dreams* his single greatest contribution, declaring, "Such discoveries occur but once in a lifetime." Analyzing your dreams is an excellent way to gain inspiration while learning from the past. In fact, it has been found that only 5 percent of dreams typically deal with the future. By analyzing your dreams, you might uncover acts of self-sabotage resulting from a fear of success or attempted derailment by disingenuous people who only pretend to offer support. Dreams can provide greater insight into long-standing problems and ideas for creative solutions.

In a landmark 1966 study, psychologists Calvin Hall and Robert van Castle collected the dreams of 1,000 individuals. They separated the dreams into various categories, including those that were directly related to mastery (Table 9.2). With a little effort, we were able to extract dream probabilities for each of the four mastery elements (self-mastery, values, support, and time). The subcategories, including those of success and failure fit under self-mastery; familiar and unfamiliar surroundings can be linked to intrinsic and extrinsic values; friendly and unfriendly environments relate to support; and past, present, and future dream imagery can be linked to time. Table 9.2 can be used as a guide for tracking as many dreams as you want. If this type of analysis interests you, keep a notebook next to your bed. Write down your dreams, as precisely as you can, right after you wake up. Once you have collected at least ten dreams, compare your percentages to those in Table 9.2.

Table 9.2. Hope-Based Dream Analysis

Mastery Themes	Hall & van Castle Findings		Number to Expect (per number of dreams)			
Self-Mastery			100	50	20	10
(30% of dreams)	Success	50%	15	8	4	2
	Failure	50%	15	8	4	2
	Dreamer succeeds	90%	14	7	4	2
	Another succeeds	10%	1	1	0	0
Support			100	50	20	10
(40% of dreams)	Providing assistance	45%	18	9	4	2
	Getting help	45%	18	9	4	2
	Collaborating	10%	4	2	1	0
Values			100	50	20	10
(Every dream)	Familiar ground	30%	30	15	6	3
	Distorted surroundings	50%	50	25	10	5
	Unfamiliar territory	20%	20	10	4	2
Time and Movement			100	50	20	10
	Situated in the past	30%	12	6	2	1
Time	Situated in the present	50%	20	10	4	2
(40% of dreams)	Situated in the future	20%	8	4	2	1
			100	50	20	10
Movement	Dreamer moving	60%	60	30	12	6
(Every dream)	Dreamer stationary	40%	40	20	8	4

For example, starting with self-mastery, Hall and van Castle's findings suggest that themes of success and failure appear in approximately 30 percent of dreams. Moreover, their results indicate that about half of these represent success and half symbolize failure. If you decide to track 100 of your dreams, then about 15 should deal with success (50 percent of 30). However, if you are harboring feelings of ineffectiveness, you might very well experience a preponderance of failure dreams. Approximately 90 percent of your success dreams should feature you as the effective, achieving, or masterful protagonist. A much lower percentage suggests that you might not be taking ownership of a successful outcome, even when it does occur.

You may want to pay special attention to the category pertaining to values. Dreams that take place on familiar ground suggest that you are following your bliss. Myth expert Joseph Campbell commented that individuals feel most at home when they are following their higher calling and honoring the values they cherish and hold dear. This moral basis for feeling at home or in a familiar space was beautifully captured by Henry David Thoreau, who advised his readers to "dwell as near as possible to the channel in which your life flows."

Note that typically about 60 percent of dreams include some physical movement. Movement in dreams (and in imaginative exercises) suggests a readiness or potential for change, an active coping style, and a strong level of motivation. Too little movement might indicate deep feelings of stagnation, emotional paralysis, or even depression.

A number of self-help writers, including Patricia Garfield, have suggested that there may be certain universal dream symbols. In particular, Garfield has referred to the following mastery-related dream elements: driving well or driving poorly, falling down or flying high, performing well or performing poorly, missing the boat or traveling well. If you are comfortable with the idea of universal symbols, the following list of mastery-related objects and themes might be of interest to you. For greater depth of understanding, pay attention to the emotions and the general mood that permeate your dreams.

Self-mastery. Decision time (exiting or entering a cave, standing at a crossroads or on a diving platform); goal pursuits (running toward or chasing something); competence and drive (planes, trains, automobiles, horses, eagles, hawks).

Values. Moral standards (judge, jury, courtroom, lawyers); things held sacred (church, temple, synagogue, mosque); orienting or purpose-driving values (compass, road map, path in the woods).

Support. General environment: living room, kitchen, dining room, garden; social support: father, mother, teacher, mentor; financial support: money, banks; emotional support: milk, honey, hearts.

Time. Substance: changing shadow, sand in an hourglass, ticking clock; cause: father time, primetime, downtime; medium: river, road, obstacle course; direction: one-way street, going around in circles, spiral staircase.

THE VISION QUEST

Perhaps you have tried some of the above suggestions but still feel mired in the hopeless grind of an uninspired life. In reviewing your past, was it hard to recall any true moments of flow or joyful engagement? In exploring your values, was it difficult for you to achieve any sense of clarity? Do you feel as if you have hit a wall in terms of mastery development? If this is the case, then consider a vision quest.

In many indigenous cultures, it is or was common for both young and old to leave the group and venture into the wilderness in search of guidance and wisdom. In fact, within many tribal societies, such vision quests were considered an essential component of the adolescent rite of passage. Today this practice has become popular among some individuals in Western and industrialized countries as a means of achieving inner peace and a deeper clarity of purpose.

A vision quest is aimed at transforming the self through a three-step process of separation, transition, and incorporation. The first step is to pull yourself away from the forces and elements that are inhibiting your spiritual development. This can be achieved by venturing into a remote area such as an island, a forest, or a desert, where you can experience yourself free from the usual constraints of daily life.

The second step is to effect a transition from a world-centered focus to an inner-centered state. Fasting, going without sleep, and living off the land are some of the strategies that can be used to facilitate this shift. Among certain indigenous groups, there is also a reliance on special foods, herbs, or beverages. The more dramatic accounts of this spiritual migration liken it to a symbolic death of the old self.

The third step is incorporation or rebirth. This is often facilitated by a spiritual guide who imparts new beliefs and values. Additional support may be provided by a group of like-minded individuals who uphold a similar vision. In this manner, individuals can fashion a new image of themselves, the world, and the future.

Circles of Air, Circles of Stone is a Vermont-based organization that specializes in four-day vision quests. Journeys are conducted in Vermont as well as various parts of the American Southwest and Mexico. Several different forms of a vision quest are offered, including those rooted in the traditions of Native North Americans, the Mayans of Central America, and Australian Aborigines. For mastery development, we recommend two of their programs, *Journey of the Soul* and *The Medicine Walk*. For a more immediate primer, you may want to try psychologist John Suler's mini vision quest. The following guidelines are adapted from his Internet posting (http://www.rider.edu/~suler/vquest.html).

For a period of at least four hours, leave your home and go out somewhere. Don't plan ahead. Just follow your instincts and go where your intuition leads you. Do this alone. If you encounter a friend or acquaintance, limit your time with them to just a few minutes.

As you move about, reflect on one or more big questions that you would like to answer such as "Who am I?" "What is important to me?"

and "What do I want from life?" Try to balance thinking and reflecting with moments of unfocused drifting.

Frequently remind yourself that you are on a quest, a search mission. Expect to find something and trust that insights will occur. Stay open to any sign or symbol that might provide you with inspiration. It could be something that happens to you or something you see or hear. Bring a notebook and a pen. Every half hour or so, sit down and write. Note your reactions, including your thoughts, your feelings, and your insights. If you're feeling anxious, frustrated, or bored, ask yourself why and write about this aspect of your experience. If nothing important has happened, you should reflect and write about this as well.

For some, the call to mastery will reflect a universal tune such as the impulse to be a good parent, teacher, artist, plumber, farmer, or business owner. For others, it may consist of a more personal "mission in life." In addressing your particular mastery needs, you must look deep within, far ahead, and everywhere around. Only then will you be able to summon the discipline and inner truth, vision, and time perspective, as well as support and inspiration needed, to achieve a meaningful sense of mastery. In the final analysis, only you can evaluate your success in life.

10

Hope for Health

*[Healing] is an art: and if it is to be made an art, it
requires an exclusive devotion, as hard a preparation
as any painter's or sculptor's work; for instead of
working with dead canvas or dead marble, we are
working with the living body, the temple of God's spirit.*

—FLORENCE NIGHTINGALE, *NURSING PIONEER*

In this chapter we examine how hope can support health, foster healing, and facilitate wellness. We begin with a summary of the best evidence linking hope-related thoughts, feelings, and behaviors to research on health and healing. We underscore the health implications of balanced and unbalanced forms of mastery, attachment, and survival. A comprehensive hope-based health plan is provided—consisting of specific prescriptions for facilitating empowerment, connection, and self-regulation—as well as a more general philosophy of healing. The chapter ends with suggestions for wellness, focusing on hope-based fitness and hopeful aging. As Nightingale's remarks suggest, healing with hope is akin to an art form that goes well beyond mere positive thinking.

TONY'S STORY

In the past, I frequently suffered from gastrointestinal (GI) symptoms. These problems always seemed to "sneak up" on me, with little apparent warning. These "flare-ups" lasted weeks, and sometimes months. My quality of life was significantly impacted. I could only tolerate certain foods. I could not enjoy a beer or a glass of wine. I had to keep a strict eating schedule. From time to time, I would request a diagnostic check-up to rule out anything serious. The frequency, intensity, and apparent randomness of the symptoms were demoralizing. Like the plumber who fixes everyone else's leaky faucets but his own, or the chef who has no time to prepare a healthy meal for herself, I was neglecting to use my own resources, especially my growing knowledge about the power of hope.

A few years ago, I finally decided to adopt a more hopeful approach to my GI problems. To be honest, my motivation for doing this was partly the result of treating several patients in a fairly short period of time who were experiencing similar but not identical stress-related GI problems. Given the large number of people who suffer from irritable bowel syndrome (IBS), inflammatory bowel disease (IBD), Crohn's disease, and other related intestinal issues, researching this topic seemed like a wise investment of time. I might address my own nagging health issues while learning about a set of ailments that plague many others, including those prospective clients who might someday seek me out for psychological help.

Relying on my mastery and attachment resources, I consulted with traditional healthcare providers as well as practitioners of complementary medicine. I also researched the medical and psychological literature.

I sought expert advice but maintained a collaborative stance, determined to fashion a personal recipe for wellness. I learned that too much stress and too little exercise were strongly associated with GI imbalances. I also purchased a great book, *Digestive Wellness* by Elizabeth Lipski, and started to keep a journal with notes about various probiotics, digestive enzymes, and other forms of nutritional support for the GI system. In addition, I began to track my occasional flare-ups and discovered that they typically occurred in the spring, when I was wrapping up a year of intense, often sedentary, professional work. My symptoms waned and often disappeared during the summer when I was not teaching, doing less work on the computer, and spending more time working outdoors or going to the gym. Balance is the key to everything. When I ate at a more leisurely pace, slept more restfully, and got more physical activity, my GI system was happy, and I was happy.

HENRY'S STORY

Although I will soon enter my eighth decade, I have been fortunate to remain strong and healthy, attributes for which I am extremely grateful. In my own experience, hope and health are inseparable. I have always been a hopeful, future-oriented person, and this has clearly played a large part in my active, playful approach to life. At the same time, while I derive great enjoyment from the process of daily exercise, I must admit that I also view it as a means to an end, a hope booster that will prolong my sense of mastery, allow me more time and opportunities to nurture my relationships, and enhance my survival skills.

My physical self has been a fundamental part of my identity for all of my life, even though it might not seem that relevant to my professional career as a psychologist. My health regimen may seem unusual for someone my age. Simply put, my attitude is to "play every day." Play is subject to different definitions, but for me it comes down to a variety of activities that are pleasurable and stimulating, activities that I can look forward to on a daily basis.

People who don't know me well often act surprised or dumbfounded. They asked me, "Do you work out like this every day?" "No," I reply, "I don't work out, I play. When you were a kid, did you ever pass up an opportunity to play because it was 'not your day to play'? Would you consider eating or sleeping only on certain days of the week or hugging your loved ones only on weekends?" "What about your other responsibilities?" they might ask. I often reply, "If I'm not feeling right, I will not be right with my family, friends, or work responsibilities." Yes, I prefer to play in the early morning hours, but if I have other pressing duties, I'll get up even earlier or divide my playtime. In any event, I will find a way to play every day.

My everyday play routine begins with several miles of running, followed by a wide variety of resistance and stretching exercises done at a very brisk pace. In life, you have to know how much is too much and how much is not enough. I strive for moderation. Clearly, moderation is a subjective term. What I find moderate may seem light or heavy for someone else. I also realize that a healthy lifestyle goes beyond daily exercise. I make sure to eat and sleep well, to minimize my stress level, and to seek out daily contact with loved ones.

JAIME'S STORY

Jaime was diagnosed with thyroid cancer in her midtwenties. A few years ago, Tony spoke to Jaime on the phone about her condition. She found it both amusing and infuriating when she was told by others that she had the "good cancer."

"Let me tell you," she said, "I run a support group for thyroid cancer survivors. We had a woman attending for her husband, who had thyroid cancer. Well, a short time later this poor man died. Now tell his wife," she added sarcastically, "that he had the 'good cancer.'"

In pursuit of healing, Jaime relied on a strong will to live as well as her previous training in teacher education. "You have to take action and do your own research," she said. "No one is going to be as concerned about your health as you. I use the mind-set of a teacher and a learner to gather as much information as possible. I subscribe to a number of medical journals. I keep up on the progress of new clinical trials. I also rely a great deal on the Thy-CA website, which includes a listserv and other great resources."

Jaime discovered that there was not a single support group for thyroid cancer survivors in her community. Drawing on her background in education, she started her own group. "I have been running the group for nearly three years," she reports. "I have about eighty cancer survivors in my database. We do a lot of fund-raising and awareness activities, including participating in the American Cancer Society's Relay for Life. I get as much as I give during the support group's meetings. The sense of camaraderie is unbelievable. Plus, you can only do so much research on your own. When you have certain symptoms and experiences and a doctor tells you that something is not possible, yet thirty people validate you with their own similar testimonies—that's powerful."

In dealing with healthcare providers, Jaime took a collaborative approach. "I worked with a team of doctors, including some fantastic nuclear medicine physicians. I also had a great endocrinologist who is really on top of things. We traded e-mails on a daily basis. My surgeon was also excellent. She would not 'blow smoke up your ass' but at the same time was always confident."

From the start of her healing journey, Jaime garnered a tremendous amount of support. "My partner and my parents have been wonderful. They come to my appointments, help in caring for my seven-year-old son, and share the burden of running a household." Jaime's attachments have strengthened her resolve to stay positive and strong. "Knowing my son needs a mom makes the fight more bearable. I can't abandon him. In fact, I feel as if all my connections have a purpose."

Jaime is big on having options. "Although I was being treated at one of the most respected medical centers in the country, I wanted a second opinion. I took my chart to Sloan-Kettering in New York and asked them to review my records. They told me that I should continue with my treatment back home, that no one would know my neck better than my own doctors, and that my previous treatment had, in their opinion, been excellent. This gave me a great deal of reassurance."

Jamie noted that hope requires time and patience. "From all I've read on preparing for surgeries, I know it's important to relax. I do a great deal of meditating. I take breaks. I try to deal honestly with what is going on without dwelling on it nonstop." Jaime felt that time was on her side. "This is a slow-growing cancer, and new technologies are being developed all the time. This is another source of hope for me, that time will bring more answers."

Like many cancer survivors, Jaime found meaning in the midst of her suffering. "I am no longer self-conscious about my scars. I used to cover them with turtleneck sweaters and elaborate scarves. Now I view them as my badges of courage. Each scar serves to tell a story. Each scar is part of the journey I have traveled."

Jaime derived great comfort from her religious and spiritual beliefs. "I'm Roman Catholic. I buy candles with pictures of the saints like St. Jude (the patron saint of hope) and St. Peregrine (the patron saint of cancer patients). I light the candles. I use my rosary and pray. I do not believe that God is vindictive. I do not believe He would have put me through all this and allowed me to recover from all these surgeries, just to abandon me and let me die. God put me here for a reason."

ROOM FOR HOPE

To understand God's thoughts we must study [the data], for these are the measure of His purpose.

—FLORENCE NIGHTINGALE

A hopeful attitude can promote healing. Table 10.1 lists notable mind-body advocates throughout the ages. It begins with the sage advice of Hippocrates and concludes with the immunologist-psychologist team of Ronald Glaser and Janice Kiecolt-Glaser. Note that across the centuries, the very best minds in philosophy, medicine, and biology have presumed that the mind plays a vital role in maintaining health and facilitating healing.

Table 10.1. Notable Proponents of Mind-Body Healing

Mind-Body Advocate	Credentials	Quote or Contribution
Hippocrates (400 BCE)	The founder of medicine; author of the Hippocratic Oath.	"It is more important to know what kind of patient has a disease than what kind of disease a patient has."
Galen (200 CE)	Greatest healer of antiquity; described the cranial nerves, the valves of the heart, and the kidneys.	Temperament is a factor in health and disease; healing dreams can aid in diagnosis and treatment.
Avicenna (1000)	Prince of physicians; his *The Canon of Medicine* was the physician's primary textbook for 500 years.	Emotions are one of the six determinants of health; positive thinking is a powerful healer.
Paracelsus (1500)	Greatest chemist of the Middle Ages; founder of pharmacology.	"Imagination is a great factor in medicine; the spirit is the master, and imagination is the tool."
Sir William Osler (1900)	Dubbed "world's greatest physician" at the turn of the twentieth century.	The role of hostility in heart disease, the impact of stress on arthritis, coping, and chronic illness.
Herbert Benson (1985)	Professor, Harvard Medical School; proponent of the relaxation response.	Combining the relaxation response with a faith factor can produce beneficial changes in physiology.
Jonas Salk (1986)	Physician and medical researcher; developer of the polio vaccine.	"The mind has the power to turn the immune system around."

Mind-Body Advocate	Credentials	Quote or Contribution
Bernie Siegel (1986)	Yale-trained pediatric and general surgeon.	Chronicled the successes of exceptional cancer patients. "To give a family hope is never wrong."
Candace Pert (1999)	Neuroscientist; former division head, National Institutes of Health.	"Molecules of emotion" link the brain with the immune system and the endocrine system.
Ronald Glaser & Janice Kiecolt-Glaser (2002)	Immunologist and psychologist, Ohio State University School of Medicine.	Psychological and social interventions can boost the immune system.

Opponents of mind-body healing too often fail to give hope a level playing field in their research. Specifically, we can identify at least five potential sources of error that have plagued research on healing and the mind. When these factors are taken into account, we are left with plenty of room for hope.

- A double standard in evaluating research
- Excessive biological loads
- Lack of emotional precision
- Inadequate measurements
- Superficial approaches to the mind

The critics of mind-body medicine have been known to dismiss studies that suggest a connection between positive mental states and health because they purportedly reflect "poor research designs or fail to incorporate alternate explanations." However, these critics have not always been consistent in their own evidence gathering, at times relying on misleading studies to bolster their arguments against a mind-body connection.

Some mind-body critics focus primarily on studies where a majority of individuals have the most severe or debilitating form of an illness (such as advanced HIV or the most serious tumors). Some scientists, particularly those with less training in psychology, make the mistake of lumping together a variety of emotions under the umbrella of ineffectiveness, including wishful thinking and denial. Some investigators will invest hundreds, if not thousands, of dollars in assessing the body with sophisticated biological tests. However, when it comes to measuring the mind, they are often comfortable relying on a questionnaire of five to ten items that is completed in a few seconds. Hope must be accurately measured, and not in a superficial manner.

How Hope Heals

Just about every mind-body finding in the scientific literature seems to be associated with one or more of the motives underlying hope. Moreover, it is remarkable how well the evidence lines up in support of a hope-based approach to mastery, attachment, and survival. Do your own test. Can you think of any mind-body research, case study, or personal anecdote that you have read about or encountered that did not involve one or more of the motives underlying hope?

Before delving any further into the research that supports the hope-health connection, we would like to provide a broader philosophical framework for understanding the ways in which hope can facilitate health and healing. As you will see, a little Aristotle can go a long way in clarifying the healing power of hope.

Aristotle described four causes in nature. First, some effects can be attributed to the substance from which a cause is composed; this is the *material cause*. For example, a beam made of metal may cause injury or damage if it lands on someone or something. A second effect is made possible by the formal properties of the cause; this is the *formal cause*. Wheels permit a vehicle to move along the ground because they have a round form. A third type of effect is imparted when a cause sets a process in motion; this is the *efficient cause*. Hypertension can cause a stroke if high arterial pressure results in fat particles being dislodged and propelled toward smaller blood vessels. A fourth cause can be linked to final aims or targeted endpoints; this is the *final cause*. Among human beings, goal setting and other future-directed plans can be the cause of numerous thoughts, feelings, and actions throughout a lifetime.

Using Aristotle's approach, we can identify eight different hope-related healing pathways:

- *Systemic involvement (material cause).* Although you cannot literally touch or feel hope, it does have a biological underpinning, a substrate consisting of the mastery, attachment, and survival systems that are intimately related to health and healing.

- *Balance (formal cause).* Hope is a balanced emotional state, defined by shared power, mutual caring, and relaxed coping. At the physiological level, balance is paramount. Minor fluctuations in sugar, salt, or fluid levels can wreak havoc on an organism. Without the proper ratio of helper cells to suppressor cells, immunity is compromised.

- *Authenticity (formal cause).* Hope is fully informed by an enlarged life perspective. At the physiological level, health and healing are compromised when there is a failure to honor true feelings. Repressed anger, inhibited fear, or unresolved grief all take a toll on the body. Hope is about the full integration of experience.

- *Inclusiveness (formal cause).* Hope spans conscious and unconscious awareness. Immunologists Richard Booth and Kevin Ashbridge suggest that healing is maximized when all systems of the body (nervous, immune, endocrine) are working together. Hope heals through the unrestricted commitment of resources.

• *Openness (efficient cause)*. Openness is one of the fruits of hope. It can yield emotional and practical support from others (external openness) as well as greater informational exchange within the body (internal openness). Hope brings improved communication.

• *Flow (efficient cause)*. Hope is "wetter" and "hotter" than a "dry" or "cold" expectation. As an emotion, hope includes the limbic system, an important storage site for neuropeptides that shuttle back and forth between the brain and the immune and endocrine systems. Candace Pert and other neuroscientists propose that mind-body healing is facilitated by the flow of such informational substances. Hope permits greater emotional expression.

• *Resilience (efficient cause)*. Hopeful individuals are buttressed by the secular as well as the spiritual. They remain resilient in the face of adversity, centered in good times and bad. In contrast, physiologists refer to the wear and tear caused by stress-induced deviations as allostatic load. Hope facilitates reduced allostatic load.

• *Harmony (final cause)*. Hope is a way of being cultivated through higher aims, sacred purposes, and an eternal perspective. Booth and Ashbridge believe that the highest purpose of the mind-body connection is not defense but organism integrity secured through biological harmony. Hope contributes to harmony of purpose.

Support for Aristotle

Between 2005 and 2007, Tony coordinated two research projects to verify the Aristotelian healing hypothesis. In one study, a dozen thyroid cancer survivors were recruited to complete a comprehensive hope test, which included sections dealing with mastery, attachment, survival, and spirituality. In addition, each participant completed a health-related processes scale that represented the eight hope-healing pathways. The survivors rated their present level of physical well-being and their level of health-related distress.

The findings were strongly supportive of a hope-health connection. The total scores on the hope test were highly correlated with reports of greater physical well-being as well as fewer health-related worries. Moreover, those who endorsed more of the healing processes (the eight pathways) tended to score significantly higher in overall well-being.

In the second study, fifteen HIV-positive individuals took the hope test, and as in the first study, reported their level of physical well-being and health-related distress while also completing the questionnaire on health-related processes. For this study, it was also possible to obtain blood levels of CD4 at the beginning and the end of the study (two years later). CD4 is the master cell of the immune system and is especially critical for health maintenance among those dealing with HIV.

Again, the results supported the hope-health hypothesis. HIV-positive individuals who were higher in hope reported greater overall health and were less worried about their future well-being. In addition, those who endorsed more of the healing processes (the eight pathways) tended to report greater well-being. Equally impressive, higher hope scores were associated with greater CD4 levels at both the beginning and the end of the study. Statistically speaking, *the hope factor accounted for nearly 40 percent of the difference in immune functioning.*

In short, hope has great healing potential, particularly if we adopt a fair and balanced perspective. Hope is not a panacea or a magic bullet. However, it is a powerful ally in maintaining health and recovering from illness. As further proof, let us review the best evidence linking the motives of mastery, attachment, and survival to health and illness.

MASTERY: THE WILL TO LIVE

In Western cultures, there is a tendency to address matters of healing with fighting words. Patients and their physicians speak of *beating*, *defeating*, or *vanquishing* an illness. An infection prompts the notion of a body *under siege* and visions of recruiting the *defenses* of the immune system to *attack* the *foreign invaders*. When a loved one succumbs, it may be noted in the obituary that he or she "lost a courageous battle" with cancer or some other disease.

Gary Reisfield, a professor of medicine at the University of Florida Health Science Center, has pointed out that some physicians have become particularly enamored of what he calls the "military metaphor." In reference to cancer, he notes, "The enemy is cancer, the commander is the physician, the combatant is the patient, the allies are the health-care team, and the weapons are chemical, biological, and nuclear."

Reisfield cautions physicians against using such stark militaristic metaphors without considering the individual dispositions of their patients. For instance, Lance Armstrong was told that he was going to be *bombarded* by very high levels of chemotherapy, "high enough levels to nearly kill you as well as the cancer." Rather than feeling inspired, Armstrong was taken aback and switched doctors. From his perspective, a healing journey (not unlike a bicycle race) served as a more hopeful metaphor.

Similar concerns prompted Susan Sontag to write *Illness as Metaphor*. Sontag suggested that some disease characterizations, while intended to serve as vehicles of empowerment, may actually add to an individual's suffering. This is particularly likely when an illness myth promotes an exaggerated sense of personal responsibility for contracting a disease and results in a feeling of failure if one does not fight and overcome.

What has been learned from the research? Is it helpful to be a *fighter* when you are sick? In truth, the evidence is mixed.

On one hand, many studies have shown that perceptions of control or the assumption of personal responsibility for one's health can prolong life in the elderly and promote healing in those who are ill, including individuals dealing with cancer, HIV, or cardiovascular problems. However, there is also some seemingly conflicting data. For example, several studies have apparently failed to show any connection between the will to live and recovery from illness. Other research suggests that overengagement or excessive striving might even make matters worse. Highly hostile individuals are four to five times more likely to develop cardiovascular disease. Laboratory studies have revealed that hostility can trigger the release of five different stress hormones while also weakening the parasympathetic system, the nerves that are responsible for eliciting the relaxation response. Individuals who scored higher on a measure of aggressiveness and other antisocial tendencies were found to have lower T-cell and B-cell counts, both indicative of a compromised immune system.

Empowered Healing

We believe that hope-based mastery *can* facilitate healing through hopeful empowerment. Hope-based mastery is derived from supportive relationships as well as from a spiritual direction. This yields an experience of mediated power and a will to hope that is spiritually sanctified and emotionally charged.

A fighting spirit that is not hope-based may provide only limited opportunities for healing. Perhaps this is why data on coping with breast cancer or "making it through" holidays and anniversaries sometimes fail to support the "will to live" hypothesis. On the other hand, having a reason to live that is linked to a set of transcendent values and grounded in hope may do wonders for the body as well as the spirit.

Hope-based mastery is derived from a unified sense of purpose, a working alliance and faith in the future. Psychologists Robert Emmons and Laura King found that individuals who are less conflicted about their goal strivings reported fewer illnesses and were less likely to require the services of a healthcare center. David McClelland used a picture-story exercise to assess an individual's stressed-power index. *Stressed power* is defined as high power and high frustration. McClelland measured the participants' need for power as well as the number of times they included words in their stories such as *couldn't* or *can't*, which are indicative of greater goal frustration. Finally, McClelland collected blood samples to assess the robustness of each participant's immune system. Individuals who did not suffer from a stressed-power syndrome tended to have a greater number of natural cancer-killing cells. Moreover, the cancer-killing cells of these more at-ease individuals appeared to make them better able to track and destroy "foreign invaders."

Hope-based mastery implies a sense of spiritual sanctification. Terminally ill individuals who look forward to their next birthday as a time to reflect on past achievements and to receive positive feedback from others are significantly less likely to die in the preceding month. Similarly, those who view an upcoming religious holiday as a time to fulfill a privileged and sacred role are also less likely to die. For example, the death rates for older Jewish men are significantly lower the week before Passover. The same is true for elderly Chinese women the week prior to the Chinese Harvest Moon (an important midautumn festival). In stark contrast, consider the fate of legendary football coach Bear Bryant, who lived to prowl the sidelines on Saturday afternoons. Many were stunned when he died of cardiac arrest just thirty-seven days after retiring. A mere forty-eight hours before suffering a massive heart attack, Bryant had lamented, "There are no more Saturdays."

Death may also be hastened when individuals believe that they are spiritually finished. In the New Testament (Acts of the Apostles), there is a dramatic tale of sudden death resulting from a severed spiritual contract. When Ananias and his wife, Sapphira, sold a piece of land to secure funds for their spiritual community, they selfishly withheld a portion for themselves. When told by the apostle Peter, "You have lied not to men but to God," both of them immediately "fell down and died."

Suggestions for Mastery

What follows are a set of suggestions for maximizing your degree of hope-based mastery in a manner that is most conducive to healing. They represent our distillation of the varied, and sometimes confusing, data that relate mastery efforts to health and healing. Think of these as general guidelines for creating a healthy portable environment.

Focus your energy. Goal-related frustrations and conflicts can limit your healing potential. Are you being blocked in achieving an important life goal? How can you remove the obstacles in your path? Are you trying too hard? Have you failed to consider other avenues for reaching your goals? Perhaps the ultimate question that you can ask yourself is "Do I want to thrive or merely survive?"

Strive for authenticity. If you are sick, don't try to convince yourself, or others, that everything is just fine. However, at the same time you should not merely resign yourself to fate. Follow Norman Cousins's advice, "Do not deny the diagnosis; defy the verdict." You will probably find that the so-called odds of recovery are misleadingly low because they were derived by including those with multiple health problems, high levels of stress, and other confounding factors that do not apply to you.

Reduce hostility. Buddha was known to have a warm heart and a cool head. Follow his example. Consider a regimen of meditation and exercise to lower your baseline level of arousal. A calm body is incompatible with a hostile countenance. Learn to be effectively assertive rather than aggressive or hostile. Anger has its place, but it does not have to be fully vented or violent to be effective. Heed Aristotle's suggestion that the noble individual knows when and where, as well as toward whom and for how long, to express anger.

Foster mediated control. At every level in the healing process, mediated or shared control is crucial. Even within the immune system, there are helper cells that stimulate the B cells to produce antibodies to fight disease. Cultivate an attitude of balanced responsibility. Rather than blaming yourself or some external factor, focus on maintaining a sense of shared control and responsibility.

Suggestions for Spiritual Strength

Attending to your spiritual life is an important part of the healing process. As noted in previous chapters, spirituality does not necessarily mean a religious belief system. However, to serve as a source of hope and healing, your spiritual system must engender a deep sense of faith. It helps if you include a meditative component and nurture a collaborative relationship with one or more individuals, a group, or a higher power.

The centers of value that form the basis for a spiritual belief system afford you with a chance to ally yourself with something greater and more powerful. In addition, such belief systems tend to promote greater self-integration, thus reducing the chances of experiencing harmful goal conflicts or an immune system weakened as a result of stressed-power motivation.

A spiritual approach to healing ensures greater authenticity. Rather than pursuing recovery for the mere sake of feeling better or looking well, the individual is guided by a deeper desire for transformation of the mind and the spirit as well as the body. Instead of dismissing this as New Age psychobabble, one should honor the unity of the mind-body network. *Superficial healing* is really a misnomer.

A spiritual perspective can also help reduce the level of hostility by promoting acceptance, forgiveness, and gratitude. Hostility is a major risk factor for cardiovascular disease, whereas a more tolerant and amicable disposition can do wonders for the heart, the veins, and the capillaries. Physician Harold Koenig found that those who regularly attended religious services and prayed were 40 percent less likely to have high blood pressure.

Psychologists Robert Emmons and Michael McCullough studied adults with a neuromuscular disease. Those who practiced gratitude reported greater well-being than a similarly afflicted control group of people who did not regularly count their blessings.

Attachment: Support for Health

Two are better than one. If they fall, one will lift up his fellow; but woe to him who is alone when he falls and has not another to lift him up.

—Ecclesiastes [4:9]

The impact of attachment and social support on health is the most powerful and impressive mind-body effect found in the scientific literature. The sheer volume of this data is impressive. It consists of both human and animal studies as well as an enormous range of health-related issues, including mortality, progression of disease, and rates of recovery from illness.

Mice that are regularly petted develop fewer tumors, monkeys shocked in the presence of a buddy release less stress hormone, and HIV-positive men with stronger social support maintain higher levels of immunity.

How does social support lead to better health? Research suggests that a host of biological processes can be activated by proximity, touch, expressions of affection, and feelings of love or togetherness. The strongest evidence is of the impact of social support on three primary glands: the pituitary, the hypothalamus, and the adrenals.

For example, Swedish investigator Kerstin Uvnas-Moberg and her colleagues showed that social contact may release the hormone oxytocin, which is associated with a host of beneficial physiological reactions, including enhanced immunity. Psychologist James Coan found that women allowed to hold the hand of their spouse produced a far milder stress response when exposed to a shock. In contrast, some recent evidence suggests that social isolation may allow tumor cells to feed more efficiently on fats and sugars, thereby accelerating their growth.

Notwithstanding the considerable data on health and social support, it is not always the case that two are better than one. The quality of social interaction appears to be more important than the quantity. That is, the size of an individual's social network does not predict health status. Crowding is highly stressful and has been related to a variety of health problems in numerous species, from fish to apes to humans. Some relationships are highly toxic. Data from a study of newlyweds indicated that just thirty minutes of emotional conflict produced enough stress-hormone output to lower immune functioning for more than twenty-four hours.

Supported Healing

The key to securing wellness is depth of relatedness. Close relationships that facilitate openness and trust are essential for health and healing. By now you know that these are the same dimensions of relatedness that define hope-based attachments.

Healing relationships provide a twofold benefit: enhancing an individual's sense of self and providing outlets for emotional expression. If you are blessed with positive early family experiences, or later reparative bonds, your hopeful imprints will be empowering, trust-filled, and soothing. Individuals who fit this profile rarely feel totally helpless, completely alone, or utterly terrified. However, those who have suffered prolonged bouts of neglect or abuse are at risk for developing a sense of self that feels disenfranchised, isolated, and fragile.

Well-attached individuals are better able to weather the vicissitudes of life. They are physiologically less reactive to stressors and show a greater capacity for fighting disease. More than two dozen studies indicate that individuals with high-quality social support have lower blood pressure. Among women who are dealing with breast cancer, those with a helpful spouse and a supportive physician tend to demonstrate better cancer-killing cell activity.

Illness can be an isolating experience. Laura, a breast cancer survivor, noted, "You get that look on some people's faces that, you know, 'oh, she's got cancer.' Some of my friends stopped calling me. Some of them couldn't deal with it. And that's when I needed them the most." Christie, a twenty-four-year-old cancer survivor, had a similar experience. Some of her "best friends" just disappeared. "I don't know if having a good friend with cancer scares them or turns them off." After joining a cancer listserv, another survivor revealed, "I used to think I was an island."

In *Illness as Metaphor*, Susan Sontag referred to the "kingdom of the well" and the "kingdom of the sick." Illnesses such as AIDS, hepatitis, or cancer are especially likely to engender the feeling of being an outcast. Psychologist Oakley Ray quoted the late Mother Teresa: "Being unwanted is the worst disease that any human being can ever experience."

Openness and Trust. Psychologist James Pennebaker and his colleagues documented the health hazards of suppressing one's thoughts and feelings, particularly concerning serious or traumatic life experiences. Such containment stress can raise blood pressure, flood the body with harmful hormones, and even suppress the immune system. For example, among HIV-positive men, nondisclosure of important personal information has been related to more rapid disease progression. In particular, concealment of homosexual identity has been associated with unfavorable cellular immune changes, conversion from HIV to AIDS, and increased mortality.

For more than a decade, physician Redford Williams and his colleagues studied nearly 1,400 men and women undergoing cardiac catheterization for heart disease. At the start of their investigation, each participant was asked about his or her social support network. Those who could not list a single confidant were three times more likely to die within five years.

In one of the most cited studies pertaining to the mind-body effect, psychiatrist David Spiegel offered women who were diagnosed with advanced breast cancer a support-group experience. A control group received an identical level of medical care without a support group. On average, the survival time for the women who had participated in the support group was double that of the women in the control group. According to Spiegel, when this study was being conducted, there was not a single drug or other medical intervention that could promise the same degree of life extension. Repeatedly, the women in the support group talked about how hard it was to be strong for their husbands, their children, and other family members. At the same time, they expressed deep appreciation for having a time and a place to air their hopes and fears in a climate of trust and openness.

Suggestions for Attachment

To reduce the risk of social isolation or emotional congestion, aim for a support network that is solidly rooted in trust, provides a sense of belonging, and allows you to express your deepest hopes and fears. Here are some general suggestions:

- *Build a trust network.* Disclosure without trust may be ineffective, if not harmful. Researchers have found that highly cynical individuals who are not accustomed to opening up but who are in crisis tend to disclose too much too soon and increase their sense of vulnerability. Moreover, their immune systems are actually in a weaker state after they disclose. Seek out those with whom you can regularly and safely disclose your feelings.

- *Correspond.* Sending and receiving heartfelt letters, e-mails, or phone messages is another way to secure a measure of connected healing. Investigators have found that emotional intimacy can bring about a multitude of positive physiological changes, including lower blood pressure, decreased muscular tension, and increased immunity. James Pennebaker, who has done extensive research on writing for health, offers a number of suggestions. In particular, he discourages dry, factual summaries devoid of emotion, as well as the opposite extreme of hysterical outpourings of unprocessed feelings. According to Pennebaker, the most healing occurs when you write about the significant events in your life while expressing your deepest thoughts and feelings.

- *Join a support group.* Psychiatrist David Spiegel emphasizes that a support group should be uplifting. Attend a meeting and gauge your comfort level. Initially, you might feel a little anxious or awkward. This is normal. However, you should leave the first meeting sensing that the group is indeed a place for hope, providing empowerment, connection, and safety. According to Spiegel, "If you feel attacked or belittled, the group is doing something wrong. Find another one."

What constitutes a good support group? Would Aristotle have approved of the group's philosophy? In other words, does it revolve around the golden mean of balance? For example, while providing hope and encouragement, is the group also able to tolerate frank and honest discussions? Spiegel notes that it is doubly unfortunate if the group or leader is driven by a need to maintain an optimistic atmosphere and is therefore unable to allow the airing of realistic fears and concerns. Such a mind-set robs the members of badly needed support while also implying that some aspects of their illness are truly hopeless. Be wary of groups that promise a magic bullet rooted in simplistic positive thinking or that eschew a cynical approach to any form of traditional healing. However, also stay clear of those that blame the victim or suggest that recovery is purely a matter of adequate willpower.

There are many ways to find a support group. Your physician or local health center should be able to recommend a group that is geared toward your particular illness. You could also do an Internet search of your illness to find information on available support groups. Another option is to join a listserv or another Internet-based support group. An excellent example of online support is the Livestrong.org site associated with Lance Armstrong, where cancer survivors can share their stories and gather valuable healing suggestions.

If your attempts at finding a support group fail, consider individual psychotherapy. If you are feeling emotionally congested, seek out a therapist who is trained in either client-centered or emotion-focused therapy. Both approaches are designed to explore and clarify feelings in the present rather than facts from the past. If you are also struggling with depression or anxiety, make sure that your therapist has some familiarity with cognitive-behavioral techniques or can refer you to a professional who is skilled in modifying distress-provoking beliefs.

Monitor your authenticity. Deep healing requires an honest assessment of your inner and outer reality. Alistair Cunningham's research findings with long-term breast cancer survivors revealed three important chaerateristics: authenticity, autonomy, and support. James Pennebaker has also differentiated a superficial processing of life events, which he refers to as low-level thinking, from a mindful, fully aware coping style. The key is to move beyond denial or blind optimism to a place within you that is fully aware and resolutely committed to life.

One way to monitor your authenticity is through biofeedback. You could ask a trained practitioner to monitor one or more indicators of autonomic arousal such as skin conductance, heart rate, or finger temperature while you talk about your hopes and your fears. You may be telling yourself and others that things are just fine, but the feedback from your body might suggest otherwise. Pay particular attention to your skin conductance readings because increases can be indicative of inhibited stress responses. Authenticity will be evident when your verbal statements match your bodily feedback.

Suggestions for Spiritual Support

One of the most consistent findings in the mind-body literature is that individuals who attend a house of worship on a regular basis are healthier than those who never or rarely attend. They are less likely to suffer from cardiovascular disease or hypertension. They live longer after surgery. They have stronger immune systems. How can this phenomenon be explained?

Think about attendance at a church, temple, or mosque from the perspective of social support and health. In all likelihood, those who attend such services will derive additional reassurance and a deeper sense of belonging, as well as a consistent outlet for emotional expression. In short, regular immersion in a religious or spiritual tradition is apt to foster greater trust and openness, which in turn facilitates hope and healing.

One very obvious example of faith-based disclosure is the Catholic ritual of confession. However, every religious or spiritual tradition provides a context for some degree of emotional outpouring. The practitioners of Ifa, the Australian Dreamtimers, and the Lakota participate in vigorous singing and dancing rituals. Muslims kneel and chant openly while positioning their bodies in the direction of Mecca. The whirling dervishes of the Sufi sect spin themselves into an ecstatic embrace with God. Jews in Jerusalem pray before the Western Wall and place written prayers in its crevices; Jewish prayer in general involves swaying and chanting.

Authentic relating is another pathway through which religious or spiritual involvement can lead to better health. What makes a belief system spiritual is its centrality to an individual's sense of self. Harold Koenig found that both active involvement and deep faith are crucial for healing. If you want to enlist your spiritual beliefs in the healing process, strive for a fully authentic relationship with your centers of value (e.g., a higher power, loved ones, nature, science, or other people).

SURVIVAL: REGULATION AND LIBERATION

The physician should make every effort to ensure that all the sick should be most cheerful of soul and should be relieved of the passions of the psyche that cause anxiety.

—MAIMONIDES, *REGIMEN OF HEALTH* (1198)

Fear and anxiety can wreak havoc on the body and the mind. We noted previously that high levels of arousal can trigger the release of stress hormones, which in turn disrupt the immune system. A sense of helplessness or entrapment tends to diminish both the potency and the prevalence of cancer-fighting cells. For those who are already compromised by a serious illness or injury, fear and anxiety can retard the healing process, slowing the rate of recovery from wounds and infections. To reinforce these lessons, author Carol Orsborn has quoted from both Shakespeare ("frame your mind to mirth and merriment, which bars a thousand harms and lengthens life"), and the Book of Proverbs (17:22) ("A merry heart doeth good like a medicine; but a broken spirit drieth the bones"). Studies have shown that intense and prolonged fear or anxiety can suppress the immune system, extend hospital stays, raise blood pressure and blood sugar, and slow wound healing.

Balanced Healing

Indeed, chronic overarousal or a strong sense of entrapment can be hazardous to your health. When your sympathetic nervous system, which is responsible for the fight-or-flight response, is perpetually firing, it sabotages the healing process. However, it would be a mistake to presume that a total takeover by the competing relaxation response (parasympathetic dominance) would be ideal. On the contrary, rather than engendering a prolonged state of blissful relaxation, parasympathetic dominance can also be harmful, if not lethal. This is because there is a systemwide shutdown when humans or animals are confronted with a stressor that overwhelms their perceived resources and produces a seemingly intractable state of helplessness. In humans, such profound states of hopelessness can result in depression or even sudden death.

Although a sense of entrapment is detrimental, unpredictability can also spell disaster. For example, a great deal of research indicates that stressors exert more wear and tear on the mind and the body if they are unpredictable. In fact, sometimes the damage caused by unpredictability even trumps the stress of restraint. Physiologist Jay Weiss restrained three groups of rats in adjoining boxes. The first group was restrained but received no shocks, the second received a warning light and then a mild shock, and the third received a mild shock without a warning light. After a number of trials, the three groups were examined for ulcers. The rats that suffered only the stress of restraint showed, on average, one-millimeter-wide ulcers. The restrained rats that received a shock preceded by a warning light had two-millimeter-wide tears. However, the rats that were "shocked without warning" averaged ten-millimeter-wide tears.

Suggestions for Self-Regulation and Liberation

If you are dealing with a serious ailment but are unable to relax or free yourself from worry, then your attempts at healing might be seriously hampered. Anxiety is typically a twofold problem that consists of fearful thoughts coupled with high arousal and muscular tension. To achieve a deeper level of terror management, consider calming both your mind and body with the use of the following practices.

- *Practice focused meditation.* This is what most Westerners think of as meditation. It typically involves sitting in a cross-legged or kneeling position with eyes closed while repeating a sound or a mantra. This form of meditation is excellent for stilling and emptying an overactive mind that is cluttered with fear and doubt.
- *Don't neglect your body.* Personal terror management should be approached from the perspective of the body as well as the mind. You are less likely to worry when you are physically relaxed.

Consider some form of bodywork therapy that is designed to ease the tension and stress from your body while simultaneously massaging the psyche to unlock any negative emotions that might be interfering with healing. You can choose from a variety of approaches, including yoga, breathing-oriented meditations, or deep-tissue massages.

• *Find a "calm buddy."* We are profoundly impacted by the words, deeds, and feelings of those around us. Research by psychologist John Gottman has indicated that a single, brief dispute between spouses can cause increases in blood pressure and stress hormones for both of them that can last more than a day. In a related finding, children who passively observed their parents fighting also showed a dramatic rise in stress hormones. More recently, physiologists have identified mirror neurons in the temporal areas of the brain. When you observe an individual do, say, or feel something, these neurons fire, producing a host of physical and emotional changes that mirror what is happening to the other person. If you can surround yourself with at least one "calm buddy," you may share in the health benefits of his or her relaxed support.

• *Seek out a healer-physician.* There are numerous anecdotes about patients losing the will to live after a bad encounter with an insensitive physician. Make sure your doctor is a healer and not just a technician. Does he or she actually see "you" or are you treated merely as an object or "condition"? Would you consider him or her a "doctor of the soul," or is he or she functioning more like a passionless plumber or uninspired assembly-line worker?

To enhance your liberation beliefs, consider the following practices:

• *Practice insight meditation.* This form of meditation, which is derived from Theravada Buddhism, is becoming increasingly popular in the

West. The focus is on cultivating greater awareness, or mindfulness, rather than pure stillness. Buddhist scholar Shinzen Young describes it as the art of penetrating experience with awareness: "The awareness literally soaks into [mind and body] like water into a sponge. . . . Each phenomenon [is approached with] the six senses: hearing, seeing, smelling, tasting, the feeling body, and the thinking mind."

• *Be persistent.* Recall how Norman Cousins distilled his views on hope and healing into a simple eight-word phrase: "Do not deny the diagnosis; defy the verdict." Of course, in some cases, even a diagnosis is sometimes worth another look. Don't be shy about asking for a second or even a third opinion. You can also do your own research in a medical library or on the Internet (WebMD.com is an excellent resource). Take into account not only your specific illness but also your overall level of fitness, as well as other personal and social assets. If you have practiced a healthy lifestyle and enjoy other advantages such as good medical insurance or a large and caring network of family and friends, then your prognosis is likely to be far better than the average outcomes would indicate.

Suggestions for Spiritual Solace

A spiritual foundation can be deeply reassuring, offering a larger perspective, a trusting presence, and hope for some form of liberation, if not salvation. Dr. Harold Koenig has identified nearly three dozen scientific studies indicating that more religious individuals are significantly less anxious. For example, he reports that those who attend religious services more frequently have a diastolic blood pressure reading that is six points lower than that of nonattenders.

For decades, Dr. Herbert Benson promoted the benefits of a no-frills relaxation response. However, he later concluded that adding a "faith factor" derived from a "deeply held set of philosophical or religious convictions" could produce an even greater impact, leading to enhanced states of health and well-being. He suggested the following practice:

- Sit in a comfortable position.
- Close your eyes and relax your muscles.
- Focus on your breathing, inhaling for a count of four and exhaling for a count of six.
- Select a word or a prayer that reflects your spiritual beliefs.
- Maintain a receptive attitude.
- Practice for ten to twenty minutes, twice a day.

FINDING THE RIGHT COMBINATION

Table 10.2 lists some of the most prevalent medical conditions along with hope-based prescriptions that can aid in healing. Listed by condition, each prescription consists of recommended "dosages" of investments to be directed at strengthening one's attachment, mastery, and survival systems. Attachment activities include support groups, healing networks, couples therapy, clubs, and Internet chat rooms. Mastery activities include self-efficacy training, tai chi, Zen philosophy, and insight meditation (mindfulness). Survival activities include exercise, biofeedback, progressive muscle relaxation, breathing, meditation, and yoga. We computed the "dosages" by weighing both the quantity and the quality of mind-body research that has been conducted on a particular condition.

Table 10.2. Suggested Hope Prescriptions and "Dosages"

Condition	"Dosages" (Approximate Time & Energy Investments)		
	Attachment	Mastery	Survival
Cancer Cardiovascular disease	40%	10%	50%
Arthritis HIV or AIDS	33%	33%	33%
Diabetes Chronic pain Respiratory infections	20%	20%	60%
Gastrointestinal disorders Serious wounds or injuries	10%	10%	80%

These hope formulas might be compared to the compound strengths used to produce homeopathic remedies or the molecular formulas underlying prescription drugs. For example, if you had a headache, a doctor might recommend aspirin, which is made of nine parts carbon, eight parts hydrogen, and four parts oxygen. In contrast, if you were diagnosed with meningitis or pneumonia, the preferred treatment might be penicillin, which is composed of eleven parts hydrogen, nine parts carbon, four parts oxygen, two parts nitrogen, and one part sulfur.

Over the long run, a full hope, consisting of equal parts attachment, mastery, and survival investments, is likely to offer the most health benefits. However, when dealing with a specific medical condition, one or more of the hope motives may serve as an especially potent healing compound. For example, cancer patients seem to do best when they can lower their stress levels (survival system) and obtain high-quality social support (attachment system). Individuals who have been diagnosed with gastrointestinal problems or who are recovering from a serious wound or injury might be best served by focusing on stress reduction. HIV or AIDS patients and those dealing with arthritis should distribute their time and energy evenly across all three of the motives underlying hope. Naturally, like any good homeopath or apothecary, you may have to adjust your required "dosage" of attachment, mastery, or survival investments, depending on your particular needs.

Remember to maintain a working alliance with your healthcare provider. This should increase your sense of empowerment and connection while also providing additional degrees of freedom concerning treatment options. Regular physical exercise and the adoption of a healthy diet, along with the use of selected vitamins and minerals, can further boost your immune system.

A HEALING PHILOSOPHY

The best healer is also a philosopher.

—GALEN, 200 CE

We live in an era of highly focused treatment plans. Individuals are seen by specialists who deal exclusively with the heart or the lungs, the eyes or the throat, the bones or the tendons, the mind or the body. Indeed, it is not uncommon for a large metropolitan hospital to house several dozen clinics, each focused on a specific malady. Fyodor Dostoyevsky, one of the great "psychologists" of the nineteenth century, was frequently bemused by the cult of myopia that can often blind members of the medical profession. In *The Brothers Karamazov*, he even lampooned a physician who insisted on treating only the left nostril!

Specialized care is at its best when it offers a concentrated but comprehensive approach to treatment. In contrast, when specialization becomes fragmentation, healing is impeded. What is needed is a renewed commitment to what the ancients called the art or philosophy of healing. That is, you must complement your knowledge of hope-based healing strategies and prescriptions with an overarching set of principles. The key elements of this healing philosophy are what might be called the six *Cs* of healing: commitment, collaboration, combinations, care, connection, and courage.

Commitment

A few years ago, Tony counseled a young man whose father had died a few months after being diagnosed with cancer. In therapy, the man expressed a great deal of disappointment that his father had not "fought harder." Over time, he began to sense that his father had probably "accepted his fate" as "just punishment." A lay minister, his father had never been able to resolve his guilt over having abandoned his family for another woman. Moreover, he had repeatedly let his children down, including writing a bad check when his son first entered college.

Health and healing require a commitment to life. One of the lessons to be gleaned from the mind-body literature is that healing requires a sense of purpose. Individuals who have a life mission heal better and faster. Similarly, many survivors who have achieved unexpected recoveries from serious illnesses, such as advanced forms of cancer, have typically been characterized as authentic, autonomous, or fully involved.

Collaboration

Share the responsibility for your healing. Begin by making sure that your doctor is willing to develop a working alliance. If your condition is serious or otherwise resistant to treatment, make sure that your doctor is tenacious and persistent. Is he a true hope provider in the sense of being accessible, trustworthy, and responsive? Is she capable of instilling a sense of empowerment, trust, and reassurance? The poet Samuel Taylor Coleridge wrote, "He is the best physician who is the most ingenious inspirer of hope."

Tom Ferguson, a physician and nationally known expert on medical self-help, has recommended several strategies for cultivating an empowering doctor-patient partnership. First, plan for your visit by making a list of questions. Be assertive and, if necessary, consider getting a second opinion. Be a good observer of your symptoms and overall condition. Do not leave the doctor's office confused or with unanswered questions. If a medical test is ordered, do not be afraid to ask about the potential time involvement, risks, and implications.

Kim, a brain cancer survivor, wrote, "If someone tells you that you're not gonna survive and that they can't do anything more, find someone else. Find someone [who] will be encouraging. Even if they don't think that they can do anything, if they're willing to be there for you and encourage you. . . . I had one doctor [who] was doom and gloom, and another doctor came in and said, 'We're gonna beat it.' And I think he saved my life. I really do."

Second opinions are particularly useful when there are unexpected findings, the discovery of a very rare condition, a failure to obtain the usual treatment results, or conflicting feedback from different tests. Dr. Jerome Groopman's *Second Opinions* details eight case studies in which a second look made all the difference in the world.

Combinations

Do not limit your healing options by thinking exclusively in terms of traditional versus nontraditional therapies. There is considerable evidence that different types of interventions can complement one another to produce better outcomes. For example, meditation and other relaxation procedures can help to reduce nausea from chemotherapy, allowing an individual to tolerate the necessary dosage to destroy the cancer cells. Expand your range of healing possibilities by thinking in terms of complementary medicine as well as alternative approaches.

Alisa Gilbert, a breast cancer survivor, combined traditional chemotherapy with her own Native American detoxification rituals once her treatments had stopped. "The complementary therapies that I went through were some traditional Native ceremonial-type stuff: a purifying ceremony and this internal cleansing I did after my treatment to get the toxins out of my body. It was a turning point in the whole path to survivorship, because I could actually close that door. I was moving into wellness."

Care

Deep healing requires an investment in transforming your life. In *Care of the Soul*, Thomas Moore describes "a continuous process . . . of attending to the small details of everyday life as well as to major decisions and changes . . . to give ordinary life the depth and value that comes from soulfulness." Moore notes that the original Latin word for *cure* also means to *nurse*, in the sense of providing attention and devotion. Instead of shallow manipulations aimed at a quick fix, care for the soul involves ongoing involvement and a commitment to depth and observance.

Philosophers may have done the best job of illuminating the process of hopeful self-care. Paul Pruyser emphasized that hope should be viewed as a way of life rather than a short-term intervention. William F. Lynch stressed the importance of affirmation and acceptance. Gabriel Marcel likened hope to a form of active waiting sustained by an enlarged perspective and distinguishable from the psychic stiffening of obstinate denial. To foster your own hope-centered self-care, look beyond your symptoms for a larger lesson. Aim further than "fighting" the disease. Stay alert and informed, yet remain patient with yourself and others. With trust and openness, you will be prepared for every healing opportunity that comes your way.

Connection

You cannot heal in isolation. Remember that social support is often the most potent mind-body factor. Emotional ties rival smoking cessation in terms of reducing the odds of developing cancer. Love benefits the heart and blood vessels as much as any cholesterol-lowering drug does. Healthy attachments can serve as natural beta-blockers, calming your body while limiting the output of harmful stress hormones.

To reap the full health benefits of social support, you must strive to build relationships that are open and trusting, capable of fostering genuine emotional expression. The best support networks provide a complete hope that is empowering, loving, and reassuring. The women who took part in David Spiegel's breast cancer study found themselves discussing how best to deal with their doctors while also sharing their victories and defeats (mastery). They came to care deeply and personally about one another (attachment). The support group provided a setting in which they could face their concerns about loss and dying so that these and other fears did not dominate their lives (survival).

Courage

Confronting a serious illness often requires a heroic stance. There may be great physical pain and suffering as well as fears of permanent disability or even death. Even those who have enjoyed some degree of healing may be burdened with ongoing anxiety. In fact, many survivors may continue to feel as if the sword of Damocles is hanging overhead.

In public, some cancer survivors may quip that they have beaten the odds, but at a deeper level they may be asking themselves, "Will it recur?" or "Did the surgeon really get all of it?" or "If it does return, will it be worse?" Similarly, a heart attack survivor may anxiously wonder, "What if I have another incident and nobody is around to bring me to the hospital?" The trauma survivor may fear that another mugging, assault, or catastrophe is just around the corner.

Hope-based healing, unlike denial or blind optimism, requires true grit. It is no small feat to remain open, accepting, and engaged when confronting a frightening diagnosis, complex medical jargon, and painful procedures. Nevertheless, if you are dealing with a serious illness, there is a wealth of scientific evidence that supports an emboldened path. Perhaps Emerson put it best when he wrote, "The wise man in the storm prays to God; not for safety from danger, but for deliverance from fear."

Visit the website of the Lance Armstrong Foundation (http://www. livestrong.org). You will be able to read the personal testimonies of various cancer survivors and discover how each of them found a way to keep hope alive. Fully embodying the live-strong philosophy promoted by Armstrong's foundation, these survivors are truly profiles in courage. For example, Charles Fletcher, an octogenarian who survived two bouts of cancer, observed the following:

You know, it's just mind over matter. And if you have faith, which I have, it's a matter of saying, "Well, what is the greatest fear in the world? Dying? Well, I'm not afraid to die." So what's in between? Nothing . . . I got all kinds of medals in the hospital for walking up and down the hall with my little bottle. When I got home, I would treadmill. . . . Now I'm still lifting weights, and I'm going to keep lifting weights. . . . There's always hope.

HOPE AND WELLNESS

A desire for wellness is the great hope that lies behind every healing journey. John Keats, the frail and sickly poet of love, called health "my expected heaven." Lao Tzu labeled it "the greatest possession." The Roman Stoic philosopher Lucius Annaeus Seneca proclaimed health "the soul that animated all the enjoyments of life." Writer Thomas Carlyle wrote, "He who has health has hope."

Hope and wellness are intertwined. Being healthy is one of the key determinants of a hopeful attitude. It is far more difficult for individuals to be positive and upbeat when they are constantly fatigued or battling pain. However, it is also true that hope is essential for health. Having one or more reasons for living or, as Emerson called it, a "horizon," is a critical factor in sustaining health and wellness. Stripped of hope, human beings lose their incentive for self-care. Without dreams and forward-looking agendas, they abandon the pursuit of vitality. Rather than choosing life they opt to let themselves go.

Hope and Happiness

A true and deep experience of hope can also bring a richer and more lasting form of happiness beyond superficial or fleeting moments of "hurried excitement." Moreover, despite all the recent emphasis on "mindfulness" and "living in the moment," an exclusive focus on securing the "here and now" will never bring a lasting sense of peace or contentment. In contrast, a well-founded hope that bridges the past, present, and future can ensure joy, happiness, and pleasure for today and tomorrow, as well as for next year and beyond. In contemporary psychology, the research of Fred Bryant and Joseph Veroff on "savoring" comes the closest to our notion of a hope-centered happiness.

Hope-Based Fitness

Fitness-minded individuals tend to possess a hopeful outlook on life, because a healthy lifestyle tends to strengthen the same motive systems that underlie hope. Wellness derives from an adequate sense of mastery, loving and supportive relationships, and manageable levels of stress. These are also the pillars of hope.

At the same time, a hopeful mind-set can provide a powerful set of incentives for a regimen of healthy habits. Being fit is most compelling to an individual who values empowerment, intimacy, and self-regulation. Hopeful individuals are future-oriented. They look ahead and envision positive mastery, attachment, and survival experiences. These ever-present leaps in time propel an investment in staying fit.

Consider the impulse to exercise. What motivates an individual to begin and then maintain a regular program of exercise? One of the most important factors seems to be exercise imagery, mental pictures of present and future benefits of physical activity. Some individuals imagine becoming stronger, whereas others envision themselves more attractive or less prone to injury or disease. It is reasonable to assume that individuals who entertain a full complement of hope-related exercise imagery (benefits related to mastery, attachment, and survival) will be least vulnerable to abandoning a program of regular physical activity.

To test some of these ideas, Tony, in collaboration with Dr. Erica Checko, assessed the hopefulness of nearly 100 college students. In addition, each student was asked a series of questions dealing with exercise, diet, current height and weight, and smoking behaviors. Students who were rated as more hopeful were more likely to be involved in a regular program of exercise. In contrast, those who were the least hopeful were more likely to be in a "precontemplation" stage, which means that they were not even

thinking about beginning a program of exercise. In addition, greater hopefulness was associated with a more desirable body mass index (BMI),
greater consumption of fruits and vegetables, and fewer cigarettes smoked.

Exercise can strengthen the hope motives. Improved physical
endurance contributes to a generalized sense of mastery. When you are
feeling fresh and strong, nothing seems impossible; hope spirals forward.
In Shakespeare's *The Winter's Tale*, we read that "a merry heart goes all
day." In contrast, when you are tired, the smallest obstacles seem overwhelming. Football legend Vince Lombardi summed it up well: "Fatigue
makes cowards of us all."

Even in intellectual pursuits, the role of physical stamina should not
be underestimated. Your brain uses as much as one-fifth of all the energy
that is derived from food. The 1984 world championship of chess
between Anatoly Karpov and Gary Kasparov went on for several
months. In the process, Karpov lost more than twenty pounds. Thus,
even hope-based mastery that involves intellectual pursuits can be augmented by increasing overall fitness.

A commitment to physical health can facilitate greater emotional intimacy as well. Of course, there are various indirect social benefits from joining a neighborhood fitness center, including schmoozing around a water
fountain, or socializing before or after a group aerobics class. However,
there are deeper and more direct interpersonal gains. For example, being
more confident and comfortable in one's body makes it more likely that
you will experience contact comfort (like hugs and kisses). In addition,
regular exercise increases cardiovascular endurance and improves blood
flow, two important factors in greater sexual satisfaction.

With increased physical contact, there is a greater likelihood of releas-
ing oxytocin, the "cuddle hormone." Oxytocin release is especially
strong during sex and other forms of skin-to-skin contact, prompting

some scientists to invoke the notion of sexual healing. Oxytocin is presumed to act as a kind of stress buffer. Swedish scientists found that rats that were injected with oxytocin, compared to those that were not, demonstrated a greater tolerance for heat stress, lower blood pressure, better blood-sugar control, and increased immunity.

Exercise offers a particularly effective way to boost survival skills. Aerobic exercise can alleviate symptoms of anxiety. It can also limit allostatic load by reducing cardiovascular reactivity to stress and accelerating the return to the baseline after the introduction of an arousing stimulus. Investigators at the Cooper Institute in Dallas found that four months of aerobic activity, consisting of three to four moderate workouts per week, was effective in lowering blood pressure and stress hormone levels in hypertensive individuals.

Another way to boost your sense of mastery involves strength training. Working out with weights or engaging in other forms of muscle-building exercise can reinforce bones and joints while reducing fat and improving balance and coordination. Fitness programs can be combined with self-defense courses to provide an enhanced sense of personal safety.

Exercise is an excellent form of preventive medicine. Individuals who engage in a regular program of physical activity are less likely to have a stroke, to be diagnosed with heart disease, or to develop certain forms of cancer. When a serious illness or injury does occur, those who are in better physical condition tend to heal more rapidly and more thoroughly. For example, among individuals dealing with heart disease, diabetes, or multiple sclerosis, the best predictors of quality of life are maintaining an appropriate weight and involvement in ongoing physical activity.

The strong association among physical fitness, mental vitality, and life satisfaction is well documented in *Creative Fitness: Applying Health Psychology and Exercise Science to Everyday Life*, another book of Henry's. Countless studies deal with the benefits of an engaged and active lifestyle, including research in biology, kinesiology, health (such as sleep and nutrition findings), as well as psychology and sociology. While underscoring the importance of regular exercise and self-care across the life span, the research emphasizes that there are multiple paths to fitness (one size does *not* fit all). Those who adopt a mindful, creative approach to exercise and health will be most likely to fashion a personal training program that is able to address their particular mastery, attachment, and survival needs.

Hopeful Aging

The old who have gone before us are on a road
which we must all travel . . . it is good to
ask them about the nature of that road.

—SOCRATES, 400 BCE

Did you know that Estée Lauder launched her empire by marketing containers of a mysterious cream that she called "jars of hope"? Notwithstanding Lauder's business acumen, the true fountain of youth is not a growth hormone or Botox but an enduring sense of hope. It is normal and healthy to keep hope alive in the later years. Researchers at the Max Planck Institute of Human Development in Berlin found that even among people in their eighties and nineties, nearly three-quarters continued to add new hope domains to their life scripts. Moreover, those who stopped hoping and merely focused on maintenance concerns or fears showed a precipitous decline in life satisfaction.

Psychiatrist George Vaillant analyzed findings from the Harvard Study of Adult Development, a longitudinal study of life adaptation that began in 1938. Drawing on this extensive database, Vaillant provided a number of guideposts for successful aging, which he summarized in his book, *Aging Well*. In addition to promoting sound health habits, he underscored the following hope-sustaining processes: an ongoing curiosity, a continued emotional involvement in the life of others, and an ability to tolerate and make peace with the indignities of old age. These were among the most critical factors distinguishing the "happy-well" from the "sad-sick."

"The centrality of hope and love in lifespan development goes unchallenged," he wrote. "Regardless of the words, the melody is still the same; the last years of life without hope and love become a mere sounding brass or tinkling cymbal."

Other life-span investigators have also found that a commitment to mastery, attachment, and survival can foster positive aging as well as longevity. A research team at UCLA, headed by geriatric specialist Dr. David Reuben, found that older adults who were physically active had lower levels of Interleukin-6 and C-reactive protein, two markers of systemic inflammation. A study by gerontologist Terry Lum and his colleagues at the University of Minnesota indicated that older adults who volunteered a minimum of 100 hours a year enjoyed better health while reducing their risk of depression and premature death.

Attachments still matter. At Duke University, a group of older adults were asked to fill out a standard questionnaire that measured interpersonal trust. Eight years later, psychologist John Barefoot and his colleagues integrated this data with health and mortality findings derived from a series of follow-up studies. They found that those who had higher trust scores eight years before were more likely to still be alive and functioning well.

Religious and spiritual beliefs can bolster hope-based survival in the elderly. Psychologist Kevin Masters reported that intrinsically religious subjects sixty years and older were less likely to demonstrate a rise in blood pressure after an emotional stressor compared to their extrinsically religious counterparts. Moreover, there was no difference in stress tolerance between older and younger (eighteen to twenty-four) intrinsically religious individuals. Epidemiologist William J. Strawbridge and his colleagues studied the mortality patterns of more than 5,000 individuals who lived in Alameda, California, between 1965 and 1994. The mortality rate of those who attended religious services at least once a week was 36 percent less than that of those who never or rarely went to a house of worship.

Erik Erikson's last book, *Vital Involvement in Old Age*, dealt with the hopes of individuals in the final stages of the life cycle. Drawn from interviews with more than two dozen octogenarians, it shed light on the mastery, attachment, and survival strategies that help older adults to retain their sense of vitality. For example, to preserve a sense of mastery, some older individuals attended continuing education classes; others spent time gardening, cooking, or remodeling their homes.

Erikson and his coauthors noted some excellent examples of supported mastery. For example, a number of elders reported that they felt empowered to live more vigorous lives when they were introduced to a similarly independent roommate or community member. Many also emphasized that they were able to continue with their activities and hobbies because of the intergenerational support they received, from both children and grandchildren, in terms of assistance with household chores and paperwork as well as moral support and advice. In a rural area, an individual who was still able to drive transported his friends to a senior center. When the car was no longer big enough to accommodate everyone, he and his friends managed to buy and maintain a van; now those who still drive take turns at the wheel.

Hope-based attachments were especially cherished by these vital seniors. A common theme was absolute belief and unquestioning trust in loved ones. The family was perceived as an anchor in a world that is often tempestuous. As loved ones passed away, many of the seniors found inspiration and interpersonal security within a religious community, where, in the words of the authors, they might "find themselves looking up to the immortal heroes of religion and the timeless, infinitely trustworthy qualities they represent." Another powerful sense of attachment was derived from the preservation of residential continuity. Quite a few elders made sacrifices so they could remain in the same town or neighborhood. Part of their hope experience was rooted in a sense of place.

The survival skills of these resilient octogenarians included wise financial management as well as careful attention to diet and exercise. They also demonstrated the ability to recruit care from others, including children, grandchildren, and neighbors. Many sustained or even deepened their faith in God to fashion a sense of security in "some entity or order outside the self." Some spoke of a personalized "hope for generative confirmation . . . [a] hope to be remembered by the grandchildren after death [as] kind and loving or perhaps as a "fountain of wisdom."

On a more cosmic level, the most hopeful elders continued to express concern for the future. While proud of past contributions, such as raising healthy and productive children, they did not lose sight of present opportunities to further maintain the world. Moreover, as they passed on this torch of grand generativity, many proclaimed an unqualified faith in their children as future custodians of the world.

GOING FORWARD

Hope is about being as well as arriving. Hope is a way of life as well as a powerful tool for realizing desired endpoints. The most hopeful individuals achieve more than personal success. They answer Gandhi's challenge to be an instrument of positive change, to "become the hope of all mankind."

Earlier in this book we extolled the benefits of having a mission in life. A mission is a particularly creative way to actualize hope. It incorporates all three of the motives underlying hope: mastery, attachment, and survival. Moreover, it should be apparent that you do not have to be religious in the traditional sense to appreciate your individual gifts and learn how they might be used to create a more hopeful planet.

Underlying Aristotle's reference to the "inner design" of nature were notions of "matter" and "form." Everything in nature begins as matter but strives toward form. Over time, lower forms become the matter for higher forms. This upward spiral occurs because everything in nature is moved by an inner urge to become something greater than it is. Similarly, Ernest Becker wrote that the "heroic individual" willingly participates in a "metaphysic of hope" by "fashioning something . . . and dropping it into the forward momentum of life." In one way or another, all the great spiritual traditions have brought forth this same message: that men and women, young and old, rich and poor, must each do their part in repairing, strengthening, and upholding the world.

Erik Erikson's notion of "generativity" was rooted in secular humanism. Rick Warren's "purpose driven life" is Christian-based and God-centered. However, the basic premise is the same. *One of the best things you can do is to share your talent (mastery) in the service of others (attachment) while doing something of enduring value (survival).* In the same vein, we noted earlier in this book how Emerson encouraged his readers to view the universe as "the property of every individual in it."

In conclusion, we have repeatedly emphasized the role of empowerment, collaboration, and relationships in building and maintaining hope. With this in mind, we would like to offer some additional resources for you to consider. For those of you who wish to share your reactions to this book, please visit our website at: http://www.gainhope.

com. Our contact information is provided on page 413. On our website you will also find two extensive versions of the hope test: one that will help you to assess your current state of hope and another to gauge your general level of hopefulness. Your results will be automatically scored, and you will get a detailed report, explaining each of your subscores (mastery, attachment, survival, spirituality, etc.).

You may also want to read our earlier book, *Hope in the Age of Anxiety*, to learn more about the evolutionary, historical, cultural, and religious foundations of hope, as well as previous theories advanced by other scientists and scholars. This book also includes information for parents and other childcare providers (e.g., the development of hope and spirituality, and suggestions for nurturing hope) as well as a chapter on helping children suffering from hopelessness or helplessness.

EXERCISE 10: Take the Hope Post-Test

Now that you have reached the end of this book, we suggest that you complete the hope post-test below. When you finish the last question, you will find a self-scoring key that will help you to evaluate your current hope profile. The post-test will allow you to gauge how much of the "power of hope" you have absorbed, and which sections, if any, you might want to review. Specifically, we suggest you do a pre-test versus post-test comparison for your total hope score as well as your subscores for mastery, attachment, survival, a positive future, and spirituality.

Reflect on how you think, feel, and act most of the time. In other words, you should answer the questions below according to what is generally true of you. For example, if you have had an unusually good or bad week, put those thoughts and feelings aside and focus on your typical ways of thinking, feeling, and doing things.

Please use the following scale to answer each question.

Not Me	A Little Like Me	A Lot Like Me	Exactly Like Me
0	1	2	3

_____ 1. I can succeed in ways that are important to me.

_____ 2. I have a friend or family member who really listens to me.

_____ 3. I have ways of reducing my fears and worries.

_____ 4. Spiritual experiences are possible with the right attitude.

_____ 5. I depend on a committed parent, friend, or mentor for advice.

_____ 6. My spiritual beliefs provide me with a feeling of safety.

_____ 7. I'm hopeful about the future.

_____ 8. I believe in a benevolent (kind) higher power.

_____ 9. I'm uncomfortable around strangers.

_____ 10. My spiritual beliefs have empowered me to succeed in life.

_____ 11. I feel safe knowing there are people I can call in a time of crisis.

_____ 12. In the right environment, I can feel the presence of a spiritual force or a higher power.

_____ 13. I have made (or will make) a difference in this world.

_____ 14. When we die, there is a part of us that continues to live.

_____ 15. I will find ways to make my dreams come true.

_____ 16. There are people in my life that I completely trust.

_____ 17. I can stay calm under almost any set of circumstances.

_____ 18. I cannot imagine ever having a spiritual experience.

_____ 19. I do some of my best work when inspired by others.

_____ 20. I could never imagine relying on spiritual beliefs to manage fear or stress.

_____ 21. The future will bring opportunities for a better life.

Not Me	A Little Like Me	A Lot Like Me	Exactly Like Me
0	1	2	3

____ 22. There is a higher intelligence that guides life in a positive direction.

____ 23. I view life as an adventure and welcome new experiences.

____ 24. My goals can be achieved without prayer or "spiritual" assistance.

____ 25. I've had good success when seeking help from others.

____ 26. It's unlikely that I will ever experience a spiritual force or a "higher power."

____ 27. I have a reason to live.

____ 28. Immortality is a myth.

Scoring Your Hope Test

Step 1: Reverse the values for questions 9, 18, 20, 24, 26, 28 (i.e., if you put down 0, change it to 3; if you put 1, change it to 2; if you put 2, change it to 1; if you put 3, change it to 0).

Step 2: Calculate your Mastery Score: questions 1 + 5 + 15 + 19 = ____

Step 3: Calculate your Attachment Score: questions 2 + 9 + 16 + 23 = ____

Step 4: Calculate your Survival Score: questions 3 + 11 + 17 + 25 = ____

Step 5: Calculate your Positive Future Score: questions 7 + 21 = ____

Step 6: Calculate your Spiritual Hope Score:

questions 4 + 6 + 8 + 10 + 12 +

13 + 14 + 18 + 20 + 22 + 24 + 26 + 27 + 28 = ____

Step 7: Calculate your Nonspiritual Hope Score:

Mastery + Attachment + Survival + Positive Future = ____

Step 8: Calculate your Total Hope Score: Spiritual + Nonspiritual = ____

Interpreting Your Scores

HOPE Score	Average	Low Range	Medium Range	High Range
Mastery	8	0–6	7–8	9 and higher
Attachment	9	0–7	8–9	10 and higher
Survival	8	0–6	7–8	9 and higher
Positive Future	4	0–2	3–4	5 and higher
Spiritual Hope	34	0–30	31–37	38 and higher
Non-spiritual	27	0–23	24–31	32 and higher
Total Hope	60	0–53	54–67	68 and higher

References

Aaron, H. (1991). *I had a hammer: The Hank Aaron story*. New York: HarperCollins.

Abboud, S. K., & Kim, J. (2005). *Top of the class*. New York: Berkley Books.

Abdel-Khalek, A. M. (2002). Why do we fear death? The construction and validation of the reasons for death fear scale. *Death Studies*, 26(8), 669–680.

Abramson, L. Y., Metalsky, G. I., & Alloy, L. B. (1989). Hopelessness depression: A theory-based subtype of depression. *Psychological Review*, 96(2), 358–372.

Abramson, L. Y., Seligman, M. E. P., & Teasdale, J. (1978). Learned helplessness in humans: Critique and reformulation. *Journal of Abnormal Psychology*, 87, 49–74.

Ader, R., & Cohen, N. (1975). Behaviorally conditioned immunosuppression. *Psychosomatic Medicine*, 37(4), 333–340.

Alberti, R. E. & Emmons, M. L. (2008). *Your perfect right: Assertiveness and equality in your life and relationships*. Atascadero, CA: Impact Publishers.

Allport, G. W., & Odbert, H. S. (1936). Traitnames: A psycho-lexical study. *Psychological Monographs*, 47, (211), 171.

Alverson, H. (1994). *Semantics and experience: Universal metaphors of time in English, Mandarin, Hindi, and Sesotho*. Baltimore, MD: Johns Hopkins University Press.

American Psychiatric Association. (2000). *Diagnostic and Statistical Manual of Mental Disorders*. 4th ed. Arlington, VA: Author.

Ames, R. T., & Rosemont, H. (1999). *The analects of Confucius*. New York: Valentine Books.

Aquinas, T. (1989). *Summa theologiae*. Allen, TX: Christian Classics.

Armstrong, L. (2001). *It's not about the bike*. New York: Berkley Trade.

Arrington, R. L. (2001). *A companion to the philosophers*. Malden, MA: Blackwell Publishers.

Asanti, M. (1996). *African intellectual heritage*. Philadelphia: Temple University Press.

Associated Press. (2002). *Nine alive: The miraculous rescue of the Pennsylvania miners*. Champaign, IL: Sports Publishing LLC.

Averill, J. R. (1968). Grief: Its nature and significance. *Psychological Bulletin*, 70 (6), 721–748.

Averill, J. R., Catlin, G., & Chon, K. K. (1990). *Rules of hope*. New York: Springer-Verlag.

Averill, J. R., & Nunley, E. (1992). *Voyages of the heart: Living an emotionally creative life*. New York: The Free Press.

Bakhtiar, L. (1999). *Avicenna's canon of medicine*. Chicago: Abjad Book Designers and Builders.

Bandura, A. (1994). *Self-efficacy: The exercise for control*. New York: Freeman.

Bannister, R. (2004). *The four-minute mile*. Guilford, CT: Globe Pequot.

Barefoot, J. C., Maynard, K. E., & Beckham, J. C. (1998). Trust, health and longevity. *Journal of Behavioral Medicine*, 21 (6), 517–526.

Bassett. L. (1996). *From panic to power*. New York: HarperCollins.

Bean, W. B. (1968). *Sir William Osler, Aphorisms from his bedside teachings and writings*. Springfield, IL: Charles Thomas.

Beck, A. T. (1976). *Cognitive therapy and the emotional disorders*. New York: International Universities Press.

Beck, A. T., Weissman, A., Lester, D., & Trexler, L. (1974). The measurement of pessimism: The hopelessness scale. *Journal of Clinical and Counseling Psychology*, 42, 861–865.

Beck, J. (1995). *Cognitive therapy: Basics and beyond*. New York: Guilford.

Becker, E. (1973). *The denial of death*. New York: The Free Press.

Benson, H. (1985). *Beyond the relaxation response*. New York: Berkeley Books.

Besant, A. (2006). *Auguste Comte: His philosophy, his religion and his sociology*. Whitefish, MT: Kessinger.

Bethune, M. M. (1996). My last will and testament. In M. K. Assante & A. S. Abarry, *African intellectual heritage: A book of sources* (pp. 671–673). Philadelphia: Temple University Press.

Biller, H. B. (1971). *Father, child, and sex role: Paternal determinants of personality development*. Lexington, MA: Lexington Books.

Biller, H. B. (1974). *Paternal Deprivation: Family, school, sexuality and society*. Lexington, MA: Lexington Books.

Biller, H. B. (1993). *Fathers and families*. Westport, CT: Auburn House.

Biller, H. B. (2002). *Creative fitness*. Westport, CT: Auburn House.

Biller, H. B. & Meredith, D. L. (1974). *Father Power: The art of effective fathering and how it can bring joy and freedom to the whole family*. New York: David McKay.

Biller, H. B., & Solomon, R. (1986). *Child maltreatment and paternal deprivation: A manifesto for research, prevention, and treatment*. Lexington, MA: Lexington Books.

Biller, H. B., & Trotter, R. (1994). *The father factor: What you need to know to make a difference*. New York: Pocket Books (Simon & Schuster).

Binswanger, L., Mendel, W. M., & Lyons, J. (1958). The case of Ellen West: An anthropological clinical study. In R. May, E. Angel & H. F. Ellenberger, *Existence: A new dimension in psychiatry and psychology* (pp. 237–364). New York: Basic Books.

Bloch, E. (1970). *Man on his own: Essays in the philosophy of religion*. New York: Herder & Herder.

Bloch, E. (1986). *The principle of hope* (Vol. 3). Cambridge, MA: MIT Press.

Bodhi, B. (2005). *In the Buddha's words: An anthology of discourses from the Pali Canon*. Somerville, MA: Wisdom Publications.

Bolletino, R., & Leshan, L. (1997). Cancer. In A. Watkins, *Mind-body medicine: A clinician's guide to psychoneuroimmunology* (pp. 87–112). New York: Church-Livingstone.

Booth, R. J., & Ashbridge, K. R. (1993). A fresh look at the relationship between the psyche and immune system: Teleological coherence and harmony of purpose. *Advances*, 9(2), 4–23.

Borg, M. J. (1995). *Meeting Jesus again for the first time*. New York: HarperCollins.

Boswell, J. (1993). *The life of Samuel Johnson*. New York: Random House.

Boteach, S. (2006). *Parenting with fire*. New York: New American Library.

Boucher, S. (2000). *Hidden spring: A Buddhist woman confronts cancer*. Somerville, MA: Wisdom Publications.

Branden, N. (2008). *The psychology of romantic love: Romantic love in an anti-romantic age*. New York: Tarcher.

Breathnach, S. (1995). *Simple abundance: A daybook of comfort and joy*. New York: Warner Books.

Brehm, S. S. (1988). Passionate love. In R. J. Sternberg & M. L. Barnes, *The psychology of love* (pp. 232–263). New Haven, CT: Yale University Press.

Brodbeck, S., & Mascaro, J. (2003). *The Bhagavad-Gita*. New York: Penguin.

Brokaw, T. (2001). *The greatest generation*. New York: Random House.

Brooks, R., & Goldstein, S. (2002). *Raising resilient children: Fostering strength, hope, and optimism in your child*. New York: McGraw-Hill.

Browning, E. B. (2005). *The complete poetical works of Elizabeth Barrett Browning*. Whitefish, MT: Kessinger.

Bryant, F. B., & Veroff, J. (2006). *Savoring: A new model of positive experience*. Philadelphia, PA: Taylor and Francis.

Bulfinch, T. (1998). *Bulfinch's mythology*. New York: Modern Library.

Burns, D. D. (1999). *Feeling good: The new mood therapy*. New York: Harper.

Cahill, T. (1999). *The gift of the Jews*. New York: Random House.

Campbell, J. (1991). *The power of myth*. New York: Anchor Books.

Camus, A. (1958). *Exile and the kingdom*. New York: Knopf.

Carnegie, D. (1998). *How to win friends and influence people*. New York: Pocket Books.

Carson, R. (1964). *Silent spring*. New York: Fawcett Crest.

Carson, R. (1998). *Lost woods: The discovered writings of Rachel Carson*. Boston: Beacon Press.

Checko, E. R., & Scioli, A. (2007, March). *Hope, self-determination, stages of change, and health*. Paper presented at the annual midwinter meeting of Division 36 of the American Psychological Association, Philadelphia, PA.

Chopra, D. (2001). *How to know God*. New York: Random House.

Christy, R. (1893). *Proverbs, maxims and phrases of all ages*. New York: Putnam.

Cicero, M. (2005). *Tusculan disputations: On the nature of the gods and the commonwealth*. New York: Cosimo Classics.

Circles of air; Circles of stone. Information was retrieved March 5, 2007 from http://www.questforvision.com.

Cleary, T. (2004). *The Qur'an: A new translation*. Chicago: Starlatch.

Coan, J. A., Schaefer, H. S., & Davidson, R. J. (2006). Lending a hand: Social regulation of the neural response to threat. *Psychological Science*, 17(12), 1032–1039.

Cohen, K. (1999). *The way of qigong: The art and science of Chinese energy*. New York: Wellspring (Ballantine).

Cohen, K. (2006). *Honoring the medicine: The essential guide to Native American healing*. New York: Ballantine.

Coleman, G., Jinpa, T., and Dorie, G. (2007). *The Tibetan book of the dead*. New York: Penguin.

Coles, R. (1967). *Children of crisis: A study of courage and fear*. Boston: Little, Brown & Company.

Collison, D., Plant, K., & Wilkinson, R. (2000). *Fifty Eastern thinkers*. London: Routledge.

Comte, A. (2001). *Systems of positive polity.* Bristol, UK: Thoemmes Press.

Cook, J., Deger, S., & Gibson, L. A. (2007). The book of positive quotations. Minneapolis, MN: Fairview Press.

Cooper, I. (2008). *Up close: Oprah Winfrey.* New York: Puffin

Cousins, N. (1989). *Head first: The biology of hope.* New York: E. Dutton.

Covey, S. (2004). *The seven habits of highly effective people.* New York: The Free Press.

Crider, T. (1996). *Give sorrow words: A father's passage through grief.* Chapel Hill, NC: Algonquin Books.

Csikszentmihalyi, M. (1991). *Flow: The psychology of optimal experience.* New York: HarperPerennial.

Cunningham, A. J., Philips, C., Lockwood, G. A., Hedley, D. W., & Edmonds, C. V. I. (2000). Association of involvement in psychological self-regulation with longer survival in patients with metastatic cancer: An exploratory study. *Advances in Mind-Body Medicine,* 16(4), 276–286.

Cunningham, A. J., & Watson, K. (2004). How psychological therapy may prolong survival in cancer patients: New evidence and a simple theory. *Integrative Cancer Therapies,* 3(3), 214–229.

Dalton, D. (1996). *Mahatma Gandhi: Selected political writings.* Indianapolis, IN: Hackett Publishing Co.

Darabont, F. (2004). *The Shawshank Redemption: The shooting script.* New York: Newmarket Press.

Darwin, C. (2004). *The descent of man.* New York: Penguin.

Davidson, R. J., Pizzagalli, D., & Nitschke, J. B. (2002). The representation and regulation of emotion in depression: Perspectives from affective neuroscience. In I. H. Gotlib & C. L. Hammen, *Handbook of Depression* (pp. 219–244). New York: Guilford.

Davis, M., McKay, M., & Robbins-Eshelman, E. (2000). *The relaxation and stress reduction workbook.* Oakland, CA: New Harbinger.

De Becker, G. (1997). *The gift of fear.* New York: Dell.

De Bono, E. (1999). *Six thinking hats.* Boston: Back Bay Books.

Denson, E., Tattersall, I., van Couvering, J. A., & Brooks, A. (2000). *Encyclopedia of human evolution and prehistory.* New York: Garland.

de Saint-Exupéry, A. (1995). *The little prince.* Ware, Hertfordshire (UK): Wordsworth Classics.

Dickens, C. (2002). *Great expectations.* New York: Penguin.

Dickens, C. (2006). *David Copperfield.* New York: Penguin.

Dillard, A. (1990). *Three by Annie Dillard: The writing life, An American childhood, Pilgrim at Tinker Creek.* New York: HarperPerennial.

Donne, J. (1999). *Devotions upon emergent occasions and death's duel.* New York: Vintage.

Dostoevksy, F. (2006). *Crime and punishment.* New York: Penguin.

Dostoevsky, F. (2008). *The Karamazov brothers.* New York: Oxford University Press.

Durant, W. (1961). *The story of philosophy.* New York: Simon and Schuster.

Durkheim, E. (2007). *On suicide.* New York: Penguin.

Edelman, M. (2004, May). *Liberation of a blind survivor. The Braille Monitor,* 47, 5.

Edelman, M. W. (1993). *The measure of our success.* New York: HarperPerennial.

Eliot, T. S. (1968). *Four quartets.* Orlando, FL: Harcourt.

Emerson, R. W. (1910). *Journals of Ralph Waldo Emerson.* Boston, MA: Houghton-Mifflin.

Emerson, R. W. (1983). *Essays and lectures.* New York: Library of America.

Emmons, R. A. (1999). *The psychology of ultimate concerns.* New York: Guilford.

Emmons, R. A., & King, L. A. (1988). Conflict among personal strivings: Immediate and long-term implications for psychological and physical well-being. *Journal of Personality and Social Psychology, 54,* 1040–1048.

Emmons, R. A., & McCullough, M. E. (2003). Counting blessings versus burdens: An experimental investigation of gratitude and subjective well-being on daily life. *Journal of Personality and Social Psychology,* 84(2), 377–389.

Erikson, E. H. (1950). *Childhood and society.* New York: Norton.

Erikson, E. H. (1993). *Gandhi's truth: On the origins of militant nonviolence.* New York: Norton.

Erikson. E. H., Erikson, J. M., & Kivnick, H. Q. (1994). *Vital involvement in old age.* New York: Norton.

Fatunmbi, A. F. (1994). *Ibase orisa: Ifa proverbs, folktales, sacred history, and prayer.* New York: Original Publications.

Faulkner, R. (2000). *The Egyptian book of the dead: The book of going forth by day.* San Francisco: Chronicle Books.

Fenton, W. N. (1987). *The false faces of the Iroquois.* Norman, OK: University of Oklahoma Press.

Ferguson, T. (1993). Working with your doctor. In D. Goleman & J. Gurin, (Eds.), *Mind/body medicine* (pp. 429–450). New York: Consumer Reports.

Fischer, C. S. (1982). *To dwell among friends: Personal networks in town and city.* Chicago: University of Chicago Press.

Fowler, J. (1981). *Stages of faith.* San Francisco: HarperCollins.

Fowler, J. W. (1996). Pluralism and oneness in religious experience: William James, faith development theory, and clinical practice. In E. Shafranske (Ed.), *Religion and the clinical practice of psychology* (Vol. 1, pp. 165–186). Washington, DC: American Psychological Association.

Frank, J. (1968). The role of hope in psychotherapy. *International Journal of Psychiatry,* 5, 383–395.

Frankl, V. (1985). *Man's search for meaning.* New York: Washington Square Press.

Freud, S. (2008). *The interpretation of dreams.* New York: Oxford University Press.

Fromm, E. (1941). *Escape from freedom.* New York: Rinehart and Co.

Fromm, E. (1970). *The revolution of hope.* New York: Harper and Row.

Fromm, E. (2000). *The art of loving.* New York: HarperPerennial.

Fulghum, R. (2004). *All I really need to know I learned in kindergarten.* New York: Ballantine.

Fuller, R. C. (1996). Erikson, psychology, and religion. *Pastoral Psychology,* 44 (6), 371–384.

Garfield, P. *The universal dream key: The 12 most common dream themes around the world.* New York: HarperOne.

Garrett, D. (1995). *The Cambridge companion to Spinoza.* Cambridge, UK: Cambridge University Press.

Gates, H. L., & West, C. (2002). *The African-American century: How black Americans have shaped our country.* New York: The Free Press.

Gibran, K. (1970). *Sand and foam.* New York: Knopf.

Gibran, K. (1983). *The prophet.* New York: Knopf.

Gibson, W. (2002). *The miracle worker.* New York: Pocket Books.

Godfrey, J. J. (1987). *A philosophy of human hope.* Dordrecht: Martinus Nijhoff.

Goodall, J., & Berman, P. (2000). *Reason for hope.* New York: Grand Central Publishing.

Gorer, G. (1955, October). The pornography of death. *Encounter,* pp. 49–52.

Gottman, J. M. (1999). *The seven principles for making marriage work.* New York: Three Rivers Press.

Gottman, J. M. (2001). *The relationship cure.* New York: Three Rivers Press.

Gottschalk, L. A. (1974). A hope scale applicable to verbal samples. *Archives of General Psychiatry, 30,* 779–785.

Gottschalk, L. A. (1985). Hope and other deterrents to illness. *American Journal of Psychotherapy,* 39(4), 515–525.

Gotz, I. (1998). On inspiration. *Crossroads,* 48(4), 510–517.

Gould, S. J. (1982, June). The median isn't the message. *Discover,* 40–42.

Gray, F. C. & Lamb, Y. R. (2004). Born to win. *The authorized biography of Althea Gibson.* Hoboken, NJ: Wiley and Sons.

Greenberg, J., Solomon, S., & Pyszczynski, T. (1997). Terror management theory and self-esteem and cultural worldviews. In M. Zanna (Ed.), *Advances in experimental social psychology* (pp. 61–139). San Diego, CA: Academic Press.

Greer, S. (1999). Mind-body research in psycho-oncology. *Advances in Mind-Body Medicine,* 15(4), 236–244.

Griffith, G. (2005). *Will's choice.* New York: HarperCollins.

Groopman, J. (2001). *Second opinions.* New York: Penguin.

Hadas, M. (1982). *The complete plays of Sophocles.* New York: Bantam Classics.

Hafen, B. Q., Karren, K. J., Frandsen, K. J., & Smith, N. L. (1996). *Mind-body health.* Boston: Allyn & Bacon.

Hall, C. S., & Van De Castle, R. L. (1966). *The content analysis of dreams.* New York: Appleton-Century-Crofts.

Hall, G. S. (1897). A study of fears. *American Journal of Psychology,* 8(2), 147–249.

Hamilton, M. B. (1998). *Sociology and the world's religions.* New York: St. Martin's Press.

Hanh, N. T. (2002). *Looking deeply: Mindfulness and meditation.* Berkeley, CA: Parallax Press. [Audio CD].

Harlow, H. F. (1958). The nature of love. *American Psychologist,* 13(12), 673–685.

Hart, T. (2000). Inspiration as transpersonal knowing. In T. Hart, P. L. Nelson, & K. Puhakka (Eds.), *Transpersonal knowing: Exploring the horizon of consciousness* (pp. 31–53). Albany, NY: State University of New York Press.

Hartmann, F. (1902). *The life and doctrines of Paracelsus.* New York: The Theosophical Publishing Co.

Havel, V. (1995). The need for transcendence in the post-modern world. *The Journal for Quality and Participation,* 18(5), 26–29.

Havel, V. (2004). An orientation of the heart. In P. R. Loeb (Ed.), *The impossible will take a little while* (pp. 82-89). New York: Basic Books.

Hegel, G. W. F. (1979). *Phenomenology of the spirit.* New York: Oxford University Press.

Heinrich, B. (2003). *Winter world: The ingenuity of animal survival.* New York: HarperPerennial.

Helminski, K. (1998). *The Rumi collection.* Boston: Shambhala Publications.

Hemingway, E. (1995). *A farewell to arms.* New York: Scribner's.

Hendrix, H. (1993). *Keeping the love you find.* New York: Pocket Books.

Herman, J. L. (1997). *Trauma and recovery.* New York: Basic Books.

Herrigel, E. (1999). *Zen in the art of archery.* New York: Vintage.

Herth, K. (1991). Development and refinement of an instrument to measure hope. *Scholarly Inquiry for Nursing Practice,* 5(1), 39–51.

Hesse, H. (1977). *Steppenwolf.* New York: Bantam.

Higgins, G. O. (1994). *Resilient adults.* San Francisco: Jossey-Bass.

Hill, N. (2004). *Think and grow rich*. San Diego, CA: Aventine.

Holmes, L. (1967). *More than a game*. New York: MacMillan.

Homes, H. A. (2003). *Alchemy of happiness*. Whitefish, MT: Kessinger.

Hooker, R. (1995). Building unbreakable units. *Military Review*, 75(4), 23–25.

Horner, M. (1972). Toward an understanding of achievement-related conflicts in women. *Journal of Social Issues*, 28(2), 92–95.

Hume, R. E. (1921). *The thirteen principal Upanishads: Translated from the Sanskrit with an outline of the philosophy of the Upanishads and an annotated bibliography*. London: Oxford University Press.

Humez, J. M. (2003). *Harriet Tubman: The life and the life stories*. Madison, WI: University of Wisconsin Press.

Jacobus, L. A. (1983). *A world of ideas*. New York: St. Martin's Press.

James, W. (1961). *The varieties of religious experience*. New York: Collier Books.

James, W. (2007). *What is an emotion?* Radford, VA: Wilder Publications.

Jarovsky, B. (1996). *Hoop dreams: The true story of hardship and triumph*. New York: Harper.

Joiner, T. E. (2002). Depression in its interpersonal context. In I. H. Gotlib & C. L. Hammen, *Handbook of Depression* (pp. 295–313). New York: Guilford.

Joseph, L. (1999). *Little girl lost*. New York: Random House.

Jowett, B. (1999). *The essential Plato*. New York: Quality Paperback Book Company.

Jung, C. G. (1968). *Man and his symbols*. New York: Dell.

Kabat-Zinn, J. (1990). *Full catastrophe living: Using the wisdom of your body and mind to face stress, pain, and illness*. New York: Dell Publishers.

Kant, I. (1957). *Perpetual Peace*. Upper Saddle River, NJ: Bobbs-Merrill.

Kant, I. (2001). *Lectures on ethics*. Cambridge, UK: Cambridge University Press.

Keating, T. (2006). *Open mind open heart: The contemplative dimension of the gospel*. New York: Continuum International Publishing Group.

Kiecolt-Glaser, J. K., & Glaser, R. (1993). Mind and immunity. In D. Goleman & J. Gurin, (Eds.), *Mind/body medicine* (pp. 39–59). New York: Consumer Reports.

Kirkpatrick, L. A. (1999). Attachment and religious representations and behavior. In J. Cassidy & R. Shaver (Eds.), *Handbook of attachment* (pp. 803–822). New York: Guilford.

Kirkpatrick, L. A., & Shaver, R. (1992). An attachment-theoretical approach to romantic love and religious belief. *Personality and Social Psychology Bulletin*, 18(3), 266–275.

Kirshenbaum, M. (1997). *Too good to leave, too bad to stay*. New York: Plume.

Kobasa, S. C. (1979). Stressful life events, personality, and health: An inquiry into hardiness. *Journal of Personality and Social Psychology*, 37(1), 1–11.

Koenig, H. G. (2001). *The healing power of faith*. New York: Simon & Schuster.

Koenig, H. G., & Cohen, H. J. (Eds.). (2001). *The link between religion and health: Psychoneuro-immunology and the faith factor*. New York: Oxford University Press.

Kohut, H. (1971). *The analysis of the self*. New York: International Universities Press.

Kovic, R. (1990). *Born on the fourth of July*. New York: Pocket Books.

Kushner, H. S. (2002). *Living a life that matters*. New York: Anchor Press.

Lamott, A. (1995). *Bird by bird: Some instructions on writing and life*. New York: Anchor Press.

Langer, E., & Rodin, J. (1976). The effects of choice and enhanced personal responsibility for the aged: A field experiment in an institutional setting. *Journal of Personality and Social Psychology*, 34(2), 191–198.

Larson, R. W. & Bradney, N. (1988). Precious moments with family members and friends. In T. Lewis, F. Amini, & R. Lannon, (2001). *A general theory of love*. New York: Vintage.

Lifton, R. J. (1991). *Death in life: Survivors of Hiroshima*. Chapel Hill, NC: University of North Carolina Press.

Lifton, R. J. (1996). *The broken connection: On death and the continuity of life*. Arlington, VA: American Psychiatric Publishing.

Linehan, M. (1993). *Cognitive-Behavioral Treatment of Borderline Personality Disorder*. New York: Guilford Press.

Link, M. S. (1998). *The pollen path: A collection of Navajo myths*. Walnut, CA: Kiva Publishing.

Lloyd, G. E. R. (1984). *Hippocratic writings*. New York: Penguin.

Lum, T. Y., & Lightfoot, E. (2005). The effects of volunteering on the physical and mental health of older people. *Research on Aging*, 27 (1), 31–55.

Lynch, W. F. (1965). *Images of hope: Imagination as healer of the hopeless*. Baltimore, MD: Helicon Press.

Maddi, S. (2004). Hardiness: An operationalization of existential courage. *Journal of Humanistic Psychology*, 44(3), 279–298.

Maddox, B. (2003). *Rosalind Franklin: The dark lady of DNA*. New York: HarperCollins.

Marcel, G. (1962). *Homo viator: Introduction to a metaphysic of hope*. New York: Harper and Row.

Masters, K. (2005). *Role development in professional nursing*. Sudbury, MA: Jones and Bartlett.

Masters, K. S., Hill, R. D., & Kircher, J. C. (2004). Religious orientation, aging, and blood pressure reactivity to interpersonal and cognitive stressors. *Annals of Behavioral Medicine*, 28(3), 171–178.

Maxwell, J. C. (2006). *Winning with people*. Nashville, TN: Thomas Nelson Publishers.

May, R. (1950). *The meaning of anxiety*. New York: The Ronald Press.

May, R. (1999). *Freedom and destiny*. New York: Norton.

May, R. (2007). *Love and will*. New York: Norton.

McCain, J., & Salter, M. (2008). *Why courage matters: The way to a braver life*. New York: Ballantine Books.

McCasland, D. (2004). *Eric Liddell: Pure gold*. Grand Rapids, MI: Discovery House Publishers.

McClelland, D. C. (1961). *The achieving society*. New York: Macmillan.

McClelland, D. C. (1986). Some reflections on the two psychologies of love. *Journal of Personality*, 2, 334–353.

McClelland, D. C. (1989). Motivational factors in health and disease. *American Psychologist*, 44(4), 675–683.

McClelland, D. C., & Krishnit, C. (1988). The effects of motivational arousal through films on salivary immunoglobulin A. *Psychology and Health*, 2(1), 31–52.

McEwen, B. S. (1999). Protective and damaging effects of stress mediators. In I. Kawachi, B. Kennedy, & R. G. Wilkinson (Eds.), *The society and population health reader* (pp. 379–392). New York: The New Press.

McKeon, R. (1941). *The basic works of Aristotle*. New York: Random House.

Mellor, C. M. (2006). *Louis Braille: A touch of genius*. Boston: National Braille Press.

Menninger, K. (1959). Hope. *Bulletin of the Menninger Clinic*, 51(5), 447–462.

Meriwether, J. (2004). *William Faulkner: Essays, speeches and public lectures*. New York: Random House.

Merton, T. (1999). *Thoughts in solitude*. New York: Farrar, Straus & Giroux.

Metcalf, L. (2007). *The miracle question: Answer it and change your life*. Carmarthen, Wales: Crown House Publishing.

Mikulincer, M., Florian, V., & Hirschberger, G. (2004). The terror of death and the quest for love: An existential perspective on close relationships. In J. Greenberg, S. L. Koole, & T. Pyszczynski (Eds.), *Handbook of Experimental Existential Psychology* (pp. 287–304). New York: Guilford Press.

Miller, A. A. (1996). *Death of a salesman.* New York: Viking.

Milton, J. (2003). *Paradise lost.* New York: Penguin.

Mishra, R. (2002, September). Trials continue in a different form. *The Boston Globe*, A1.

Moberg, K .U. (2003). *The oxytocin factor: Tapping the hormone of calm, love, and healing.* Cambridge, MA: Da Capo.

Moberg, K. U., Arn, I., & Magnusson, D. (2005). The psychobiology of emotion: The role of the oxytocinergic system. *International Journal of Behavioral Medicine, 25*(2), 59–65.

Moffat, M. J. (1992). *In the midst of winter.* New York: Vintage.

Moltmann, J. (1993). *Theology of hope.* Minneapolis, MN: Augsberg Press.

Money, J. (1988). *Lovemaps.* New York: Irvington.

Monte, C., & Sollod, R. (2003). *Beneath the mask: An introduction to theories of personality.* New York: Wiley.

Montville, L. (2005). *Ted Williams: The biography of an American hero.* New York: Broadway Books.

Moore, T. (1992). *Care of the soul.* New York: HarperCollins.

Musa, M. (2003). *The portable Dante.* New York: Penguin.

Netherlands Institute for War Documentation. (2003). *The diary of Anne Frank: The revised critical edition.* New York: Doubleday.

Nietzsche, F. (1996). *Human, all too human: A book for free spirits.* Cambridge, UK: Cambridge University Press.

Nietzsche, F. (2006). *Thus spoke Zarathustra.* Cambridge, UK: Cambridge University Press.

Oden, M. B. (1995). *One hundred meditations on hope.* Nashville, TN: Upper Room Books.

O' Hahn, C. (2001). Be the change you wish to see: An interview with Arun Gandhi. *Reclaiming Children and Youth, 10*(1), 6.

O' Hanlon, B. (2000). *Do one thing different.* New York: Harper.

Olson, J. M., Vernon, A., Harris, J. A., & Jang, K. (2001). The heritability of attitudes: A study of twins. *Journal of Personality and Social Psychology, 80*(6), 845–860.

Ordoubadian, R. (2006). *The poems of Hafiz.* Bethesda, MD: IBEX.

Ornstein, R. (1992). *Evolution of consciousness: The origins of the way we think.* New York: Simon and Schuster.

Orwell, G. (1961). *The Orwell reader.* Orlando, FL: Harcourt-Brace & Co.

Pardee, M. B. (1979). The friendship bond. *Psychology Today,* 13(4), 43–54.

Pargament, K. I. (2001). *The psychology of religion and coping: Theory, research, and practice.* New York: Guilford Press.

Peale, N. V. (2007). *The power of positive thinking.* New York: Fireside Press.

Pennebaker, J. W. (1990). *Opening up: The healing power of confiding in others.* New York: Avon Books.

Perkins, D. N. (1981). *The mind's best work: A new psychology of creative thinking.* Cambridge, MA: Harvard University Press.

Pert, C. (1999). *Molecules of emotion: The science behind mind-body medicine*. New York: Simon & Schuster.

Philips, D. P., Ruth, T. E., & Wagner, L. M. (1993). Psychology and survival. *Lancet, 342*, 1142–1145.

Pogrebin, L. C. (1988). *Among friends: Who we like, why we like them, and what we do with them*. New York: McGraw-Hill.

Pope John Paul II (1994). *Crossing the threshold of hope*. New York: Alfred A. Knopf.

Poussaint, A. F., & Alexander, A. (2000). *Lay my burden down*. Boston: Beacon Press.

Prabhavanada, S., & Manchester, F. (2002). *The Upanishads: Breath of the eternal*. New York: Signet Classics.

Pruyser, W. (1986). Maintaining hope in adversity. *Pastoral Psychology, 35*, 120–131.

Pruyser, W. (1990). Hope and despair. In R. J. Hunter (Ed.), *Dictionary of pastoral care and counseling* (pp. 532–534). Nashville, TN: Abingdon Press.

Rampersad, A. (1994). *Days of grace (a memoir)*. New York: Ballantine Books.

Rand, A. (1996). *The fountainhead*. New York: Penguin.

Rand, A. (1999). *Atlas shrugged*. New York: Penguin.

Rando, T. (1984). *Grief, dying and death*. Champaign, IL: Research Press.

Rando, T. (1991). *How to go on living when someone you love dies*. New York: Bantam.

Rappaport, H., Fossler, R. J., Bross, L. S., & Gilden, D. (1993). Future time, death anxiety and life purpose among older adults. *Death Studies, 17*(4), 369–379.

Ray, O. (2004). How the mind hurts and heals the body. *American Psychologist, 59*(1), 29–40.

Reisfield, G. M., & Wilson, G. R. (2004). Use of metaphor in the discourse on cancer. *Journal of Clinical Oncology, 22*(19), 4024–4027.

Reuben, D. B., Judd-Hamilton, L., Harris, T. B., & Seeman, T. E. (2003). The associations between physical activity and inflammatory markers in high-functioning older persons. *Journal of the American Geriatrics Society, 51*(8), 1125–1130.

Richardson, C. (2003). *Stand up for your life*. New York: The Free Press.

Richter, C. (1959). The phenomenon of unexplained sudden death in animals and man. In H. Feifel (Ed.), *The meaning of death* (pp. 302–316). New York: McGraw-Hill.

Robbins, A. (1992). *Awaken the giant within*. New York: Fireside.

Rogers, C. (1951). *Client-centered therapy: Its current practice, implications and theory*. London: Constable.

Rokeach, M. (2000). *Understanding human values*. New York: The Free Press.

Rosen, G. (1971). History in the study of suicide. *Psychological Medicine, 1*(4), 267–285.

Rothbaum, F., Weisz, J. R., & Snyder, S. S. (1982). Changing the world and changing the self: A two-process model of perceived control. *Journal of Personality and Social Psychology, 42*(1), 5–37.

Russell, B. (1967). *Why I am not a Christian and other essays on religion and related subjects*. New York: Simon & Schuster.

Russell, B. (1972). *Unpopular essays*. New York: Simon & Schuster.

Russell, B. (2000). *The autobiography of Bertrand Russell*. London: Routledge.

Ryan, R. M., & Deci, E. L. (2000). Self-determination theory and the facilitation of intrinsic motivation. *American Psychologist, 55*(1), 68–78.

Sagan, C. (1985). *Cosmos*. New York: Ballantine.

Sagan, C. (1996). *The demon-haunted world: Science as a candle in the dark*. New York: Ballantine.

Sartre, J. (1989). *No exit and three other plays*. New York: Vintage.

Schwartz, M. (1997). *Morrie: In his own words*. New York: Delta.

Scioli, A. (1990). The development of hope and hopelessness: Structural and functional aspects. *Dissertation Abstracts International*, 52(1-B), 544–545.

Scioli, A. (2007). Hope and spirituality in the age of anxiety. In R. Estes (Ed.), *Advancing quality of life in a turbulent world* (pp. 135–152). New York: Springer.

Scioli, A. (2009). *Hope, emotional regulation, and transcendent time perspective*. Poster presented at the annual mid-winter meeting of Division 36 of the American Psychological Association, Loyola College, Columbia, MD, April 1.

Scioli, A., & Biller, H. B. (2009). *Hope in the age of anxiety*. New York: Oxford.

Scioli, A., McNeil, S., & Partridge, V. (2008). *Hope, HIV, and immunity*. Paper presented at the Annual Meeting of the American Psychological Association, Boston, MA.

Scioli, A., Chamberlin, C. M., Samor, C. M., Lapointe, A. B., Campbell, T. L., & Macleod, A. R. (1997). A prospective study of hope, optimism, and health. *Psychological Reports*, 81, 723–733.

Scioli, A., McClelland, D. C., Weaver, S. L., & Madden, E. M. (2000). Coping strategies and integrative meaning as moderators of chronic illness. *International Journal of Aging and Human Development*, 5(2), 115–136.

Scudder, V. D. (1892). *Shelley's Prometheus unbound: A lyrical drama*. Boston, MA: Heath & Co.

Seligman, M. E. (1975). *Helplessness*. San Francisco: Freeman Press.

Shakespeare, W. (1997). *The complete works of William Shakespeare*. London: Wordsworth.

Shipler, D. K. (2005). *The working poor: Invisible in America*. London: Vintage.

Shneidman, E. (1999). Perturbation and lethality: A psychological approach to assessment and intervention. In D. Jacobs (Ed.), *The Harvard Medical School guide to suicide assessment* (pp. 83–97). San Francisco: Jossey-Bass.

Siegel, B. S. (1986). *Love, medicine, and miracles*. New York: Harper & Row.

Siegel, B. S. (1993). *How to live between office visits*. New York: HarperCollins.

Simonton, D. K. (1994). *Greatness: Who makes history and why*. New York: Guilford.

Simpson, J., & Weiner, E. (Eds.) (1989). *The Oxford English Dictionary*. New York: Oxford University Press.

Singer, P. N. (1997). *Galen: Selected works*. New York: Oxford University Press.

Skinner, B. F. (2005). *Walden two*. Indianapolis, IN: Hackett Publishing Co.

Smith, H. (1986). *The religions of man*. New York: Harper and Row.

Smith, H. (2001). *Why religion matters*. New York: HarperOne.

Snyder, C. R. (1989). Reality negotiation: From excuses to hope and beyond. *Journal of Social and Clinical Psychology*, 18(2), 130–157.

Snyder, C. R. (1994). *The psychology of hope*. New York: The Free Press.

Snyder, C. R., Harris, C., Anderson, J. R., Holleran, S. A., Irving, L. M., Sigmon, S. T., Yoshinobu, L., Langelle, C., & Harney, P. (1991). The wills and ways: Development and validation of an individual differences measure of hope. *Journal of Personality and Social Psychology*, 60(4), 570–585.

Solomon, A. (2002). *The noonday demon: An atlas of depression*. New York: Touchstone.

Somers, J. M., Goldner, E. M., Waraich, P., & Hsu, L. (2006). Prevalence and incidence studies of anxiety disorders: A systematic review of the literature. *Canadian Journal of Psychiatry*, 51 (2), 100–113.

Sontag, S. (2002). *Illness as metaphor and AIDS and its metaphors*. New York: Penguin.

Spence, J. (1998, April 13). Mao Zedong. *Time*, 151(14), 148–150.

Spiegel, D. (1993). Social support: How friends, family, and groups can help. In D. Goleman & J. Gurin, (Eds.), *Mind-body medicine* (pp. 331–349). Yonkers, NY: Consumer Reports Books.

Spiegel, D., Bloom, J. R., Kraemer, H. C., & Gottheil, E. (1989). Effect of psychosocial treatment on survival of patients with metastatic breast cancer. *Lancet, 2,* 888–891.

Spinoza, B. (2005). *Ethics.* London: Penguin.

Spradlin, S. (2003). *Don't let your emotions run your life: How dialectical behavior therapy can put you in control.* Oakland, CA: New Harbinger Publications.

Stein, B. (2007). *On being moved: From mirror neurons to empathy.* Amsterdam, Netherlands: Johns Benjamin Publishing Company.

Steinbeck, J. (2002). *East of Eden.* New York: Penguin.

Steinbeck, J. (2002). *The grapes of wrath.* New York: Penguin.

Stone, I., & Stone, J. (1995). *Dear Theo: The autobiography of Vincent van Gogh.* New York: Penguin.

Stotland, E. (1969). *The psychology of hope.* San Francisco: Jossey-Bass.

Strawbridge, W. J., Shema, S. J., & Cohen, R. D. (2001). Religious attendance increases survival by improving and maintaining good health behaviors, mental health, and social relationships. *Annals of Behavioral Medicine, 23*(1), 68–74.

Stroebe, M., Gergen, M., Gergen, K., & Stroebe, W. (1996). Broken hearts or broken bonds? In D. Klass, P. R. Silverman, & S. L. Nickman (Eds.), *Continuing bonds: New understandings of grief* (pp. 31–44). Philadelphia: Taylor & Francis.

Styron, W. (1992). *Darkness visible: A memoir of madness.* New York: Vintage.

Sutich, A., & Vich, M. A. (1969). *Readings in humanistic psychology.* New York: The Free Press.

Swann, B. (1996). *Coming to light: Contemporary translations of the native literatures of North America.* New York: Vintage.

Taylor, S. E., Repetti, R. L., & Seeman, T. (1999). What is an unhealthy environment and how does it get under the skin? In I. Kawachi, B. Kennedy, & R. G. Wilkinson (Eds.), *The society and population health reader* (pp. 351–378). New York: The New Press.

Tennyson, A. L. (1973). *Selected poems.* New York: Oxford University Press.

Teresa, M. (2002). *No greater love.* Novato, CA: New World Library.

Terkel, S. (2003). *Hope dies last: Keeping the faith in difficult times.* New York: The New Press.

Tiger, L. (1979). *Optimism: The biology of hope.* New York: Simon & Schuster.

Tillich, P. (2001). *Dynamics of faith.* New York: HarperPerennial.

Tolle, E. (1999). *The power of now.* Novato, CA: New World Library.

Tolstoy, L. (1981). *The death of Ivan Ilych.* New York: Bantam.

Tolstoy, L. (1987). *A confession and other religious writings.* New York: Penguin.

Tolstoy, L. (1997). *War and peace.* Lincolnwood, IL: NTC Contemporary Publishers.

Tolstoy, L. (2006). *The death of Ivan Ilych.* West Valley City, UT: Waking Lion Press.

Torricelli, R. G., & Carroll, A. (2000). *In our own words: Extraordinary speeches of the American century.* New York: Washington Square Press.

Troyat, H. (2001). *Tolstoy.* New York: Grove Press.

Tzu, S. (2003). *The art of war.* New York: Barnes and Noble Classics.

Vaillant, G. (1993). *The wisdom of the ego.* Cambridge, MA: Harvard University Press.

Vaillant, G. (2003). *Aging well: Surprising guideposts to a happier life from the landmark Harvard study of adult development.* Boston: Little, Brown.

Vygotsky, L. (1986). *Thought and language.* Cambridge, MA: MIT Press.

Waley, A. (1958). *The way and its power: Lao Tzu's Tao Te Ching and its place in Chinese thought*. New York: Grove Press.

Walker, A. (1982). *The color purple*. Orlando, FL: Harvest Books.

Walter, T. (1996). A new model of grief: Bereavement and biography. *Mortality*, 1(1), 7–25.

Warren, R. (2002). *The purpose driven life*. Grand Rapids, MI: Zondervan.

Washington, J. (1990). *A testament of hope: The essential writings and speeches of Martin Luther King, Jr*. New York: HarperOne.

Weiss, J. M. (1970). Somatic effects of predictable and unpredictable shock. *Psychosomatic Medicine*, 32 (4), 397–408.

West, C. (1999). *Restoring hope*. Boston: Beacon Press.

White, R. W. (1959). Motivation reconsidered: The concept of competence. *Psychological Review*, 66, 297–333.

Wilder, T. (2003). *Our town: A play in three acts*. New York: HarperPerennial.

Williams, R. B. (1993). Hostility and the heart. In D. Goleman & J. Gurin (Eds.), *Mind/body medicine* (pp. 65–83). Yonkers, NY: Consumer Reports Books.

Williams, T. (1988). *My turn at bat: The story of my life*. New York: Simon & Schuster.

Wood, J. (1893). *Dictionary of quotations from ancient and modern English and foreign sources*. New York: Warne.

Wordsworth, W. (2008). *William Wordsworth: The complete works*. New York: Oxford University Press.

Yancy, P., & Stafford, T. (1992). *The new student bible (NIV)*. Grand Rapids, MI: Zondervan Publishing House.

Zuess, J. G. (1999). *The wisdom of depression: A guide to understanding and curing depression using natural medicine*. New York: Three Rivers Press.

Electronic Sources

American Association of Suicidology. U.S. statistics on suicide were retrieved October 29, 2007 from http://www.suicidology.org.

American Foundation for Suicide Prevention. Statistics on suicide were retrieved December 17, 2009 from http://www.afsp.org/

American Film Institute. List of one hundred greatest romantic films was retrieved December 8, 2008 from http://www.afi.com/tvevents/100years/passions.aspx.

Angelou, M. Quote on love and hope was retrieved July 7, 2009 from http://www.thinkexist.com.

Arabian proverb. Passage on friendship was retrieved July 28, 2007 from http://www.friendship.com.

Australian "Dreamtime." Passages were retrieved March 29, 2007 from http://www.dreamtime.net.au/dreaming/storylist and http://www.crystalinks.com/dreamtime.

Bacon, F. Quote on friendship was retrieved July 20, 2007 from p. 79 [digitized version] of The Essays at http://www.NuVision.com.

Braveheart. Film details and quotes were retrieved October 18, 2007 from http://www.imdb.com.

Buck, P. Quote regarding hope and freedom was retrieved January 6, 2010 from womens history.about.com/od/quotes/a/pearl_buck.htm.

Carlyle, T. Quote on health and hope was retrieved February 4, 2005 from http://www.whatquote.com.

Cicero. Quote on "nothing better" than friendship was retrieved October 15, 2007 from p. 34 [digitized version] of his collected works at http://www.books.google.com.

Cicero. Quote on friendship as "good hope" was retrieved July 14, 2007 from p. 35 [digitized version] of his collected works at http://www.books.google.com.

Coleridge, S. Quote on health was retrieved February 4, 2005 from http://www.whatquote.com.

Collins, J. Lyrics were retrieved October, 28, 2007 from http://www.rhapsody.com

Cosby, B. Quote was retrieved October 26, 2007 from http://www.msnbc.msn.com/id/5345290/.

Cunningham, G. Biographical information was retrieved October 10, 2009 from http://bleacherreport.com/articles/198249-forgotten-stories-of-courage-and-inspiration-glenn-cunningham.

Day, L. Biographical information was retrieved November 7, 2008 from www.drday.com/.

Earhart, A. Biographical information was retrieved from http://www.ameliahearhart.com/about/quotes.html.

Ebert, R. Review of *Hoop Dreams* was retrieved August 12, 2007 from http://www.rogerebert.suntimes.com.

Ederle, G. Historic swim was reported in a *Sports Illustrated* article (August 6, 1926). It was retrieved February 24, 2007 from vault.sportsillustrated.cnn.com/vault/article/ magazine/MAG1017808/index.htm.

Edrich, A. Quote about hope chests was retrieved January 15, 2009 from http://www.theparentsite.com/parenting/hopechests.asp.

Einstein, A. Quote on the mystical was retrieved September 24, 2008 from http://www.spaceandmotion.com/albert-einstein-god-religion-theology.htm.

Emerson, R. W. Quote regarding fear of death was retrieved September 18, 2007 from http://www.quoteworld.org.

Epicurus. Quote on living and dying was retrieved September 20, 2007 from http://www.quotationsbook.com.

Epicurus. Quote on friendships was retrieved September 29, 2008 from http://www.thinkexist.com.

Gallup Poll. Results were retrieved November 6, 2007 from http://www.galluppoll.com.

Gandhi, M. Quote regarding thoughts and destiny was retrieved September 14, 2008 from http://www.quotationspage.com.

Goethe, J. W. Quote on talent and character was retrieved March 3, 2007 from http://www.quoteworld.org.

Great Spirit Prayer. Retrieved October 18, 2007 from http://www.firstpeople.us/html/ An-Indian-Prayer.html.

Heraclites. Quote was retrieved March 3, 2007 from http://www.forums.philosophyforums.com/threads/heraclitus-and-parmenides.

Herbert, A. Quote was retrieved April 26, 2009 from http://www.thinkexist.com.

Holdt, J. Quote on self-blame among African Americans was retrieved October 20, 2007 from http://www.american-pictures.com.

Hoop Dreams. Details on the film *Hoop Dreams* were retrieved August 12, 2007 from http://www.imdb.com.

James, W. Quote on the greatest use of life was retrieved September 20, 2007 from http://www.quotationspage.com.

Keats, J. Quote on health was retrieved February 4, 2005 from http://www.whatquote.com.

King, M. L. Felicia H. quote was retrieved from a Google search. The site has apparently been removed.

Kingsolver, B. Quote retrieved January 10th, 2010 from http://en.wikiquote.org/wiki/Hope.

Kralik, D., & Telford, K. Booklet information on "transition in chronic illness" was retrieved March 14, 2007 from rdns.org.au/research_unit/documents/Booklet%2010%20-%20 Self-care.pdf.

Kung Fu quote was retrieved September 4, 2007 from kungfu-guide.com/addendum/addendum_tlc.html.

Lombardi, V. Quote "we'd go through fire for him" was attributed to former Packer Henry Jordan. It was retrieved December 10, 2008 from http://www.washingtonpost.com/wp-srv/sports/longterm/general/povich/launch/lombardi.htm.

Lombardi, V. Quote regarding fatigue was retrieved February 6, 2006 from http://www.world ofquotes.com.

Mandela, N. Quote was retrieved October 23, 2007 from http://www.info.gov.za/speeches/1999/990617935a1003.htm.

McGeary, J. The story about Laetitia appeared in *Time* (February, 12, 2001) and was retrieved October 16, 2007 from http://www.time.com.

Melville, H. Quote was retrieved February 20, 2007 from http://www.quotationsbook.com.

Moody Blues. Lyrics for the song "Question" were retrieved September 5, 2009 from http://www.allspirit.co.uk/question.html.

Moody Blues. Lyrics are from the song "Say What You Mean" and were retrieved May 10, 2007 from http://www.poemhunter.com.

Nigerian Proverb. Quote regarding love and acceptance is attributed to the Kanuri ethnic group and was retrieved May 12, 2008 from http://www.famous-proverbs.com.

Nigerian proverb. Passage about "both hands" was retrieved July 28, 2007 from http://www.quotationspage.com.

Nightingale, F. Quote regarding God and statistics was retrieved Janary 8, 2010 from http://www.thinkexist.com/.../to_understand_god...thoughts_we_must_study/182578.html.

Orsborn, C. Quotes related to hope and healing were retrieved November 28, 2007 from http://www.beliefnet.com.

Poitier, S. Quote on hopelessness was retrieved January 5, 2010 from http://theotherpages.org/quote/quote-27op.html.

Pali Canon. Passages were retrieved January 10, 2007 from http://www.accesstoinsight.org/tipitaka/index.html.

Pew Research Council. Statistics about believers and atheists retrieved June 7, 2008 from http://www.adherents.com/.

Qur'an. Passages were retrieved January 12th, 2007 from http://www.hti.umich.edu/relig/qur'an.

Rig Veda. Passages were retrieved March 24, 2007 from http://www.sacred-texts.com/hin/rigveda/index.htm.

Rousseau, J. J. Quote was retrieved October 14, 2003 from http://www.qoutationspage.com.

Rumi. Quote was retrieved October 24, 2008 from http://www.mevlana.net.

Torah. Passages were retrieved March 14, 2007 from http://www.shechem.org/etorahsr.html.

Scottish proverb. Proverb was retrieved September 9, 2008 from http://www.englishproverbs.org/.

Seneca, L. A. Quote on health was retrieved February 4, 2005 from http://www.whatquote.com.

Teresa, M. Quote on her care for the dying and destitute was retrieved August 7, 2009 from http://nobelprize.org/nobel_prizes/peace/laureates/1979/presentation-speech.html.

Two Towers. Film lines were retrieved November 4, 2009 from http://www.imdb.com/title/tt0167261/.

Tzu, L. Quote on health was retrieved February 4, 2005 from http://www.whatquote.com.

Weinberg, G. Quote was retrieved October 28, 2007 from http://www.brainyquote.com.

White, R. For more information on Ryan White's legacy and the national youth conference, visit http://www.ryanwhite.com.

Whittier, J. G. Quote on regret was retrieved October 4, 2007 from http://www.quotes.net.

Wong, P. Comments were from his December 14, 2002 keynote address at the Conference on Life and Death Education at the National Changhua University of Education, Taiwan. They were retrieved September 14, 2007 from http://www.meaning.ca.

Yamasaki, T. Ryan White story was retrieved August 10, 2007 from http://www.digitaljournalist.org/issue0106/voices_yamasaki.htm.

Young, S. Young's reflections on meditation were retrieved November 10, 2009 from http://www.shinzen.org/shinsub3/artMantra.htm.

Yutang, L. Quote referring to hope as a road was retrieved August 14, 2007 from http://www.greatquotes.com.

Index

389

About the Authors

Tony Scioli, Ph.D., is professor of clinical psychology at Keene State College as well as a member of the graduate faculty at the University of Rhode Island. He is licensed as a psychologist in the state of Massachusetts. He was a Phi Beta Kappa, Magna Cum Laude graduate of the University of Massachusetts/ Amherst, and received his Ph.D. from the University of Rhode Island in 1990. Dr. Scioli completed Harvard fellowships in human motivation and behavioral medicine, and is listed in *Who's Who in America*. He coauthored the chapter on emotion for the *Encyclopedia of Mental Health* and has served on the editorial boards of the *Journal of Positive Psychology* and the *Psychology of Religion and Spirituality*. Considered one of the world's leading authorities on hope, Dr. Scioli is the coauthor of *Hope in the Age of Anxiety*. Dr. Scioli has consulted to various NBC and CNN affiliates as well as WebMD on matters such as depression, coping, and trauma, and psychological adjustment in the aftermath of 9/11.

Henry B. Biller, Ph.D., is professor and codirector of externship training in clinical psychology at the University of Rhode Island. He was a Phi Beta Kappa, Magna Cum Laude graduate of Brown University and received his Ph.D. from Duke University in 1967. A fellow of both the American Psychological Association and the Association for Psychological Science, he is also listed in *Who's Who in America*. He has been involved in training mental health professionals for more than forty years. Dr. Biller has authored or coauthored eleven previous books, including *Hope in the Age of Anxiety*, *Fathers and Families*, and *Creative Fitness: Applying Health Psychology and Exercise Science to Everyday Life*. His groundbreaking work on the role of the father led to appearances on *Phil Donahue* and *Today* as well as a feature article in *Life* magazine.